Early China

First published in the United Kingdom in 2007 by
Sutton Publishing, an imprint of NPI Media Group
Limited · Cirencester Road · Chalford · Stroud ·
Gloucestershire · GL6 8PE

British Library Cataloguing in Publication Data
A catalogue record for this book is available from the
British Library.

ISBN 978-0-7509-4729-9

Typesetting and origination by
NPI Media Group Limited.
Printed and bound in England.

Early China

From Beijing Man
to the First Emperor

J.A.G. ROBERTS

SUTTON PUBLISHING

Contents

Introduction

In 1901 Edward H Parker, Professor of Chinese at the University of Manchester, described the history of China as 'wearisome', 'insipid' and 'downright stupid'. The human interest in Chinese history, he declared, only began in the nineteenth century, when contacts with Europe began to play a major part in the country's development.

Today no historian would dream of describing China's early history in those terms. In the 1970s astonishing archaeological finds brought early Chinese history to life. They included

1974   The terracotta army of the First Emperor – the most remarkable discovery since the opening of Tutankhamen's tomb
1975   Early Chinese law recorded on bamboo strips found in the grave of a Qin official

| 1976 | Shang culture illustrated by the contents of the grave of Princess Fu Hao, who died c. 1250 BCE |
| 1977 | Chinese musical instruments found in the grave of Marquis Yi of Zeng, *c.* 433 BCE |

It is not only archaeology which has enriched our understanding of early China. The teachings of the philosophers, among them Confucius and the Daoists, are now given renewed attention. Issues relating to Chinese medicine and diet have been related to Western concerns on matters of health. In these, and in many other topics, the history of early China has a greater significance today than ever before.

On the Chinese Language

Chinese is a tonal language, which means that words which have the same sound may be pronounced in different tones and have a variety of different meanings. The official language of China, the language known in the West as Mandarin, has four tones. A common sound like *ma* in the first tone may mean a mother, in the second tone hemp, in the third tone a horse and in the fourth tone to scold.

Chinese is also written in characters. Each character has its own meaning and its own pronunciation. The famous eighteenth-century Kangxi dictionary listed 47,000 characters, a good dictionary may contain up to 8,000 characters and to be able to read Chinese one has to know at least 3-4,000 characters.

In this book Chinese characters have been transliterated into *pinyin*, the official system of romanization, rather than the traditional Wade-Giles system. *Pinyin* is now used in newspapers and is being adopted generally in scholarly works. All Chinese personal and place names have been transliterated into *pinyin*. Thus Mao Tse-tung is rendered as Mao Zedong and Peking is transliterated as Beijing.

For the most part, *pinyin* spelling approximates to the phonetic values of English, with the following notable exceptions:

c	is pronounced 'ts' as in Tsar
i	is pronounced 'ee', except when it follows c, ch, r, s, sh, z and zh, in which case it is pronounced approximately 'er'
ian	is pronounced 'ien'
q	is pronounced 'ch' as in cheap
r	is similar to the English 'r' but is pronounced with the tongue behind the front teeth
x	is pronounced 'sh' as in sham
z	is pronounced 'ds' as in hands
zh	is pronounced 'j' as in jasmine

When citing Chinese names, the family name is given first, followed by the given name. Following the usual practice, Chinese emperors are designated by their reign titles, not by their personal names.

Prehistoric man in China

The fossil remains of early man in China were found in the 1920s at Dragon Bone Mountain, Zhoukoudian, thirty miles from Beijing. These were of *homo erectus*, who lived between 500,000 and 200,000 years ago, who was a predecessor of *homo sapiens*, that is modern man. At this time north China had a relatively mild climate, buffalo, deer and sheep grazed the grasslands and wild pig and rhinoceros could be found in the undergrowth. Beijing man was a hunter gatherer who made tools of quartz and greenstone and could use fire. He had a flat skull, protruding mouth and a relatively large brain. In 1941, when China was at war with Japan, these finds were removed for safety and then disappeared under mysterious circumstances.

Many thousands of years later *homo sapiens*, who had probably come from Africa, began to occupy sites in China. Three skulls, found in the Middle Cave at

Zhoukoudian gave an unconfirmed radiocarbon date of 16,922 BCE. Deposits of stone tools made by *homo sapiens* have been found in various places in northern Shaanxi.

From about 8,000 BCE the climate of East Asia became warm and moist. North China was covered with dense forests, elephants roamed the land and crocodiles could be found in the rivers. Neolithic cultures, marked by the cultivation of crops and the domestication of animals, began to appear.

In 1973 an example of an early Neolithic settlement was found at Hemudu in south-east China. Finds included terracotta pottery, the remains of pigs and buffaloes and articles made of wood and bone. The bone articles included whistles made from the bones of birds. These whistles, which emit a very high note, may have been used to lure birds rather than to make music. A notable feature of the Hemudu settlement was that its people were cultivating wet rice.

The best-known Neolithic site is the village of Banpo near Xi'an, which was occupied from about 4,500 BCE. Its inhabitants cultivated millet using polished stone hoes and knives. They had domesticated animals, the most common being pigs and dogs, but the remains of sheep and cattle have also been found. They supplemented their diet with fish and they also went hunting, killing deer and other animals. They clothed themselves with a fibre made from hemp and possibly with silk, as silkworm cocoons have been found on the site.

Banpo had a residential area comprising some one hundred houses and other buildings. The earlier houses were half underground, while the later houses stood on ground level and had a wooden framework. Each house had a central pillar to support a thatched roof, a fire pit and a door which faced south. Some of the floors were dressed with white clay and clay was used to make ovens, cupboards and benches. This part of the village was surrounded by an artificial moat for protection from wild animals. There was a cemetery, where adults were buried in individual graves, often with a ceramic vessel beside the body. Infants who had died were placed in pottery jars and buried near the houses.

In another sector of the village was the pottery. Six kilns have been found and over half a million fragments of pottery have been dug up. The kilns made pots for drinking, cooking, storage and burial. One type of pottery, a coarser variety made out of grey clay, was decorated with cord marks, or incised patterns. Some pots have scratch marks on them, which have sometimes been interpreted as an early form of writing. Finer pots, made out of red clay, have human or animal designs painted on them using manganese dioxide for black and iron oxide for red designs. The pots were then fired at a temperature of 1000-1400 degrees centigrade. The most famous piece of painted pottery is a basin which bears a drawing of a fish on its side and a human face in the bowl. The human face was very rarely depicted, one of the few other examples being that of a modelled human head with a painted mask on the lid of an urn found on a site to the west of Banpo. A snake appears to run up the back of the head and the person depicted appears to be wearing a collar or ruff round his or her neck.

The people of Banpo belonged to the Yangshao culture, Yangshao being the name of a village in the province of Henan which was excavated in the 1920s by the Swedish archaeologist J Gunnar Andersson. Yangshao culture, which spread over Henan and Shaanxi between 5,000 and 3,000 BCE, was marked by the appearance of villages defended by moats, which had sophisticated methods of producing and storing food and which had a well-organized society, possibly headed by women.

Soon after Andersson made his discoveries at Yangshao, archaeologists found a completely different type of Neolithic pottery at Longshan in Shandong province. Longshan pottery was black and decorated with rings and grooves. It was much finer than Yangshao ware, was elevated on a circular foot or on legs and may have been made on a potter's wheel. Longshan culture, which seemed more advanced than that of Yangshao, spread along the middle and lower Yangzi valley. When an excavation at Miaodigou in Henan found that Yangshao ware was found *below* Longshan pottery, it was suggested that Longshan had developed from Yangshao culture. However no links have been found between the two cultures and the modern theory is that they developed separately, but gradually Longshan spread westwards and overtook the Yangshao culture which was already dying out.

From legends of China's origin to the beginning of history

According to Chinese legend, the world was created by the giant Pangu. When he died his flesh became the earth, his blood the rivers, his bones the mountains and his hair the stars in the sky. From the parasites on his body came the different races which inhabit the earth. Many years after Pangu's death the Three Emperors were said to have ruled China. The first was Fuxi, who introduced fishing, writing and music. He married his sister, to whom one can trace the institution of marriage. To this day portraits of Fuxi may be found in Daoist temples, with him holding a picture of the eight trigrams, used for fortune-telling. He was followed by Shennong, who instituted agriculture, trade and medicine. The third emperor was the Yellow Emperor, to whom was credited the invention of medicine, ceramics and the calendar. His wife developed sericulture, that is the breeding of silkworms.

Some centuries later, perhaps in about 2300 BCE the Emperor Yao was on the throne. He ruled wisely and introduced flood control. Believing that his own son was unworthy to follow him, he chose as his successor a humble sage called Shun. In later years the reigns of Yao and Shun were regarded as a golden age in Chinese history. Shun in turn passed the throne on to his faithful minister Yu, and it is at this point that China's prehistory begins to merge with history.

According to Chinese tradition, ancient China was ruled by three dynasties, the first being the Xia, followed by the Shang and then the Zhou. For a long time modern historians believed that the Xia dynasty was a myth but archaeological discoveries of palace-like buildings and tombs at Erlitou in Henan are now thought to be the work of the Xia dynasty which flourished between approximately 1900 and 1350 BCE. The genealogy of its rulers, preserved in the *Historical Records* compiled by Sima Qian, the Grand Historian, who lived between 145 and 90 BCE, named Yu as its first ruler.

Furnaces for smelting bronze and producing bronze vessels have been found at Erlitou. A notable example of their output was a ceremonial vessel called a *jue* which stood on three legs and had a handle and a spout.

The appearance of bronze smelting at Erlitou raises a very interesting question. Was the development of metal technology in China the result of diffusion of knowledge across Central Asia, or was it an independent discovery in China? Because bronze implements were made in Mesopotamia from about 3000 BCE and because the earliest bronze artefacts which have been found in China were made at least a thousand years later, and are quite sophisticated, it has often been assumed that the technology for their production came from abroad. However, the shapes of early Chinese bronze vessels echo Longshan pottery prototypes and the technique for casting bronze vessels, which involved the making of ceramic moulds for sections of the vessel, and then joining them together, was quite different from the 'lost wax' process used in the West. If one accepts these arguments, bronze casting was invented independently in China.

The Shang Dynasty

The traditional dates of the Shang dynasty are 1766–1122 BCE. Zhengzhou in Henan province was the Shang capital in the early and middle periods of the dynasty, and Anyang, about 150 miles to the east, was the capital from about 1300 BCE. These two cities are the most important Bronze Age sites in the whole of Asia. At about the same time, in Egypt, the New Kingdom flourished and Akhenaten and later Tutankhamen sat on the throne. As in Egypt, and again as in Mesopotamia, the Shang civilization developed along the banks of a great river. The Central Plain had been created by the Yellow River, which had spread a thick layer of fertile soil over the land, soil which could be worked using the limited technology of Neolithic and early Bronze Age farmers.

Zhengzhou had a four-mile-long city wall constructed using the 'stamped earth' technique. Stamped earth walls were made by pounding thin layers of earth within a movable wooden frame. The earth then becomes as hard as cement. Its base was sixty feet thick and it was at least twenty feet high. Within the walls were large buildings and villages which specialized in making pottery, bronze artefacts, wine and textiles. There were also several large tombs, deep pits in which coffins were placed, surrounded with bronze weapons, musical instruments and other objects indicating the status of the deceased. In some tombs there was also evidence of human sacrifice, possibly of prisoners of war.

The archaeological site at Anyang was discovered in 1899 by a doctor searching for 'dragon bones' to grind down for Chinese medicine. When full-scale excavation began in 1928 at Xiaotun, just outside the city, the remains were found of the ceremonial and administrative centre of the late Shang state. A few miles to the north eleven large cruciform graves were found, and these are believed to be the tombs of the eleven kings of the late Shang.

The 'dragon bones' which the doctor had found were in fact the shoulder blades of cattle, or the under-shells of tortoises, which had been used for scapulimancy or plastromancy, that is divining by interpreting the cracks which appeared in the bones or shells when a heated bronze tool was applied to them. Before this was done an inscription was scratched on the bone, asking questions such as whether the king should send troops against his enemies, whether a hunt should be undertaken, or whether it was the right time to start harvesting crops. One bone bears the inscription 'on a certain day it is divined whether it will rain or not rain.' The answer to the question, obtained by experts who interpreted the cracks, was 'not rain'.

The inscriptions were in Chinese characters, some of which are little different from those in use today. The language used is also unmistakeably Chinese, as it is monosyllabic, and sense is conveyed by word order, not by the use of tenses. The simplest characters are pictographs, that is drawings of actual objects, for example the moon or a tree. Others are ideographs, characters which conveyed ideas, such as the numerals or 'up' and 'down'. Some ideographs are complex, the concept 'bright' being conveyed by the combination of the characters for the sun and the moon, while 'peace' is expressed by showing a woman under a roof. A third category of characters is based on the phonetic principle, whereby a character which is pronounced in a certain way may be combined with a signifier (or 'radical') indicating a different meaning. For example the character for *an*, which can mean peace, may also be written with the character for 'hand' alongside it, whereupon it means 'to press down'. Over three thousand different characters have been found on the oracle bones, about half of which may be translated with some degree of certainty. The characters include a dating system based on a ten-day week and a sixty-day cycle.

From these inscriptions and from other archaeological finds a detailed picture has been obtained of Shang civilization. The names of the Shang kings have been found and the record agrees almost completely with the list of Shang kings compiled centuries later. The royal succession passed from older to younger brother rather than from father to son, so that although there were thirty Shang kings, they represented only eighteen generations.

Shang kings performed two functions. On the one hand they were rulers, who ruled their state with the assistance of officials. They were supported by aristocratic clans, with whom they had family connections. They headed a warlike society, with aristocrats practising military skills and fighting using war chariots. However the life of the ordinary people was very different. They cultivated the fields using wooden or stone implements, as their Neolithic ancestors had done, and lived on what they could produce or gather. If their villages were near to centres of Shang rule, they might be subject to direct rule by royal officials; if they lived further away, overlords appointed by the king might have some authority over their lives.

Shang kings were also religious leaders whose role was to promote the well-being of their people. They performed religious ceremonies and may even have played the role of shaman, or priest. One aspect of their religious duties was the regulation of the calendar, which was important for determining the right time to make sacrifices and when to plant and to harvest crops. The calendar was based on the observed movements of heavenly bodies. Ten 'heavenly stems' and twelve 'earthly bodies' were identified and these combined to produce a cycle of sixty days. This cycle, later extended for counting years, became the basis of the traditional Chinese calendar and is used for casting horoscopes to this day.

The Shang people worshipped many gods, many of whom were royal ancestors, some were nature spirits, while others were addressed as 'mother of the east' or 'lord of the south'. They also worshipped a high god called Di or Shang Di, who was the protector of towns and armies and controller of the wind and rain. The practice of veneration of ancestors, 'ancestor worship' as it has become known, remains an important part of Chinese culture to this day. Ancestors are not regarded as gods, but for Chinese it remains extremely important to honour recent ancestors, that is dead parents and grandparents, by providing for their needs in the afterlife.

When the Shang kings died they were buried in very large cruciform graves – one measured forty-three feet deep and sixty-five feet square. It has been estimated that the digging of each pit must have required at least seven thousand working days. The corpses were placed in wooden coffins and were surrounded by grave goods. On the ramps which led down to the burial chamber, which were each fifty to sixty feet long, were laid the bodies of scores of slaughtered human victims and horses. Some of the human bodies had been beheaded, their bodies laid in order in one place and their heads piled up in another. Alongside the royal tombs were other burials. Men, some holding bronze vessels, others halberds, were buried at intervals round the perimeter. Dogs were buried singly or in groups. In the central court five chariots were buried with their charioteers.

The royal tombs at Anyang were looted many years ago, but in 1976 an undamaged tomb was found outside the royal cemetery. This proved to be the grave of Princess Fu Hao, a consort of a Shang king, who died in about 1250 BCE. The tomb was modest in size, about eighteen feet by thirteen feet at the mouth. The floor level housed the princess's body, beneath her corpse six dogs were buried and around it the remains of sixteen human bodies were found. In the burial chamber there was a lacquered coffin, which has since rotted away, and an extraordinary collection of grave goods, which have been listed as follows:

> 468 bronze objects including 130 weapons, 23 bells, 27 knives, 4 mirrors, and 4 tigers or tiger heads;
> 755 jade objects;
> 63 stone objects;
> 5 ivory objects;
> 564 bone objects, including 500 bone hairpins and over 20 bone arrowheads;
> 11 pottery objects;

6,900 pieces of cowry shell.

The bronze objects weighed 1.6 metric tons, an extraordinary weight, indicative of Fu Hao's very high status. They included bronze ritual vessels, among them a pair of vessels of the type called a *zun*, which was used for heating wine and which stood on three legs. These were in the form of owls, the two legs of the birds forming two legs of the tripod and the third leg being the birds' tails. Another bronze object was a very fine axe, decorated on one side with a human face flanked by two tigers. Axes of this type may have been used to decapitate the sacrificial victims placed in the tombs of members of the royal family and of other important people.

Bronze vessels served a variety of ritual functions, including the preparation of sacrificial meats and the heating of the wine used in religious ceremonies. They were covered with stylized surface decoration, often depicting animals. Many vessels carry the famous motif, the *taotie*, a monster mask with two large staring eyes which was believed to avert evil. Mirrors made of bronze, which were polished on one side and bore a design on the other, were often placed in graves to provide light for the dead.

The jade and ivory items found in Fu Hao's tomb are also of great interest. Jade, which is found in western China, had been used for weapons and jewellery since Neolithic times. Many of the pieces of jade found in the tomb are in the shape of animals, often of tigers. One piece of jade, carved in the shape of a phoenix, made long before Fu Hao's time, may have been passed down to her as an antique.

The ivory used came from elephant tusks. Skeletons of an elephant and of a rhinoceros have been found near Anyang, which suggests that the court may have had a menagerie. One of the most beautiful objects found in the tomb was a drinking cup made out of ivory which had been inlaid with turquoise.

The production of bronze in the Shang state was controlled by the king. The mining of copper and tin, and the manufacture of bronze, was a major industry employing large numbers of skilled craftsmen. Bronze was also used for the manufacture of weapons, including swords and halberds, and for the fittings of war chariots and the harness used for the horses which pulled them.

The war chariots were light two-wheeled constructions drawn by two horses. The wheels had eighteen to thirty spokes and the rectangular chariot box had a floor made of planks or leather strips – the latter perhaps to minimize bouncing when travelling at speed. A Shang war chariot has been excavated near Anyang. Its two charioteers and its two horses had been killed and the whole assemblage had been buried in a pit.

These weapons, and these chariots, indicated that the Shang state was on a war footing. Aristocrats went through a formal process of investiture and in return for receiving grants of land they had to promise the king that they would perform military duties when required. The Shang kings waged wars of aggression against their neighbours, thereby obtaining prisoners and loot. They seized new land for farming and commissioned the establishment of new towns. In this way the Shang state extended its territory from along the Yellow river into the Wei valley.

It was long supposed that the Shang dynasty was the only significant Bronze Age culture which had become established in China. However, this assumption has been contradicted by recent archaeological finds. In 1986, at

Sanxingdui, a settlement just north of Chengdu, two underground caches of bronzes were found which were quite different in character from those of the Shang. Among the items unearthed were a life-sized statue on a pedestal and some very large trees bearing peach-like fruits. On the branches were birds and a dragon. Three years after this discovery, a tomb was found at Xin'gan in Jiangxi which proved to be the second richest Bronze Age burial yet discovered – second only to that of Fu Hao, described above. The contents of the tomb were of such good quality the conclusion must be reached that in the vicinity there was a significant state with rulers able to command the labours of a large number of craftsmen.

The Zhou Dynasty –
the Western Zhou

The Zhou dynasty is traditionally dated from 1122 to 256 BCE, and this immensely long period is divided into the Western Zhou, from 1122 to 771 BCE, and the Eastern Zhou, the latter age being further subdivided into the Spring and Autumn period, from 771 to 481 BCE, and the Warring States period, from 481 to 221 BCE.

Long before the fall of the Shang, the Zhou had emerged as a powerful state somewhat to the west of the main centre of Shang activities. The origin of the Zhou people is not clear. According to Mencius, a follower of Confucius, 'King Wen was a Western barbarian', and there is a theory that the Zhou were of Turkish origin. A more plausible suggestion is that they originated in the Fen valley in Shanxi and later migrated to the Wei valley to the west of Xi'an. There, in proximity to the Shang state, the Zhou people adopted many features of Shang culture. They established their capital at Hao, not far from the modern city of Xi'an.

According to the *Book of Documents,* one of the earliest surviving Chinese historical sources, the fall of the Shang came about because of the evil deeds of the last Shang ruler. He lost the protection or mandate of heaven which was transferred to the rulers of Zhou. Of these, King Wen was a paragon of virtue, and his son King Wu, who overthrew the Shang after a great battle at Muye, north of the Yellow River, was an outstanding warrior. The *Book of Documents* recorded that the Zhou headed a coalition of eight nations which included Shu, and that the Zhou and their allies gained the victory because the Shang troops were driven to mutiny by the cruelty of their ruler, who was beheaded after the battle. These events probably took place *c.* 1045 BCE, nearly eighty years later than the traditional date for the overthrow of the Shang.

Shortly after the conquest, perhaps in 1043 BCE, King Wu died. His son succeeded him, but as he was a minor, authority was wielded by his uncle, the Duke of Zhou, one of the most famous figures in early Chinese history. The duke established Zhou rule over Shang territory, defeated a rebellion headed by survivors of the Shang royal family and extended Zhou influence to the Huai valley. Later, Zhou colonies were established as far north as the vicinity of present-day Beijing and as far south as the Yangzi valley.

Chinese historians in the past explained why one dynasty fell and was replaced by another, the succession of events called the 'dynastic cycle', by stressing the shortcomings of the last rulers of the previous dynasty and the virtues of the first rulers of the new dynasty. The last kings of the Shang were accused of being overbearing and cruel. The Duke of Zhou was praised for re-establishing the rule of law and for purifying the morals of the people.

How important was the difference between the culture of the Shang and that of the Zhou? One way of answering that question is to look at the contents of a group of tombs found near Xi'an which have been dated 950-900 BCE, soon after the Zhou conquest. One tomb contained the body of the Count of Yu and his wife, and the next tomb the body of his concubine. The tomb of the Count and his wife also contained seven human sacrifices – far fewer than the numbers sacrificed when Shang rulers or their followers died. The victims had not been decapitated and some had been placed in coffins with their own grave goods, which suggests that they were servants, not prisoners of war. The first tomb contained bronze vessels which resembled those made by the Shang, but some of the shapes were new and the animals which were depicted were more lifelike. The interests of the count were illustrated by jade pendants in the form of stags and four musical instruments. However the most plentiful of the objects which have survived were weapons and fittings for chariots.

Early Zhou society has been described as a 'feudal' society. The term 'feudal' was coined to describe features of European society in the Middle Ages when grants of land were made by a king to his followers, who in return promised to fight for him and to lead their followers in his support. Certainly in China at this time there was something like feudalism. In the famous early text, the *Book of Songs* it says:

Everywhere under vast Heaven
There is no land that is not the king's.
To the borders of those lands
There are none who are not the king's servants.

The nobility were carefully arranged in ranks, with five titles, duke, marquis, earl, viscount and baron. Grants of land to nobles were accompanied by the presentation of gifts, including a jade sceptre as a symbol of authority and a tablet bearing the terms on which the rank had been conferred. The occasion when the king had presented land was often recorded on bronze vessels. Nobles were not allowed to trade and in warfare they were expected to obey a code of conduct which had some similarities with the chivalric code observed by knights in the West. But whereas in Europe grants of land were normally made to military allies, in China they were usually made to members of the king's family – indeed the entire nobility was treated as if it was part of an extended family sharing a common ancestor.

Marxist historians have argued that the labour used by the king and the aristocrats was slave labour and that China at this time was a slave society. They point to the evidence of the human sacrifices which accompanied royal burials and by references in oracle inscriptions. Other historians have argued that the bulk of the population were not slaves, because they were not bought or sold, nor were they deprived of their personal freedom. Nevertheless they had to do forced labour, building city walls and performing agricultural tasks, and they were conscripted for military duties. Much later the gap between the aristocratic warriors who ruled and the masses who served them was expressed in the saying, 'The ritual does not extend down to the common people; punishments do not extend up to the great officers.'

The Spring and Autumn Period, 771-481 BCE

The early Zhou kings had wielded considerable authority over their supporters, even though they had been given grants of land and had been allowed to govern the people who lived in their territory as they chose. It was recorded that King Yi, the Zhou king who reigned between about 865 and 858 BCE, had the Duke of Ai boiled to death for criticizing him. But that the duke dared to criticize the king was perhaps an indication that central authority was declining. This situation was made worse when the Rong, non-Chinese nomadic peoples who lived on the steppe to the north and west of Zhou territory, began to make raids. When the Rong attacked, the king would order the lighting of beacon fires to summon his vassals to assist him. However, he began to light the fires to amuse his favourite concubine and when a major attack threatened Hao, his capital city, there was no response from Zhou's supporters. The city was overrun and the king was forced to move his capital eastwards to Luoyang.

After this demonstration of weakness the Zhou state began to break up into separate kingdoms which offered only symbolic allegiance to the Zhou kings. At one point Zhou territory was divided into about 170 states, but by the end of the Spring and Autumn period the number of states had been reduced to seven. In an attempt to settle disputes and to resist attacks from nomads, one of the rulers of these states was chosen as the senior king. He was given the privilege of fighting campaigns on behalf of the Zhou ruler, who still had his capital and a small amount of territory at Luoyang. This system was at its most effective when Guan Zhong, chief minister of the state of Qi, which occupied the territory of modern Shandong province, was in power. Among the achievements credited to him was the development of the production of salt, a vital ingredient in the diet, which was made a state monopoly. Under Guan Zhong, Qi dominated the central area of north China. This area became known as the Zhongguo, or Middle Kingdom, the name still used for China.

It has been calculated that throughout the whole Spring and Autumn period only thirty-eight years were peaceful! During that time the pattern of warfare changed. Whereas in the past battles had been fought by nobles and their supporters, now states began to make ordinary people serve as soldiers. The use of bronze became more widespread and bronze weapons came into more general use. In one of the states, the state of Wu, the king employed a general named Sunzi. His book, *The Art of War* has become one of the world's most famous handbooks on military strategy, and is still used as a training manual. Sunzi advised that if possible war should always be avoided, but if it became inevitable, then the general might use any means to secure a victory. One passage from the book reads:

All warfare is based on deception.

Hence, when able to attack, we must seem unable;
When using our forces, we must seem inactive;
When we are near, we must make the enemy believe we are far away;
When far away, we must make him believe we are near.

Hold out baits to entice the enemy.
Feign disorder, and crush him.

The Spring and Autumn period also saw important changes in society. Whereas in the past senior members of aristocratic families had played a dominant role, constant warfare had led to many casualties. Now rulers of the states began to employ junior members of the aristocracy who were educated, or who had particular skills, to manage affairs. This was the beginning of a permanent decline in the aristocracy of China, which was never to exercise as much influence as the nobility of Europe.

Changes were also taking place in the lower ranks of society. Up to this time Chinese farmers had probably practised a form of communal agriculture, which was called the 'well-field' system. Under this arrangement plots of land were divided into nine holdings in a pattern like that used for noughts and crosses. The eight outside plots of land were farmed by individual families, and the ninth was farmed communally and the produce delivered to the lord. This arrangement began to decline, perhaps because of the spread of the iron plough, which increased productivity, perhaps because of the introduction, in 594 BCE in the state of Lu, of a system of land taxation which required peasants to pay taxes rather than to provide labour service. Now individual ownership and a free market in land began to appear. Accompanying this change was a growth in commerce and the appearance of coinage. In the Shang period, cowry shells and pieces of cloth had been used to make purchases. By the late Spring and Autumn period a metallic currency had been introduced, early coins being in the form of spades or knives.

Some vivid insights into the lives of people living in the Spring and Autumn period may be found in the collection of anonymous poems known as *The Book of Songs*. According to tradition, Confucius himself chose the 305 poems which make up this anthology. The songs were in rhyming verse and were probably sung to tunes, now long forgotten. Their subject matter ranges from hunting and feasting to a description of the tasks of the farming year. Two themes are particularly common, the hardships of life and the pleasures of love. Here the farmers of the state of Wei complain about the king's tax officials

Big rat, big rat,
Do not eat my millet!

Three years I have served you,
But you will not care for me.
I am going to leave you
And go to that happy land;
Happy land, happy land,
Where I will find my place.

And here a woman recalls making love in the open air

Mid the bind-grass on the plain
that the dew makes wet as rain
I met by chance my clear-eyed man,
then my joy began.

Mid the wild grass dank with dew
lay we the full night through
that clear-eyed man and I
in mutual felicity.

The Warring States Period
481-221 BCE

The Warring States period, which dates from 481 to 221 BCE, is named after an historical work written at that time. In fact wars were no more frequent in that period than in the preceding Spring and Autumn period, but the nature of war was changing, with larger armies in the field and more sophisticated weapons in use. When the Zhou states were fighting for survival, regular infantry and cavalry became more important than patrician charioteers. Now horsemen wore barbarian boots, Scythian caps, and gilded belt buckles, all quite un-Chinese and suggestive of influence from the north.

Weapons included the bronze halberd and by the fifth century BCE swords made from a bronze alloy, with a higher tin content for the cutting edge, were in use. A few iron swords have also been found. The key weapon, however, was the crossbow. This had a bronze mechanism, including a cocking device, and it shot bolts with triangular bronze heads which could pierce armour. The first recorded instance of its use was in 341 BCE at the battle of Maling, between the states of Qi and Wei. One night Qi soldiers lay in wait in a defile with their crossbows cocked so as to make no noise to reveal their presence. The Wei army was surprised and massacred, the Wei general committed suicide and the state of Wei never fully recovered its power.

The economic and social changes which had begun in the Spring and Autumn period accelerated. In agriculture, iron tools were more readily available and the application of fertilizer and the use of irrigation became more common. The number of walled towns increased and some of these developed commercial quarters. Many towns had markets and there is evidence of extensive inter-regional trade. The names of a few merchants have been preserved, including that of Lü Buwei, whose career in the state of Qin will be noted shortly.

Nevertheless the way of life of the majority of the population had not changed greatly. For peasants in the north millet cakes were the staple diet with vegetables such as beans, turnips, melons when in season and for flavour onions, ginger and basil. The basic style of costume, a long tunic with a belt or sash, topped by jacket had been established by the sixth century BCE. The Chinese were proud of wearing shoes, for they regarded this as distinguishing them from the barbarians. Peasants wore straw sandals, members of the upper classes fine cloth slippers made of damask or brocade. At the end of the Zhou period fashion in costume was modified by the influence of northern nomads – underpants, leather trousers, shoes, belts with golden and jewelled hooks in the 'animal style' of the steppes, all became popular. From peasant to king, all lived in houses of the same basic construction. Each had a courtyard with the main gateway facing south – the direction of holiness. The courtyard was surrounded by a wall made of rammed earth. The buildings inside were on a rectangular plan, the roofs, now often made of tiles, were supported by wooden pillars set on stone plinths.

The Age of the Philosophers

More than a century before Plato and Aristotle established the basis of Western philosophy, China had its own age of the philosophers. Pre-eminent amongst these was Master Kong, known in the West as Confucius who lived approximately 551-479 BCE. Confucius was born in the small north-eastern state of Lu and his parents probably belonged to the minor aristocracy. His father died when he was very young and he was brought up in poverty by his mother. He obtained a post with the state government as keeper of granaries and director of public pastures. He was ambitious and hoped to achieve high office where he could restore proper standards in public life. Believing that he had no chance of promotion in his own state, he began to travel. He became an expert on ceremony, genealogy and ancient lore and this qualified him to give advice. He visited a number of states and held office in Wei before returning to Lu for his last years. There he became a teacher and he acquired a number of followers, who recorded his sayings in a compilation known as the *Analects*. Little else is known of his life, except that he had a son and a daughter, and that his son died before he did.

Central to Confucius's teaching was his perception that he lived in troubled times. He believed that in the early Zhou period China had experienced a golden age and he frequently cited the actions of Kings Wen and Wu, and those of the Duke of Zhou, as examples of appropriate behaviour. They had followed the *dao* or Way, which in this context meant 'the Way of running a state so that good order and harmony can prevail among men'. To achieve that, the king should select good officials, set a moral example and treat his people with benevolence.

Confucius made frequent reference to standards of conduct and to the ideal of the *junzi* or princely man, a term often translated as 'gentleman'. He distinguished between the gentleman, who was superior not because of his ancestry but because of superior moral accomplishments, and the small man. 'The gentleman', he said, 'understands what is moral. The small man understands what is profitable.' He emphasized the importance of education and of self-cultivation. 'At fifteen', he said, 'I set my heart on learning.' Through his teaching he established a respect for book-learning which was to last throughout the imperial period and to the present day. Self-cultivation was not only a matter of scholarship, it was also a commitment to learning how to behave. The essential quality was *jen,* a term often translated as benevolence, but which also meant dealing with other human beings as a man ideally should. If there was a sentence which could be a guide to conduct throughout one's life it would be: 'Do not impose on others what you yourself do not desire.'

He believed in the importance of ceremony and the value of politeness. The correct performance of ritual was an essential part of the government of a state. Within the family it was important to observe the niceties of behaviour and to apply restraint with regard to eating, drinking and dress. Confucius stressed the importance of filial piety, which implied obedience to one's parents during their lifetime and care for them as they grew old. After their death it was essential to provide them with a proper funeral and to observe mourning over a period of three years. There was also an obligation to make the correct sacrifices to the dead, in particular to male ancestors. Though referred to as 'ancestor worship', these ceremonies did not imply that one's ancestors were gods.

Confucius was fond of music. He played two stringed instruments, the zither and the lute. Music was certainly important in the society of his day and in Chinese the words for 'music' and 'enjoy' are written with the same character. But the playing of music, and listening to it, was not simply a matter of enjoyment. At royal courts it was used to maintain cosmic harmony, that is harmony between heaven and earth, but for this to be achieved, the ruler had to be virtuous. A tale was told of a ruler who lacked virtue, but who insisted on hearing a particular piece of music. Black clouds came up in the west, there was a violent storm and tiles were torn from the roof of the palace. For the next three years, the country suffered a drought and sores broke out all over the king's body!

In 1977 the tomb of Marquis Yi of Zeng was dicovered. It contained a collection of musical instruments, including a set of 65 bronze bells. The bells would have been played by five musicians who struck them with wooden mallets. One bell bore an inscription indicating it was a gift to Marquis Yi from the King of Chu in

433 BCE. There were also stone chimes, three types of stringed instruments, panpipes and an instrument made out of a gourd.

In modern times Confucius has been criticized for his views on the subordination of women. In the *Book of Rites*, he said that 'to be a woman means to submit', that 'a wife's words should not travel beyond her own apartment', and that 'a woman does not discuss affairs outside the home.' A woman was expected to obey her father, her husband and her son. If her husband died, it was shameful for her to remarry.

Confucius's most famous opponent was Mozi, who lived approximately 470-391 BCE. Mozi's family may have come from a class of prisoners or slaves, for he attacked Confucius for supporting the aristocracy. Confucius had talked of 'graded love', meaning to have more concern for one's family than for other people. Mozi urged men to practise universal love, by which he meant looking after the needs of all. He objected to costly funerals and prolonged mourning and had no time for music. But like Confucius he condemned war:

Among all the current calamities, which are the

worst? I say that the attacking of small states by large states, the plundering of the weak by the strong, the oppression of the few by the many, the deception of the simple by the cunning, the disdain of the noble towards the humble – these are some of the calamities in the world.

Mencius, who lived between 372 and 289 BCE re-stated Confucius's main themes, but he added two key ideas. The first concerned human nature, on which Confucius had merely observed: 'Men are close to one another by nature. They diverge as a result of repeated practice.' Mencius believed that what set men apart from animals was their moral nature. An opponent of Mencius had likened human nature to running water, saying that if you gave it an outlet to the east it would flow east, and if you gave it an outlet to the west it would flow west. Mencius responded by asking whether water showed the same indifference to high and low? 'Human nature is good, just as water seeks low ground. There is no man who is not good; there is no water that does not flow downwards.'

Like Confucius, Mencius had much to say on the subject of good government. The important thing for a ruler was to look after the welfare of his people and he recommended a return to the 'well-field system', which he believed had existed early in the Zhou period. But he then added that if a ruler did not look after his people they had the right to rebel.

Xunzi, who lived between 298 and 238 BCE was much more critical of human nature. 'The nature of man is evil; his goodness is acquired.' Man is born with desires and passions, which if not curbed will lead to disorder:

Crooked wood needs to undergo steaming and bending by the carpenter's tools; then only is it straight. Blunt metal needs to undergo grinding and whetting; then only is it sharp. Now the original nature of man is evil, so he must submit himself to teachers and laws before he can be just; he must submit himself to the rules of decorum and righteousness before he can be orderly.

Xunzi therefore emphasized education and the study of books which he regarded as classics. It was at this time that the five classics of Confucian literature were identified. For centuries to come any young man who hoped to pass the examinations and become an official in the imperial government would memorize them. The classics were: the *Book of Changes,* a book of divination; the *Book of Documents,* a collection of writings ascribed to the Shang and early Zhou periods; the *Book of Songs,* an anthology of poetry and folksongs; the *Spring and Autumn Annals* and the *Book of Rites,* works on conduct to which Confucius may have contributed. Later four books became the basic texts for primary education. These were the *Analects* of Confucius, the sayings of Mencius and two sections from the *Book of Rites,* the *Great Learning,* an essay on self-cultivation and the ordering of the family and society, and the *Doctrine of the Mean,* which is concerned with how man and his actions may be brought into harmony with the universe.

Other thinkers at this time were concerned not with morality but with nature. This was the keynote of the ideas known in the West as Daoism (Taoism). The *dao,* which means 'the way' is described, though not explained, in the opening lines of the oldest Daoist text, the *Daodejing* or *The Way and Power Classic,* which was supposedly written by Laozi, a contemporary of Confucius. It is now generally accepted that there was no such person and that the text dates from the fourth century BCE.

The way that can be spoken of
Is not the constant way;
The name that can be named
Is not the constant name.
The nameless was the beginning of heaven and
earth;
The named was the mother of the myriad creatures.

The Way and Power Classic reflected the troubled times in which it was composed. The ideal ruler was the sage, who had acquired enlightenment and who then applied it to the art of government. The most important principle was *wuwei,* which meant that the ruler should avoid interfering in people's lives. 'Do that which consists in taking no action, and order will prevail.' Governing a great state, he said, was like cooking small fish, a task which must be done gently.

The other main Daoist text is attributed to Zhuangzi who lived *c.* 369-286 BCE. His constant theme in the text is how man might free himself from earthly constraints. Zhuangzi once dreamed that he was a butterfly,

a butterfly fluttering about, enjoying itself. It did not

know that it was Zhuangzi. Suddenly he awoke with a start and he was Zhuangzi again. But he did not know whether he was Zhuangzi who had dreamed that he was a butterfly, or whether he was a butterfly dreaming that he was Zhuangzi.

During the Warring States period other key ideas were developed. According to the theory of *yin* and *yang*, all matter may be classified either as *yin,* which is dark, passive, downward, cold, contracting and weak, or as *yang,* which is bright, active, upward, hot, expanding and strong. These two principles are regarded as complementary and their relationship is necessary for cosmic harmony. The idea is often represented by a disc, half of which is black and half of which is white. However, the black part contains a small disc of white and the white part a small disc of black, symbolising that all *yin* contains a trace of *yang* and vice versa. Another idea which attempted to explain the order of nature is the theory of the 'five elements', which are wood, fire, earth, metal and water. These elements are the five active principles of nature and are related to the five directions, the five seasons, the five metals and the five atmospheric influences. 'Five element' theory was applied to medicine, with wood associated with the liver, fire with the heart, earth with the spleen, metal with the lungs and water with the kidneys. It was extended to cover food and nutrition, on the grounds that good health depended on a balance being struck between the five elements. It was also incorporated into the divination techniques of the *Book of Changes*.

The Rise of Qin

The furthest west of the seven Warring States was Qin, situated on the Wei River. Qin's history began in 897 BCE, when a petty chieftain named Feizi, in return for supplying horses for the Zhou royal house, was given a small fief some 190 miles west of modern Xi'an in central China.

Qin was regarded by the other states as non-Chinese. They claimed that its people had the same customs as the Rong and Di, non-Chinese groups living to the west and north of their territory: 'Qin has the heart of a tiger or a wolf. . . It knows nothing about traditional customs, proper relationships and virtuous conduct.' Cultural differences between the Qin and other Chinese states are evident in archaeological finds. Over 600 Qin tombs, the earliest dating from the eighth century BCE have been excavated. Some of these tombs were found in the original territory of the state of Qin, in present-day Shaanxi and Gansu, and others in the larger area of eastern expansion after the Qin conquest in 221 BCE. The early tombs are characterized by rectangular vertical shafts, but later tombs have side-chambers. Qin burial customs differed from those of the other Zhou states in that bodies were laid with their lower limbs bent up rather than laid flat. Some large tombs were sealed with a coat of charcoal and green lime clay. Many artefacts, including bronze and pottery vessels, were placed in the tombs, and it was common for human victims to be buried alongside the person for whom the grave was built. The largest number of victims found in one tomb was eighteen, some of whom had shackles round their necks and some of whom had been dismembered.

According to the *Historical Records*, Qin music was regarded as barbaric. It consisted of 'the beating on earthen jugs, knocking on jars, plucking of the *zheng* (a twelve-stringed guitar) and striking on the thigh, while crying Wu! Wu!' The instruments at the Qin court were classified not by the way that they were played, but by the eight materials from which they were made. These were gourd, bamboo, wood, silk, clay, metal, stone and skin. Each material was connected with a season and with an aspect of nature. Chimes of bells, which were tuned to the notes of musical stones, were played and their tones were used to tune instruments throughout the empire.

Qin early expansion was achieved at the expense of the Rong, who were finally subdued in the fourth century BCE. Meanwhile Qin was modernizing its government and adopting practices from other parts of China, for example in 408 BCE a land tax payable in kind rather than in labour was introduced.

Qin was keen to employ able men from other states. The ruler of the state of Wei had been warned about a young man named Yang Gongsun '[he] has marvellous talents, – if he is not employed in an official post, it would be better to put him to death, lest another kingdom obtain his services!' In about 361 BCE Yang Gongsun was attracted to Qin, where Duke Xiao, the ruler of Qin, gave him the title of Lord Shang and placed him in control of a reform programme. Lord Shang was the first exponent of the ideas and practices later to be known as Legalism. Whereas the Confucianists had urged that rulers should rule through benevolence for the benefit of their people, Legalists argued that the interests of the state came first and that it should be organized rationally to maximize its power against that of its rivals. To achieve this, Lord Shang supported the use of war and even led a campaign against his own state. He also implemented a wide range of reforms. One of his objectives was to abolish feudalism, by ending the devolution of power to hereditary landowners in favour of direct state administration. An agrarian reform abolished the 'well-field' system and replaced it with a free market in land. This improvement in peasant status and the opportunity to prosper encouraged settlers from other states to migrate to Qin, thereby increasing agricultural output and taxation and providing more soldiers for the army. Farmers were honoured for increasing their productivity, whereas traders, whose activities were regarded as of no benefit to the state, were discriminated against.

Strict laws and punishments were instituted and fixed administrative procedures were introduced. The population was divided into groups of five or ten families and individuals were held responsible for the wrongdoing of any member of the group (a system of control often used throughout China's history). All adult males were registered and were liable to a poll tax. A law code was introduced which prescribed severe punishments for offences.

In 338 BCE, Lord Shang was accused of plotting rebellion and put to death. However, his ambitions and those of his master Duke Xiao were not forgotten. The scholar Jia Yi wrote

> Duke Xiao cherished the idea of rolling the empire up like a mat, of lifting the whole world in his arms and of tying up the four seas in a sack. At this time Lord Shang assisted him; in the interior he fixed models and measures, gave his attention to farming and weaving, and made the necessary preparations for defence and attack; abroad he extended the territory in an uninterrupted way from west to east and fought with the feudal lords.

In 316 BCE, Qin started a series of campaigns against its neighbours. The first target was the state of Shu, to the southwest, in the area of present-day Sichuan. The Shu dynasty was overthrown, many thousands of colonists were sent from Qin to consolidate control and a major transformation of the territory began. According to an inscription dated 309 BCE, land was to be redistributed and a survey was to be made setting out regular plots, paths and embankments, which would enable irrigation to be used.

There followed a series of campaigns against the other states, all marked by victories for Qin and reports of very heavy casualties. Qin's success in each of these campaigns may be explained by its location in the west which gave it a secure base, by its strict social discipline which enabled it to mobilize its manpower, and by its strong economy which provided ample resources. However the theory that Qin won because it had better weapons, in particular iron swords, has not been supported by archaeological evidence. According to the *Historical Records* Qin fought 15 major campaigns and inflicted nearly 1.5 million casualties on its enemies. The same source asserted that in 224-223 BCE in its campaign against Chu, Qin put an army of 600,000 men into the field. Undoubtedly, the Qin military forces were very large and very effective, but the figures given for the size of its armies and the casualties they inflicted appear excessive.

In 256 BCE the remaining territory of the Zhou was annexed and the dynasty extinguished. Qin was now on the verge of becoming the dominant state, but its triumph was to be delayed for a generation. In those years three individuals emerged who were to play key roles in the final victory. The first was Han Fei, whose book the *Hanfeizi* contains the most coherent expression of the ideas of Legalism. Han Fei rejected Confucian idealization of the past, and accepted something of Mozi's utilitarian view of the function of the state. He also agreed with the idea of *wuwei* as expressed in the *Laozi,* arguing that if a state has effective laws, laws which reward the people for good behaviour and punish them severely for transgressions, then there is no need for the ruler to play an active role in government.

The second individual was a wealthy travelling merchant named Lü Buwei. When trading in the state of Zhao he had befriended Zichu, a son of the ruler of Qin, who had been sent there as a hostage. As a mark of his friendship he gave the prince his favourite concubine who, according to the account of Sima Qian, the Grand Historian, was already pregnant by Lü Buwei. The latter persuaded the heir to the Qin throne, who was childless, to accept Zichu as his heir. In quick succession the Qin ruler and his heir died, to be succeeded by Zichu, who himself died in 247 BCE after a reign of only three years. Zichu had appointed Lü Buwei as his chancellor and Lü continued in that post until 237 BCE, during the minority of King Zheng, who was supposedly his son. Lü Buwei strengthened Qin by encouraging the construction of canals and by sowing dissension between the other states. He was also a patron of the arts, commissioning a compilation known as the *Spring and Autumn Annals of Mr Lü,* which summarized existing knowledge on a wide variety of matters.

King Zheng took control in 238 BCE and shortly afterwards he learned that his mother, with the connivance of Lü Buwei, was having an affair with a man named Lao Ai. The latter raised a rebellion, which was crushed. Later Lü Buwei was dismissed and in 235 BCE he committed suicide.

By now Li Si had appeared on the scene. Whereas Han Fei was a theoretician, Li Si was a practical politician who had come to Qin because he considered that the career prospects in his native state of Chu were poor. He attached himself to Lü Buwei, and would probably have fallen with him had he not presented to King Zheng a key document entitled *Memorial on Annexation of Feudal States.*

In 231 BCE Qin started the series of campaigns that unified China and within a year it had defeated Han. The other states tried to form an alliance to resist Qin and in 227 BCE Yan sent an assassin, Jing Ke, to murder the Qin king. To gain an audience he took with him the head of a Yan general and a box containing a map of Yan and a dagger. In a dramatic scene, which became the subject of a famous Han-period tomb relief sculpture, he was overpowered before he could stab the king. The king's response was to attack Yan and annex the state. In 219 BCE, a friend of Jing Ke gained access to the court by becoming a musician, but failed to kill his victim. Finally, in 218 BCE Zhang Liang of Han, to avenge the defeat of his state, attempted to murder the king, but he attacked the wrong chariot. By then it was too late, for Qin had triumphed over all the states.

Daily life in China at the time of the Qin

In China, in the third century BCE, average temperatures were much colder than today, though the climate was warming up. In 238 BCE it was so cold that people froze to death. Three years later, there was a great drought and in 226 BCE there was a snowstorm with accumulations measured at two feet five inches.

By now much of the forest which once covered China had been felled and the timber extracted had been used for building and fuel. Deforestation had affected the climate and had also caused erosion and flooding, which increased the need for river control. Elephants and rhinoceroses, as well as tigers and leopards were still to be found in parts of central China. By this time, oxen were domesticated and used for ploughing, horses were harnessed to war chariots, and dogs were trained for hunting. Pigs, goats and poultry, including ducks and geese, were reared for food. Fishponds were maintained for rearing carp and other varieties of fish and turtles, frogs and snails were obtained from rivers and ponds.

The vast majority of the population of the state of Qin and that of the rest of China was engaged in agriculture. In the north of the country the main crops cultivated were millet, wheat, hemp and beans, including soya beans. According to the *Spring and Autumn Annals,* the land was ploughed several times to break up the soil and the farmer then dug a series of furrows four feet six inches apart. Seeds were scattered on the ridges between the furrows and after sprouting the seedlings were thinned out. Multicrop rotation was practised and fertilizers were used. Ploughing might be done using oxen, but all other agricultural tasks were performed by hand. Iron-tipped ploughs and iron tools were now in use, though still comparatively rare.

Qin inherited a very strict class structure from the Zhou period. A hierarchy of ranks descended from the Son of Heaven, the term used to denote the emperor, to the feudal lords, the ministers, the senior officials, the knights, and finally to the common people. The ranks above the upper stratum of knights belonged to the ruling class, those below, who comprised the vast majority of the population, belonged to the ruled class. The title system had twenty levels and had complex regulations relating to promotion. An individual's official status could rise or fall according to his accomplishments or failures, but the focus of the award of titles was on military merit in battle. Qin rulers attempted to replace status by birth with a ranking system entirely under their own control. However some titles remained hereditary and others could be purchased.

The ruled class included peasants, merchants, craftsmen, and slaves of various kinds. Although merchants were discriminated against, some of them achieved high status. Many craftsmen were employed in government-managed industries. They formed their own organizations and were responsible for training others in their crafts.

Slaves were either privately owned or owned by the government. Private slaves were bought and sold and regarded as property just like livestock. Government slaves included criminals and prisoners of war who were used as labourers. Some persons were born into slavery or into the condition of a serf. Others were designated bondsmen and bondswomen and lived under a variety of social and legal restrictions. Bondservants were often the children of poor families who had contracted debts to their masters. If the debts were not paid back within three years, they became permanent slaves. Many convicts, persons captured in wars and destitute people were used as forced labour on state projects. In the Zhou period slaves and servants had often been sacrificed at the time of their master's death. This practice had died out by the time of the Qin Empire, with the notable exception of Qin Shihuang's interment, when many of the labourers who had constructed his tomb were buried with him.

The family has traditionally been the core unit of Chinese society. The family name passes from generation to generation through the male line and the group is held together by the practice of ancestor worship and the obligations of filial piety. These ideas were strongly endorsed by Confucius, but for the Legalists the strength of the family was a challenge to the authority of the state. In the mid-fourth century BCE Lord Shang had ordered that second or later sons should live separately from their fathers when they were grown up and that only the first son could remain in the father's household. However, Qin law endorsed the importance of the bond between husband and wife and it regulated the dissolution of marriage. For a male to initiate a divorce was fairly simple, but women were not allowed to divorce husbands, and women who absconded were punished. The influence of Confucianism was apparent in the convention that childless widows could remarry, but widows with children were forever bound to their husband's family. A fragment of Qin law shows that a father could ask permission to punish a son for unfilial behaviour, but if he wished to kill or mutilate his son for his misconduct, he had to ask the state to carry out the penalty or risk severe punishment. The infanticide of a healthy child was prohibited, but the killing of a deformed newly-born child was not a crime.

A division of labour existed between men and women. According to the *Spring and Autumn Annals* a man did not weave and a wife did not plough. Under Qin law the value of the labour of men and women was assessed on different scales. In agricultural work, the labour of one male bondservant was equal to that of two women. This scale did not apply to textile work, particularly embroidery, where the value of the labour of a woman was regarded as equivalent to that of a man.

Not a great deal is known about the clothing worn by ordinary people at this time. Silk was used and there is a record of a brocade garment with a silk lining worn by a rankless person. Stone engravings of the later Han dynasty, depicting scenes during the Qin Empire, show persons of rank wearing long flowing robes, whereas male servants are dressed in close-fitting breeches and jackets and female servants wear skirts. The soldiers of the First Emperor's terracotta army display a variety of caps and hairstyles, in some cases their hair being plaited into complicated patterns. Models of dancers, musicians and acrobats display other styles of dress. Ordinary people wore clothes made from the fibre of hemp or from ramie grass.

In northern China the staple diet was a porridge made out of millet and wheat, barley, rice and red beans were also consumed. Soya beans and a wide variety of vegetables were grown and various roots, herbs, and fungi supplemented these. Meat was obtained from pigs, cattle, sheep, goats and dogs. Also on the menu were chickens, geese, pheasants and quail and fish, turtles, frogs and snails were eaten. At least four alcoholic beverages were brewed and drunk. Sophisticated recipes were devised for consumption by the rich. Ribs of fatted ox and stewed turtle, and roast kid with yam sauce are among the dishes mentioned in contemporary poetry. Cooking vessels were made of bronze or pottery, with precise regulation of which vessels should be used to cook which dishes.

The main principles of Chinese medicine had been established long before the Qin Empire was founded. The basic cause of illness was held to be an imbalance between the forces of *yin* and *yang* and the way to maintain health was to prevent an imbalance occurring. This involved personal hygiene, appropriate diet and various exercises. If illness did occur, two main forms of therapy were available. One was the use of acupuncture or moxibustion (the burning of the herb mugwort) to restore the body's balance. The other was the use of drugs derived from the Chinese materia medica. Knowledge of herbs with antimalarial qualities indicates the presence of malaria, but diseases such as smallpox had not yet reached China.

In 1973 seven medical manuscripts were found in a tomb at Mawangdui in Hunan. These texts, which date from 168 BCE, contain discussions of physiological theories and pathology, recipe manuals for the treatment of ailments, and sexual treatises and hygienic exercises. In the remnants of Qin law that have survived there is a reference to a woman who specialized in gynaecology, clear evidence that the practice of medicine was a recognized profession.

In the Warring States period each state had had as its centre a walled town of some size, which functioned both as an administrative and as a trading centre. When military expeditions were dispatched to extend Qin control to other parts of China, one of their tasks was to establish new commanderies, military areas which centred on walled towns. It is difficult to estimate the population of these towns. It was claimed in 323 BCE that the capital of the state of Qi had a population of over 350,000 individuals, but this was a gross over-estimate. Apart from Xianyang and a few important provincial cities, for example Taiyuan in present-day Shanxi, which became a key point in the defence of northern China against incursions of nomadic peoples, most towns probably only had a population of a few thousand persons.

The Qin capital was at Xianyang, about twelve miles northwest of present-day Xi'an. The city was surrounded by a wall thiteen miles long. Excavations have revealed the remains of two palaces, several tombs and many buildings with tiled roofs. The most significant architectural remains found at Xianyang are those of the palaces. Palace site number 1, built on very high and large compressed earth platforms, extended over a site 197 feet long and 150 feet wide. It had symmetrical partitions, hallways, stairs, and gateways. Around its four sides were bays paved with bricks and under the eaves there were aprons made of river pebbles with underground ditches leading to water mains. The walls and floors of the rooms were plastered with wattle and daub and the surfaces painted red and white. About 330 feet to the southwest was palace site number 2. Its buildings included a long corridor with walls decorated with multi-coloured murals depicting ceremonial processions, human figures and plants.

Qin Shihuang, the first Qin emperor, not content with the palace his ancestors had built at Xianyang, ordered the construction of a new palace south of the river within the Shanglin Park. This became known as the Ebang, or nearby, palace. According to the *Historical Records*, the front section measured 500 paces from east to west and 500 feet from north to south. The terraces above could seat 10,000 people and there was room inside for banners fifty feet high. A labour force of more than 700,000 was drafted to build the palace and the emperor's mausoleum, which was constructed at the same time. Historians have questioned the recorded dimensions of the palace. They note that a throne room which has been excavated at Luoyang, which likewise was said to be able to accommodate 10,000 persons, only measured 262 feet by 52 feet. However, the Ebang palace project was certainly vast and the costs incurred in its construction, which was continued by the Second Emperor, are considered as one of the reasons for the fall of the empire.

In the Warring States period considerable progress had been made in the acquisition of scientific knowledge and the development of technology. By the fourth century BCE Chinese astronomers had estimated the length of the year to be 365¼ days. An observation of Halley's comet was noted in 240 BCE and by that time a systematic record of eclipses was being kept. Chinese pharmacologists knew about ephedra, a vegetable alkaloid used to treat asthma, iodine-rich seaweed for goitre, and ergot, a rye fungus, for uterine difficulties during childbirth. Other notable advances included the development of mathematical concepts, for example the concept of minus numbers. In terms of technology, compasses, the carpenter's square, the plumb line, gear wheels, and the steelyard (a balance with arms of unequal length) were all in use.

Under the Qin and subsequently under the Han scientific and technological progress continued. Among the notable achievements were astronomical observations of 'halo phenomena' (the variety of haloes which appear around the sun). Cartography had been developed and Qin Shihuang, the First Emperor, ordered that all the maps depicting his empire should be assembled.

The Qin state, and subsequently the Qin Empire, was directly involved in the production of iron. The manufacture of cast iron went back to the fifth century BCE, centuries before the technique was discovered in Europe. The conquest of the state of Shu resulted in Qin control of the best ironworking centres in the country. Regulations were enacted relating to the quality and quantity of iron produced, and officials who failed to maintain the standard required were subject to punishment. Iron objects, for example plough shares, were made from cast iron.

Under the Qin Empire important advances were made in the construction of canals. Two important canal systems were developed for irrigation. One was the Dujiang Weir project constructed in Sichuan province by Li Bing, a magistrate appointed by the Qin in 250 BCE. This system took water from the Min River and using gravity distributed it over 62 miles before returning the residue of its water to the main stream. A sophisticated system of dredging and flushing out sediment was used to prevent the system silting up. An expanded and updated version of this system is still in operation today. Another large-scale irrigation project was the Zheng Guo canal in present-day Shaanxi. Started in 246 BCE, it took heavily silt-laden water from the Jing River to the Luo River along a contour line and released water into the fields below. This system later silted up and fell into disuse.

Canals were also constructed to carry men and goods. The most famous example was the 'magic canal', engineered in 219 BCE. This canal, which still exists, is the oldest contour canal in the world. A three-mile-long cut was made through mountains to link a southern tributary of the Yangzi River with a northern tributary of the West River. The water from the river which flowed north was divided and carried along an embankment, creating a canal which was ten feet wide and three feet deep. There were thirty-six lock gates on this section of the canal. It was used to send grain south to support military campaigns and reached its peak traffic in the Former Han period, when it was used to carry troops to support the campaign against the Yue ethnic minority.

Law in the Qin Empire derived from the code formulated by Lord Shang. This had two main principles, the first of which was mutual responsibility, which meant that the lower classes were organized into groups of five or ten men who were mutually responsible for each other and obliged to denounce each other's crimes. The second principle, which was a central tenet of Legalism (the doctrine which argued that the interests of the state were paramount and that the way to control the population was to use rewards and punishments), was that the law should be so severe that no one would dare to violate it.

In 1975 the grave of a Qin official was found near Wuhan which was dated to 217 BCE. It contained a collection of 1,155 bamboo strips, 612 of which dealt with legal and administrative matters. One group of texts contained eighteen statutes referring to agriculture, stables and parks, granaries, currency and artisans. Another group comprised a series of questions and answers referring to the statutes. The statutes and the questions and answers relating to them indicate that the Qin legal system covered a very wide range of activities and that it was very sophisticated. The punishments recommended were not as severe as the reputation of Qin law might have led one to expect. Capital and mutilating punishments including tattooing were prescribed, but often the penalty for a crime was not a physical punishment, but a fine of suits of armour or shields.

Under the Qin two main forms of taxation were levied: the *fu*, the obligation to perform military service, which might be commuted or extended into various forms of poll tax, and the *zu*, taxes on the use of land and revenues derived from state monopolies. The demands for military and labour service and for state revenue were very high. According to a hostile account written a century later the exactions for frontier military service and for public labour were thirty times higher than in antiquity, and the land taxes, poll taxes and the profit margin on the production of salt and iron were twenty times greater than in the past. As a result of these taxes, farmers became impoverished and many abandoned their land. The Second Emperor imposed yet more taxes. Li Si, the chief minister, remonstrated with him about high taxation and the cost of building the Ebang palace. By that time rebellions, which in part may be ascribed to the harshness of the Qin fiscal system, had broken out leading to the end of the empire in 206 BCE.

The Rise and Fall of the Qin Dynasty, 221-206 BCE

In 221 King Zheng of Qin, having defeated the other six states, assumed the title of Qin Shihuang, the First Emperor of Qin. It was suggested to him that the newly-acquired territories should be distributed to a feudal nobility, but in an outspoken document, *Memorial on Annexation of Feudal States*, his chief minister Li Si opposed the idea. The emperor accepted his advice and the empire was divided into thirty-six commanderies and prefectures under officials appointed by central government. The emperor's and Li Si's distrust of those who served them was apparent in the arrangement in which military and civil authority was separated and a third supervisory official was appointed to each commandery, thus initiating a pattern of control through division of authority which survived through the imperial period.

After the conquest, 120,000 powerful and rich families were removed from the various states to Xianyang where they were kept under surveillance. Vast quantities of weapons belonging to these families and from all over the empire were confiscated and melted down to make bells, bell stands and twelve enormous statues. City fortifications and military constructions were levelled.

Qin Shihuang continued his drive for territorial expansion. The Qin conquered the Ordos region to the north and subjugated the Xiongnu. Chinese colonists were sent to establish a Qin presence in the region. Expeditions were sent south to modern Guangdong, Guangxi and Fujian, and settlers were sent or deported to colonize those regions. On other occasions assisted and enforced migration of families took place, either with the intention of consolidating Qin control or as a form of punishment. In 219 BCE Qin Shihuang ordered 30,000 families to move to the coast of Shandong. In return, they were given 12 years exemption from labour services. In 214 BCE in conjunction with military campaigns, convicts were sent as settlers to areas in the north and south. Later records refer to disgraced officials and fugitive peasants sent to colonize areas recently conquered.

In the Zhou period several states including Qin had constructed defensive walls to separate the agrarian population from the pastoral peoples to the north. Under the Qin Empire a much more ambitious programme of wall building was undertaken. According to Sima Qian, construction of a 'great wall' was begun by General Meng Tian in 221 BCE. This wall extended from Lintao in present-day Gansu to Liaodong, a distance of more than 3,000 miles. It took ten years to build and required the labour of 300,000 workers. Meng Tian's wall probably joined up or improved some of the earthen walls already in existence. Its course ran well to the north of that of the present Great Wall, which dates from the Ming period. The task of constructing the Qin wall, which involved complex logistics to supply the labour force with food and materials as the wall was extended, was enormous. Its route crossed long stretches of mountains and deserts, areas with only a sparse population. Although no account of the construction has survived, it may be assumed that the death toll among the labourers working on the wall was very heavy.

In 220 BCE Qin Shihuang ordered the construction of a series of imperial highways radiating from the capital

Xianyang. These roads, known as speedways, were described as being fifty Chinese double paces wide. Eight years later Meng Tian was ordered to build the Straight Road, a north-south highway from Xianyang, crossing the Yellow River and extending to Wuyuan in Inner Mongolia, a distance of about 500 miles. This road was intended to facilitate the supply of troops operating on the frontier. It has been estimated that Qin imperial highways were over 4,000 miles in length, considerably longer than the road system of imperial Rome. The roads, which were not usually paved, were constructed by cutting through hills and filling ravines or bridging rivers. Some roads which passed through mountainous regions, for example the road which crossed the mountain range which separates the modern provinces of Shaanxi and Sichuan, included long sections on wooden trestles constructed over the beds of roaring torrents, or suspended from wooden brackets driven into the cliff face above.

After the conquest Li Si, Qin Shihuang's chief minister, embarked on a series of measures which applied Legalist principles to the new state. A major effort was made to standardize weights and measures. Cups for measuring grain with seven capacities, and nine weights for use with a balance, have been found. Each cup or weight bore an inscription indicating that it had been made in compliance with the imperial edict. The width of axles was also regulated, so that the wheels of carts would fit the ruts on the roads. The correct length and width of a piece of hemp cloth was defined and cloth of poor quality was not to be traded. There was also a standardization of metal currency. Gold and copper coins were minted, but the common currency in use was a round bronze coin with a square hole, the shape which was to become standard for the next two thousand years. These measures encouraged commerce, although the emperor shared the prejudice of Legalists in favour of agriculture and against merchants, who on occasions were rounded up and settled in distant regions.

The *Historical Records* state that Li Si carried out a reform of the written language, that he 'equalized the written characters, and made these universal throughout the empire'. The probable meaning of this is that a group of scholars under Li Si's direction developed the standard script known as the Small Seal, which was used in official communications. At the same time many characters were suppressed because they had become obsolete. In the late Zhou the written languages of the various states had diverged considerably. As a consequence communication had become more difficult and the differences between the various states had become more apparent. Under the Qin Empire the standardization of the scripts used and of the characters recognized was a prerequisite for administrative efficiency and cultural unity. The Small Seal script was used for the inscriptions on the seven stone stelae erected in various parts of the empire to record the journeys made by the emperor, inscriptions which may have been composed by Li Si.

These journeys, or imperial tours, undertaken by Qin Shihuang were an important feature of his style of government. His first tour, made in 220 BCE, took him from Xianyang to southern Gansu, a distance of 300 miles. The following year he went to Shandong and on the sacred mountain, Mount Tai, he performed the *feng* sacrifice, at which he announced to heaven the glory of his dynasty. The next three tours all went to the coast, and on the last one, which was to present-day Zhejiang, he died. As part of the propaganda associated with these tours, the emperor ordered the erection of the seven stone stelae mentioned above, to record the achievements of his reign and the principles on which it was based. The inscriptions on the stones reminded the people that the emperor had brought peace to the land, had encouraged agriculture and had appointed upright officials to manage the affairs of his empire. He did not claim personal credit for these achievements, but instead invoked the genealogy of the Qin rulers, declaring that he was the descendant of many kings.

Although Legalist ideas appeared to be in the ascendant under the Qin, nevertheless Qin Shihuang, the First Emperor, continued to represent himself as a sage ruler in the Confucian mould and to cite Confucian morality as a guide to his actions. He was also deeply interested in cosmology and in particular in the theoretical concept of the Five Elements. As the Zhou dynasty had been associated with the element of fire, the Qin dynasty was identified with the element which fire does not overcome, namely water, and also with the colour black and the number six. In all garments black became the dominant colour and in measurements six was taken as the basis of calculation. Official caps had to be six inches tall, and carriages had to be drawn by six horses.

Qin Shihuang was also interested in Daoism. Daoists were much concerned with the search for the elixir of immortality. On his tours around the empire Qin

Shihuang dispatched people to collect herbs believed to grant immortality, and he sent an expedition to the island of Penglai, where immortals were believed to reside. He went three times to Langyai on the coast of Shandong and worshipped at temples dedicated to the god of the four seasons and to the lord of the sun.

The emperor's relationship with scholars was a difficult one. In 213 BCE a scholar cited the historical record to criticize the emperor for having accepted Li Si's recommendation with regard to feudal fiefs. In response Li Si presented a memorial to the emperor suggesting that scholars, other than those attached to the court, should surrender all historical records other than those of Qin and that these should be burned. Copies of works such as the *Book of Songs* and the *Book of Documents* were collected and destroyed, but the destruction was by no means complete and many books, in particular treatises on technical, medical and literary subjects, were spared the holocaust. If that incident was not enough to earn Qin Shihuang the enduring disapproval of Confucian scholars, the action he allegedly took in the following year certainly was. Having heard that certain scholars were criticizing him, he ordered that more than 460 of them should be buried alive. Descriptions of both these events are given in the account written by Sima Qian a century later. The truth of the allegations is uncertain and the latter incident may never have happened.

Even before he became emperor, Qin Shihuang had started to plan his tomb. Construction began in 212 BCE or earlier, at a site thirty miles east of Xianyang. The mausoleum consisted of an earthen mound, 385 yards long and 380 yards wide. The mound has eroded and at present it is 149 feet high, but at the time of its construction it would have been considerably higher. At the centre of the mound is a vast burial chamber. The mausoleum has been raided on at least two occasions, the first of which was within five years of the emperor's death. It has yet to be excavated completely.

According to the description written by Sima Qian a century later, the building of the tomb required the labour of 700,000 men. It contained a model of the empire that had rivers and seas of quicksilver, or mercury, and a mechanism for operating the tides. Candles made of whale fat lighted the tomb and it incorporated booby traps to shoot intruders. To guard its secrets all the designers and workers involved in its construction were also entombed. Soil samples taken recently from the vicinity of the tomb contain a high concentration of mercury, which lends support to one part of Sima Qian's description.

In 1974, some peasants digging a well 1,300 yards east of the outer wall of the mausoleum found some large fragments of pottery and some fragments of bronze weapons. This led to one of the most exciting archaeological discoveries of all time. Excavations uncovered four vast pits, three of which contained life-size terracotta figures of soldiers. The largest pit, which has an area of about 15,120 square yards, was filled with an army of 7,500 foot soldiers. The second largest pit contained 1,400 chariots and mounted soldiers. In the third pit were the officers of the headquarters of these formations. The fourth pit was empty, indicating that this part of the mausoleum had been left incomplete.

Each of the terracotta figures was distinctive and unique and each was painted in vivid colours that have now faded. From the varying physical features, it was apparent that some of the men depicted came from minority ethnic groups. The terracotta army has provided a vast amount of information about military matters at this time. The weapons carried by its soldiers included halberds, spears, crossbows and swords. They wore at least seven different styles of armour. War chariots drawn by four horses and carrying three men were used to direct the foot soldiers, who were supported by formations of bowmen and crossbowmen and units of cavalry.

In 210 BCE Qin Shihuang travelled to the coast of modern Shandong, where in response to a dream he hunted and shot a large fish. Shortly afterwards he fell ill and died. In an attempt to manipulate the situation, Li Si and Zhao Gao, the eunuch chief minister of Qin, concealed his death by keeping his body in the sleeping-carriage and disguising the smell by surrounding it with carts loaded with salted fish. By this means they procured the succession of a younger son, who became the Second Emperor.

The Second Emperor set out to rule as his father had done. In a famous memorial Li Si advised him about 'supervising and holding responsible', a method of control advocated by the Legalists. But very quickly things began to go wrong. Discontent had arisen over the heavy taxes levied to complete the Ebang palace. Before the new emperor had been on the throne a year a rebellion headed by Chen Sheng and Wu Guang, two poor farmers, had broken out in the former state of Chu. Less than a year later other uprisings had occurred and Chen Sheng's forces were within 30 miles of the capital. At court Zhao Gao intrigued against Li Si, who was executed by being cut in two at the market-place at Xianyang. Zhao Gao's political ascendancy increased to such an extent that in 207 BCE he was able to force the Second Emperor to go into retirement and then to commit suicide. Two months later the new emperor had Zhao Gao killed, but by then the empire was lost and he was forced to submit to Liu Bang, one of the rebel leaders, who became the first emperor of the Former Han dynasty.

After the Qin Empire

A century after the fall of the Qin, the poet and statesman Jia Yi wrote an essay entitled 'The Faults of Qin', an analysis of the reasons for the precipitous fall of the Qin dynasty. Jia Yi criticized Qin Shihuang for his overweening ambition, his disregard for the ways of former kings, and in particular for his burning of the books. Having pacified and fortified the empire he had supposed that it would last ten thousand generations. But the Qin Empire had a fatal flaw: it was not ruled with humanity and righteousness and it was this which enabled Chen Sheng and others to overthrow it. In recent years Marxist historians have emphasized the role of poor peasants in the fall of the dynasty, describing their rebellion as the first great popular revolt in Chinese history. Western historians have suggested that the dynasty fell because of a combination of factors, including the moral shortcomings of its rulers, the discontent brought about by their policies, and the magnitude of the task they attempted.

Although the Qin Empire only lasted for fifteen years, it left an enduring legacy. Major innovations had occurred in the fields of administration, communications, laws, writing and many other matters. From the time of the Qin, there was an expectation that China should be a unified empire, an expectation which was to survive long periods when the empire disintegrated into a number of separate states. The Han Empire built on the achievements of Qin and became one of the great centres of civilization in the ancient world, rivalling the achievements of the Roman Empire with which it was contemporaneous.

Bibliography

Caroline Blunden and Mark Elvin, *A Cultural Atlas of China* (2nd edition, Fact on File Inc., 1998)

K C Chang and Pingfang Xu, *The Formation of Chinese Civilization: An Archaeological Perspective* (Yale University Press, 2005)

Jonathan Clements, *The First Emperor of China* (Sutton Publishing, 2006)

★Arthur Cotterell, Alan Hills and Geoffrey Brightling, *Ancient China* (Dorling Kindersley Eyewitness Books, 2005)

A F P Hulsewe, *Remnants of Ch'in Law* (E J Brill, 1985)

Terry Kleeman & Tracy Barrett, *The Ancient Chinese World* (Oxford University Press, 2005)

Mark Edward Lewis, *The Early Chinese Empires: Qin and Han* (Belknap Press, 2007)

BIBLIOGRAPHY

Xueqin Li, trans. K C Chang, *Eastern Zhou and Qin Civilizations* (Yale University Press, 1985)

Michael Loewe and Edward L Shaughnessy, *The Cambridge History of Ancient China: From the Origins of Civilization to 221 BC* (Cambridge University Press, 1999)

*Jane O'Connor, *The Emperor's Silent Army: Terracotta Warriors of Ancient China* (Viking, 2002)

*Edward L Shaughnessy, *Ancient China: Myth and Art* (Duncan Baird, 2005)

Robert L Thorp, *China in the Early Bronze Age: Shang Civilization* (University of Pennsylvania Press, 2005)

*Jianwei Wang, *Ancient Civilization of China* (Mason Crest, 2006)

Frances Wood, *The First Emperor of China* (Profile Books Ltd, 2007)

* suitable for younger readers

CLEFT PALATE
AND SPEECH

BY

MURIEL E. MORLEY
D.Sc., F.C.S.T., F.A.C.S.T.

Formerly Speech Therapist-in-Charge of the Speech
Therapy Unit, the United Newcastle upon Tyne
Teaching Hospitals and the Newcastle upon Tyne
Hospital Management Committee Group; Lecturer
in Speech and Speech Pathology, King's College,
Durham University, now the University of Newcastle
upon Tyne.

SEVENTH EDITION

CHURCHILL LIVINGSTONE
EDINBURGH LONDON AND NEW YORK
1970

CHURCHILL LIVINGSTONE
Medical Division of Longman Group

Distributed in the United States of America by Longman Inc., 19 West 44th Street, N.Y. 10036, and by associated companies, branches and representatives throughout the world.

ISBN 0 443 00697 0

First Edition	1945
Second Edition	1951
Third Edition	1954
Fourth Edition	1958
Fifth Edition	1962
Sixth Edition	1966
Reprinted	1967
Seventh Edition	1970
Reprinted	1973
Reprinted	1975
Reprinted	1979

Printed in Great Britain by
T. & A. Constable Ltd., Edinburgh

FOREWORD

By Professor T. Pomfret Kilner, C.B.E., F.R.C.S.
Late Nuffield Professor of Plastic Surgery, University of Oxford

Mr Battle, in his foreword to the first edition of this excellent book, stressed the importance of a close liaison between surgeon and speech therapist. It gives me pleasure to welcome the second edition with some remarks on the surgeon's role in the production of good speech in patients afflicted with cleft lip and palate deformities. I link these two conditions because I think it is un-practical to separate them and because they are so frequently associated. The surgeon who undertakes treatment in early infancy should realise fully the immense responsibility he is shouldering for by his efforts a whole life may be made or marred. He should have before him the clear-cut objectives of making his patient look well, eat well and speak well. Of these, there can be little doubt that the last is the most important. A patient may do well in life without good looks: the dental surgeon can do much to correct deficient masticatory function: but without clear speech few will proceed far and the best efforts of the most expert speech therapist will be of no avail if the palate has been ruined by ill-planned or badly executed surgical procedures.

A cleft confined to the soft palate presents a relatively simple problem, yet it is in just these cases that the in-experienced surgeon often fails to provide a mechanism capable of producing good speech. His attention is con-centrated on the cleft itself and he fails to see the often large oronasal pharyngeal isthmus which the repaired palate will be called upon to close. He carries out a simple approximation procedure; he sometimes reduces tension on his suture line by fracturing the hamular processes and so reducing the pull of the tensor palati muscles; but he fails to produce any retroposition of the soft palate as a whole. These "simple" cases offer the best possible material for the provision of good speech and if operation is carried out on the lines described in this book and at a time before the imperfect speech mechanism has been employed and camouflage speech habits developed, there should be no need for speech training other than that available in the child's own family circle. There is little or no disturbance of tooth-development and any associated pre-alveolar lip cleft is readily repaired before or at the same time as the palate cleft. If speech therapy is required it will be concerned only with those defects dependent upon insufficiency of the oronasal sphincter.

At the other end of the scale of these deformities is the complete bilateral cleft of lip, gum and palate associated with gross skeletal deformity. Treatment in these cases is a multi-stage affair. Repair of one lip cleft and the floor of the nose (the anterior part of the hard palate cleft) reduces the condition to one of unilateral complete cleft. Repair of the other cleft on similar lines brings the case into line with the ordinary cleft palate. In most cases, however, some degree of skeletal deformity persists and partly as a result of this and partly as the result of unavoidable surgical trauma, teeth erupt irregularly and scar tissue contraction may make it difficult to obtain the requisite degree of retroposition to provide efficient oronasal "sphincteric" control. If, however, the remaining cleft is closed satisfactorily and with effective retroposition, speech should be good. In these cases, early and expert speech therapy may well make all the difference between success and failure. It is in these cases, too, that the orthodontist can give valuable help in correcting mal-position of teeth, thus improving both masticatory function and speech

Victor Veau produced radiographic evidence that there exist cases in which the conformation and dimensions of the pharynx make it well-nigh impossible to provide satisfactory oronasal closure with the palatal material available for repair. He went so far as to suggest that these cases could be diagnosed by X-ray examination and useless operation thus avoided. It is my belief, however, that careful and radical operation followed by expert speech therapy will give, even in such cases, a worth-while speech result.

The speech therapist should always be on the lookout for the submucous cleft of the palate for this is as serious a cause of defective speech as the complete cleft and calls for the same kind of surgical treatment. Usually discovered late, it almost always calls for full co-operation between surgeon and speech therapist if troublesome speech habits are to be eradicated.

The production of good speech in cleft palate cases cannot be considered a purely surgical task. The surgeon who is prepared to realise the responsibility he is accepting may reasonably take charge of the case in the beginning and aim at producing the best possible speech mechanism by the time that mechanism is required. He should, in my opinion, provide his own follow-up, training himself to diagnose faults in speech as soon as they appear and, working in the closest possible co-operation with his speech-therapist colleague, should show no hesitation whatever about handing a case over for expert speech assessment and, if necessary, training.

The demonstration to speech therapy students of the original condition of the cleft palate infant and their observation of actual operations has done much to stimulate this desirable co-operation. A further step in the right direction will have been taken when the review of all treated cases is a combined affair. The speech therapist should be the best judge of the speech result and should be in a position to indicate what defects can and what cannot be overcome by speech therapy: the surgeon, on the other hand, can indicate what further surgical measures are possible or advisable to provide the improvement for which both are striving.

OXFORD, 1951.

FOREWORD TO THE FIRST EDITION

By RICHARD BATTLE, M.Chir. (Cantab.), F.R.C.S.(Eng.).

A GREAT change has been seen in British surgery of the last twenty years. The adoption of efficient follow-up systems has meant that the surgeon's failures now live with him and cannot be forgotten or relegated to another sphere. They return to him or to his colleagues as a symbol of inexperience, or possibly of incompetence. The examination of these results has led to many advances in treatment, and the speech therapist has been to the cleft palate surgeon of the same value as an efficient follow-up system has been to surgery in general.

Miss Morley has written a book on the surgery of cleft palate that is particularly valuable in that it cements the association between surgeon and speech therapist. She enables each to understand the work of the other; and the value of her book will surely lie here just as much as in the wealth of information between its covers. Moreover, she has had the advantage of working with Mr Wardill for several years and has seen more of the practical side of palate surgery than have the majority of speech therapists. She would have failed in her duty had she not imparted her knowledge for the benefit of those of us who are attempting to solve this difficult problem.

Why is the problem difficult? Firstly, there are several different conceptions of the physiology of speech. Secondly, there may be numerous means at our disposal for the closure of a palate cleft but the results of these have never been fully investigated and co-ordinated. Thirdly, too few surgeons with an interest in the condition have a real knowledge of cleft palate speech. Miss Morley helps us to understand the mechanism of oronasal closure, teaches us to analyse our speech results and advocates a method that produces not only a sound anatomical result but also an excellent functional one. From her experience she endorses the claim put forward by the author of this method that by operating correctly at a suitable age, we may assure the development of normal speech and that, in consequence, the need for such therapy in these cases will eventually disappear.

The reader of this book will find his conception of cleft palate surgery greatly clarified and, possibly, revolutionised. He should remember that the author knows the facts and has studied the results. Veau was perfectly correct when he said:—

"La chirurgie ne vit pas que d'idées. Les faits seul doivent guider nos opinions et rester toujours les arguments de nos discussions."

PREFACE TO THE SEVENTH EDITION

FROM ITS first publication in 1945 the aim of this book has been to describe the causes of defective speech due to cleft palate and to provide practical suggestions for their treatment. An outline of the embryology, anatomy, surgery, orthodontics and prosthetics is presented to help the student and the clinician in speech pathology to understand the condition more fully and to enable him to amplify his knowledge of these subjects according to his interest and need.

The second aim continues to be to provide information which will help all those concerned in the management of this condition to understand something of the outlook and work of the others and so to assist in the total care of, and for the benefit of the patient.

It must also be remembered that it is written by a speech pathologist who does not and would not attempt responsibility for the description of the work of those who are expert in the other associated professional fields or for describing their work in all its detail. Each has a major contribution to make to the health, appearance and well-being of the patient, with all the obvious emotional implications relating to the condition.

There is at present much discussion as to the value of bone grafting. This was mentioned in the sixth edition but as the author has no direct experience of this procedure it is in no way treated fully here.

Further information has been included concerning the physiology of nasopharyngeal closure as described recently by Fritzell using cineradiography and electroencephalography, and its direct visual study by the Taub panendoscope. This can be used for direct observation or for sight-sound motion photography and does not interfere with the oral movements for articulation. Lateral cineradiography is not fully adequate as it indicates only action in two planes, in the pharynx (antero-posterior at the level of focus).

Pharyngeal flap surgical procedures have been described more fully and the surgical procedure, as practiced by Braithwaite, has been amplified and illustrated with diagrams. It is freely admitted that this is the operative technique which has provided the speech results of which the writer has had the most experience. This experience now covers the last 20 years. The speech results have been assessed critically and are the result of continuous observations at the followup clinic. Detailed results are presented on 360 children operated upon between 1949 and 1960, as summarised in 1961 and again in 1968. In this last assessment I have been helped by information provided by Miss Elisabeth Piercy, L.C.S.T., who has now succeeded me in charge of speech pathology at the cleft palate clinic at the Fleming Memorial Hospital, Newcastle upon Tyne, where this surgery is carried out. Experience of the results of other surgical procedures, even when one has travelled in countries in the world other than one's own, is naturally limited but I have not found any other consistent speech results which equal the ones described as the result of this operation. It is thought that this is mainly due to the freeing of the lateral pharyngeal walls, their inward displacement allowing the two halves of the soft palate to meet freely in the midline before suture and the muscle transplant of fibres of the superior constrictor from the medial pterygoid lamina into the palatal aponeurosis, with the identification and suture of the levator muscle fibres. The results would seem to justify a more detailed description of this surgical method in this edition.

The literature on this subject has increased enormously over recent years and continues to increase. Much of it is extremely valuable. However, I have endeavoured to maintain this as a small hand-book, indicating the most important trends which could suggest the further study in greater depth of many of the aspects of cleft palate management. Much that could have been included has therefore been excluded.

Again my thanks are due to the publishers, E. & S. Livingstone.

M. E. MORLEY.

ROTHBURY, NORTHUMBERLAND, 1970.

PREFACE TO THE FIRST EDITION

IT HAS been estimated that cleft palate and lip tends to occur approximately once in every 1,000 births. Peron, in Paris, gives the figures as 1 in 942 births, whilst Staige Davis, in America, finds the incidence to be 1 in 915 births (excluding negroes, where it is less frequent than in white races). In Denmark, Fogh-Anderson finds a somewhat higher incidence of 1.5 per thousand births, but taking into account the greater mortality among deformed infants, he acknowledges that the frequency of occurrence in the living population will be somewhat lower. It tends to occur somewhat more frequently in boys than in girls. Warren B. Davis in America gives the proportion in a series of cases as 56% boys and 44% girls. In one series of 252 cases in Newcastle upon Tyne, 55% were boys and 45% girls, whilst in 500 cases operated upon by Veau in Paris, 52% and 48% was the proportion of boys to girls. It occasionally occurs more than once in the same family. In the 252 cases in the Newcastle series it occurred twice in three families. In one family two boys, in another two girls, and in a third a boy and a girl were born with cleft palates.

Very little is known as to the cause of congenital clefts of the palate and lip, though various suggestions have been put forward, including heredity and physiological deficiency, and many mothers attribute it to some shock experienced during pregnancy. However, in these cases it is generally found that the alleged shock occurred after the tenth week of embryo life, by which time the processes involved should have been united. Staige Davis, Warren B. Davis, also

C. H. Schroder have investigated this question, and agree in thinking that heredity plays an important part in the occurrence of these clefts, although the defect in the family history is not necessarily a cleft palate, and may have been some other congenital malformation such as spina bifida, club foot, or absence of upper lateral incisor teeth (W. B. Davis). Other factors examined by Staige Davis include the age of the mother, her mentality and health, extreme difference in age of parents, their social status and environment, but he points out that there is insufficient evidence to show that any of these have a determining influence on the incidence of cleft palate.

In many cases the treatment of cleft palate requires the co-operation of the surgeon, dental surgeon and speech therapist, in spite of the fact that it is the objective of the specialist in cleft palate surgery to obviate the need for speech training. In a large proportion of cases this is now an accomplished fact, and those children submitted to successful operation before faulty speech habits have been allowed to develop acquire normal speech during natural growth without other special aid. However, until these ideal conditions become universal there will be those cases where operative procedures have been delayed, and for whom surgery alone is insufficient for the achievement of normal speech. In such cases the speech result obtained by the patient with the assistance of the speech therapist will depend to a great extent on the operative result obtained by the surgeon, and the latter will be unable to see the final result of his treatment until speech re-education has been completed.

It has been my good fortune to work for over six years under Mr W. E. M. Wardill, F.R.C.S., of Newcastle upon Tyne, who has done so much to further the progress of cleft palate surgery, and in carrying out speech therapy in connection with his cases, I owe more than I can tell to his interest, enthusiasm and guidance. In writing this book, I have tried to describe for the student of speech therapy what I have myself found interesting and useful in the study and treatment of these cases. I have, therefore, included chapters on the development of the face and the mouth in embryo, explaining the occurrence of congenital clefts of lip and palate, on the anatomy and physiology of the oropharyngeal mechanism involved in speech, and an outline story of the development of cleft palate surgery. In this connection I have tried to present the salient features in the principal methods of operation with special emphasis on the means adopted to improve the speech result.

A chapter on the development of speech has been included in an attempt to show the deviation from normal which occurs in this process in a child with a cleft palate, and to describe the way in which the speech defects associated with this malformation arise.

The suggestions for treatment are those which I myself have used and found helpful in my work with cases of cleft palate, including that carried out at the Speech Therapy Clinic at the Royal Victoria Infirmary, Newcastle upon Tyne. Some of these suggestions are original, others are in common use amongst those doing similar work, and for other ideas I am indebted to those who have published their methods, and whose help I gratefully acknowledge in the list of authorities in the bibliography.

In all work with these cases much time and patience is required. Although faulty sounds can be corrected, speech itself cannot be taught as one might teach addition or subtraction. It is rather a process of gradual development along normal lines, accompanied by a progressive elimination of the faulty habits acquired before operation. Every case of cleft palate is unique and a separate problem presenting a varying combination of difficulties, personal and otherwise. For this reason no two cases can be treated exactly alike. In presenting suggestions for treatment, it is impossible to avoid generalisations, but it will be found in practice that not all are required or found to be of use in every case. What is helpful to one patient is of no use to another, and experiments must be made, and exercises and treatment chosen which are suited to the age, interest and speech ability of the patient. Interest in speech must be aroused and sustained, fatigue and disappointment avoided.

Twenty-three case histories are quoted to demonstrate special points which may arise in connection with treatment. These cases were not all operated upon by the same surgeon, but all received operative treatment after faulty speech habits had developed. In some cases there had been one or more previous operations, rendering further surgical treatment difficult; others were classed by the surgeon as surgical failures.

In conclusion, again I would acknowledge my indebtedness to Mr W. E. M. Wardill for his help, and for the many opportunities he had given me to acquire knowledge on this subject. I am also grateful to him for reading the text of this manuscript, and for his constructive and very helpful criticisms.

I also wish to thank Mr Richard Battle, F.R.C.S., of St. Thomas's Hospital, London, for his interest and help whilst investigating the results of cleft palate surgery in Newcastle, and for some valuable suggestions in connection with this book.

To Miss M. W. Ferrie, F.C.S.T., of Liverpool, I would also express my gratitude for her stimulating enthusiasm, and for the privilege of observing her treatment of these cases; again for a reading of this book in manuscript, for her criticisms, and for permission to include some of her useful and original suggestions.

I am also indebted to those Speech Therapists who so kindly allowed me to visit their clinics and see their cases, and to Miss Cummings, late Matron of the Babies' Hospital, Blagdon Hall, Newcastle upon Tyne, for information concerning the methods adopted for artificial feeding in cases of cleft palate.

Finally, I wish to thank Dr Anne H. McAllister of Glasgow, for her assistance in the preparation of this book for publication.

The greater part of this work was originally approved by the British Society of Speech Therapists, now incorporated in the College of Speech Therapists, as a thesis for the diploma of Membership of that Society.

MURIEL E. MORLEY.

NEWCASTLE UPON TYNE,
    1944.

CONTENTS

CHAPTER I

DEVELOPMENT OF THE FACE AND MOUTH IN CONGENITAL CLEFTS OF LIP AND PALATE

Growth in embryo

Classification of clefts of lip and palate

Incidence

Ætiology

1

DEVELOPMENT OF THE FACE AND MOUTH IN CONGENITAL CLEFTS OF THE LIP AND PALATE

GROWTH IN EMBRYO

ALTHOUGH very little is known as to the cause of congenital clefts of the lip and palate, the stages in the development of the face and mouth of the human embryo have been described, and it is known that if, at some stage in prenatal life, there is interference with normal

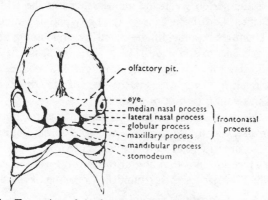

Fig. 1.—Formation of the face in a human embryo of the 6th week.

development, due to whatever cause, some type of cleft will result. Wood Jones (1946) has described how during the fifth, sixth, seventh and eighth weeks the whole character of the embryo undergoes a transformation from being "mere prophetic rudiments into actual definitive parts and organs." These are the weeks of formation. During this

3

period "the embryo has one main activity; its whole function is that of formation." In post natal life disturbance of the state of well-being of the body may manifest itself in a disturbance of function. "Upset of embryonic well-being is therefore liable to manifest itself in derangement of this function and so lead to malformation." The following is a brief outline of the development of the face and mouth in the human embryo.

The first three weeks of growth is a period before the establishment of the intra-embryonic circulation. The embryonic period, from the beginning of the fourth week to the end of the eighth week, is the period of differentiation. This is the period when the main systems of the body are established, and the organs of the body and the main external features become differentiated. The remaining period, from the end of the eighth week until birth, is the fœtal period, the time of growth, although slow changes still occur relating to variations in the rates of growth of certain parts in relation to that of others.

In the early stages of growth the gut has no outlet at either end, but by the fourth week an external depression near the anterior end of the gut deepens, and eventually breaks through into that end of the gut to form the stomodaeum. Five processes surround this opening. They are:—

1. A central frontal process;
2. Two maxillary processes; and
3. Two mandibular processes (Fig. 1).

The mandibular processes grow towards the centre to meet and fuse about the end of the fourth week, eventually forming the lower lip and jaw. Simultaneously, two specialised patches, or placodes, on either side of the central frontal process become thickened. These placodes soon become depressed and continue to deepen to form the olfactory pits, which, at the end of the sixth week, divide the frontonasal process into a median nasal process, situated between the olfactory pits, and two lateral nasal processes (Fig. 1). Changes during the second month are therefore mainly concerned with the formation of the nose.

The maxillary processes develop from the base of the mandibular processes and grow forward towards the centre, above the stomodeum, during the fifth and sixth weeks to separate the eyes from the mouth. They then fuse on each side with the corresponding lateral nasal processes to form the continuity between the sides of the nose and cheeks,

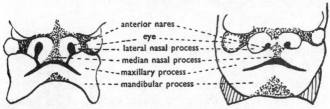

anterior nares
eye
lateral nasal process
median nasal process
maxillary process
mandibular process

Fig. 2a.—Upper lip in 6th week.   *Fig. 2b.*—Upper lip in 7th week.

and subsequently, with the median nasal process to form the upper lip and also to form the floor of the nose, alveolus and primary palate, thus dividing the stomodeum into nasal and oral cavities anteriorly (Figs. 2a, 2b).

Simultaneously, during the sixth week, a palatal plate arises from the maxillary process on each side and begins to grow inwards to form the hard palate (Figs. 3 & 4). Each plate fuses in the seventh week with the premaxilla, and finally, about the tenth week, with the corresponding plate on the opposite side, thus separating the oral from the nasal cavities and forming the roof of the mouth and the floor of the nose.

Parallel with the development of the palatal plates, beginning about the sixth week, the olfactory pits, at first

merely shallow depressions, become deeper, and by the
seventh week are open at the posterior end into the mouth
just behind the premaxilla. As the nostrils deepen, that

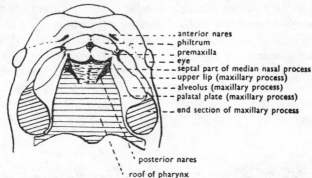

Fig. 3.—Showing the ingrowth of the palatal plates at the end of the
6th week.

part of the median nasal process lying between them forms
a partition, which, during the inward growth of the palatal
plates (Fig. 4), increases in length to form the nasal septum,

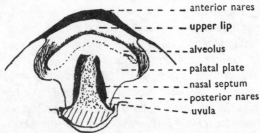

Fig. 4.—Development of the maxillary plates. Stage reached in the
9th week.

and, until the palatal plates fuse, its lower margin lies in
contact with the upper surface of the tongue (Fig. 5a).

Initially the developing palatal plates turn or hang downwards on either side and lie on each side of and below the

tongue, but towards the ninth week the forward growth of the premaxilla raises the nasal septum, the tongue gradually takes up a lower position in the mouth and allows the palatal plates to grow towards the centre (Fig. 5b) and to fuse with the nasal septum and with each other (Fig. 5c). This process of fusion continues from behind the premaxilla and spreads

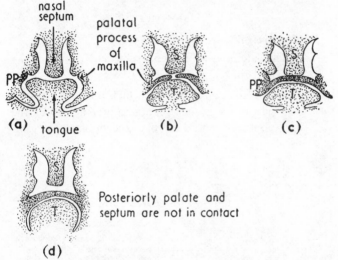

Fig. 5.—The relationship between the tongue and nasal septum during the inward growth of the palatal plates.

forwards and backwards, but the posterior part of the nasal septum is left free, only the anterior three-fourths being attached to the upper surface of the palate (Fig. 5d). Thus the three structures, the two palatal processes and the lower edge of the nasal septum, fuse in the mid-line to form the hard palate, now partially separating the oral and nasal cavities.

The soft palate is derived from folds which arise from each of the palatal plates as a prolongation backwards towards the pharynx. Before the end of the third month, the hard and soft palates form a complete septum between the nasal and oral cavities.

It should be realised that both the lips and palate are developing simultaneously at certain stages of growth, therefore both are subject to the same factors influencing growth.

SUMMARY

The frontonasal process gives rise to:—

(*a*) The lateral nasal processes, which form the side parts of the nose.

(*b*) The median nasal process which forms the central part of the nose, septum and premaxilla (*i.e.* the philtrum, central alveolus and primary palate).

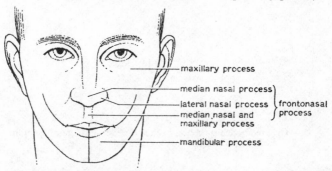

Fig. 6.—Showing the parts of the face formed from the nasal, maxillary and mandibular processes.

The two maxillary processes form the cheeks and unite with the median and lateral nasal processes to form the upper lip, the floor of the nose, the lateral alveolus, and the hard and soft palates.

The two mandibular processes form the lower jaw; and the lower lip (Fig. 6).

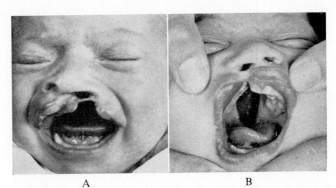

A.   B.

A.—Single harelip + cleft palate with narrow bridge of skin.
B.—Single harelip + cleft palate with broad bridge of skin.

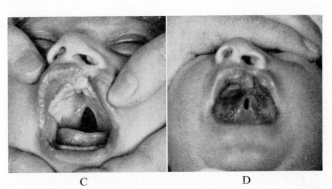

C.   D.

C.—Single harelip + cleft palate in the soft and half of the hard palate.
D.—Single harelip + cleft palate in the soft and a fistula in the hard palate.

Fig. 7.

Clefts showing bridges.

(Fogh-Anderson, P. (1942). *Inheritance of Harelip and Cleft Palate.* Copenhagen: Busck.)

At one time it was thought that clefts of the lip and palate were due to arrest of growth during the second and third months of fœtal life with a failure to *unite* of the various processes surrounding the primary oral cavity. This time having passed the defect remained and the child was eventually born with some malformation. However, Veau and others have pointed out the occurrence of incomplete clefts, that is clefts with bridge formations, or clefts which are not continuous. Varying forms of such conditions are shown in photographs by Fogh-Anderson (1942) (Fig. 7). This would seem to indicate that the partially united processes were being separated from each other. The cause of clefts is therefore explained by Frazer (1940) as follows. As the various processes come together they are at first separated from each other by epithelial septa. These membranes which unite the adherent parts disappear in normal development at about the seventh week as mesoderm grows inward from each side to penetrate this epithelial wall. The cleft is then due to a failure of growth and penetration of the epithelial wall by the mesoderm, wholly or in part, with an eventual breakdown of the tissues, and is due to a separation of the parts of the lip or palate, complete or partial. This matter is not, however, proved and there is still some diversity of opinion as to the true explanation.

In cleft palate a failure to unite, or a breakdown, occurs (1) between the frontonasal processes (median and lateral) forming the primary palate, and the maxillary processes, or (2) between the palatal plates from each side formed from the maxillary processes, and normally forming the secondary palate. Other failures may occur, but are much less frequent.

Thus it will be apparent that whatever the causes of interference with development, they must occur during the first twelve weeks of pregnancy, and most probably during the second month. The type of cleft with which the child is born is then determined by the stage development has reached when normal development of those parts which combine to form palate and lip fails to occur.

CLASSIFICATION OF CLEFTS OF LIP AND PALATE

One of the first attempts to classify clefts of the lip and palate was that of Davis and Ritchie (1922). The various conditions are divided into three groups according to the position of the cleft relative to the alveolar process, or that part of the maxillary process which forms the teeth ridge:—

> **Group I. Prealveolar (process) cleft.**—Lip cleft; alveolar process complete.

> **Group II. Postalveolar (process) cleft.**—Palate cleft; alveolar process complete.

> **Group III. Alveolar (process) cleft.**—Cleft follows incisor sutures through the alveolus.

Group I. Prealveolar (process) cleft.—When the palatal plates fuse normally with each other and with the pre-

Fig. 8.—Prealveolar (process) clefts.
A.—Right unilateral.   B.—Left unilateral.   C.—Bilateral.

maxilla there may be a cleft in the lip, or a prealveolar cleft. Although in this case there is no complete interruption in the continuity of the alveolar process there may be some distortion, the centre of the process being displaced to one side in conjunction with a deflected septum, or there may be a partial cleft extending into the alveolus associated with the cleft lip. The cleft may be unilateral (Group I, Figs. 8A and B) or bilateral (Group I₃, Fig. 8C), and occasionally median (Group I₂). This last condition is, however, rare. In each case the extent of the cleft may vary. The lip margin only may be notched, or the cleft may extend from the lip margin into the floor of

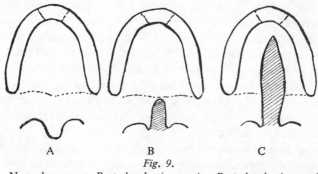

A

B
Fig. 9.

C

Normal process
and palate.

Post alveolar (process)
cleft. Soft palate only.

Post alveolar (process)
cleft. Soft and hard
palate.

the nasal cavities. In some cases a vertical groove may be seen in the lip under the skin, indicating that the muscles beneath have failed to unite normally.

Cleft of the palate may be associated with this group.

Group II. Postalveolar (process) cleft, or incomplete cleft of the palate, results when fusion occurs on each side between the maxillary process and the premaxilla, but the further process of fusion between the palatal plates is arrested at some point between the premaxilla and the uvula. The cleft is, therefore, median, and may then involve (1) anything from a bifid uvula to a cleft of the whole of the soft palate (Group II₁. Fig. 9B), or (2) the whole of the soft palate and some part of the hard palate (Group II$_2$. Fig. 9c).

A cleft of the lip may be associated with this group, but there is no cleft of the alveolus. Should the palatal plate on one side fuse with the nasal septum, then the postalveolar cleft may be unilateral.

It is sometimes found that the muscular tissues of the soft palate are cleft, this cleft extending in some cases into the bone of the hard palate, but the covering of mucous membrane is intact, or there may be some abnormality in the development and growth of the muscle elements. This is known as a **submucous cleft,** and may cause the soft palate to be immobile. The mucous membrane overlying the cleft tissues may have a somewhat transparent appearance, and the cleft in the hard palate may sometimes be felt as an indentation or notch underlying the mucous membrane, detected by feeling with the finger. (Group II$_3$).

If, in a darkened room, a bright light from a small torch is shone up either nostril in turn, it may sometimes be possible to see a translucent glow through the membranes of the palate when looking into the open mouth of the child.

Group III. Alveolar (process) cleft.—This is one in which the alveolus is cleft. The cleft may be complete or incomplete and is usually associated with a cleft of the lip and palate. The cleft may be right or left unilateral, bilateral or median.

Group III$_1$. *A unilateral alveolar cleft* occurs when the cleft extends through the lip and alveolus, on one side or the other, and through the palate. One half of the latter is usually attached to the nasal septum (Fig. 10A and B).

Group III$_2$. *In a median cleft* the premaxilla is frequently absent. The cleft in the lip is central and both halves of the palate fail to unite with the nasal septum.

Group III₃. *A bilateral cleft* results when the lip and alveolus are cleft on each side. The nasal septum is not attached to either half of the palate, and lies centrally in the cleft. The premaxilla is attached to the anterior end of the nasal septum and is abnormally prominent, being deflected upwards in the absence of the restraining influence of the upper lip (Fig. 10c).

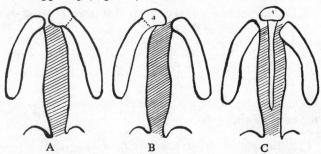

A   B   C

Fig. 10.—Alveolar (process) clefts. A.—Right unilateral alveolar cleft. B.—Left unilateral alveolar cleft. C.—Bilateral alveolar cleft with pre alveolar cleft in each case.

To summarise, congenital clefts may be classified as follows:—

Group I. Prealveolar (process) cleft:
　　　　1. unilateral, left or right.
　　　　2. median.
　　　　3. bilateral.

Group II. Postalveolar (process) cleft:
　　　　1. soft palate only, or part thereof.
　　　　2. soft and hard palate, or part thereof.
　　　　3. submucous cleft.

Group III. Alveolar (process) cleft:
　　　　1. unilateral, left or right.
　　　　2. median.
　　　　3. bilateral.

Though the foregoing is a useful classification it is by no means universal. Veau (1931) divided his cases into four groups:—

I. Cleft of soft palate only.

II. Cleft of soft palate and hard palate to the incisive foramen.

III. Complete unilateral alveolar cleft (usually associated with cleft of the lip).

IV. Complete bilateral alveolar cleft (usually associated with bilateral clefts of the lip).

Dorrance (1946) used a similar classification, but divided the cases into six groups:—

I. Congenital submucosal cleft, or congenital insufficiency of the soft palate.

II. Cleft of the soft palate.

III. Cleft of the soft and hard palates to the premaxilla.

IV. Single complete cleft (unilateral lip-jaw-palate cleft).

V. Double complete cleft (or bilateral lip-jaw-palate cleft).

VI. Complete bilateral cleft with rudimentary vomer.

Fogh-Anderson (1942) uses a somewhat different classification. He suggests that genetically there are two distinct types of deformity, namely, isolated cleft palate, and harelip with or without a cleft of the palate. These constitute the great majority of congenital clefts of the face, but more rarely there may be transverse and oblique clefts of the cheek, median clefts of the upper lip or of the lower lip and mandible. He classifies clefts of the lip and palate as follows:—

1. **Hare lip** (single or double).

2. **Hare lip** (single or double) **and cleft palate.**

3. **Isolated cleft palate.**

Group 1 here includes partial clefts of the alveolus, and varying degrees of hare lip, either single or double, and corresponds to Group I (1, 2 or 3), as previously described (Fig. 11), or clefts of the primary palate.

In Group 2 the cleft of the palate may be complete, or there may be narrow or wider bridges uniting the two parts of the lip. There may also be a cleft of the soft palate with the hard palate intact, or the cleft may be limited to a fistula in the palate (Fig. 12), clefts of Primary and Secondary palates.

The clefts in Group 3 may be of the uvula, or soft palate, or may extend forward to the alveolus. This group also includes the submucous cleft of the soft palate, or of the posterior part of the hard palate and of the soft palate (Fig. 13). Clefts of the Secondary palate.

Stark (1954) considers that, from the developmental point of view, the incisor foramen, and not the alveolus, can best be used to define the type of cleft. Kernahan and Stark (1958) classify the clefts in three groups as follows:—

Group I, clefts of the primary palate (lip and alveolus only).

1. **Unilateral,** right or left side.

2. **Medial.**

3. **Bilateral.** (Fig. 11).

Group II, clefts of secondary palate only.

    1. **Total** (to incisive foramen).
    2. **Subtotal.**
    3. **Submucous.** (Fig. 13.)

Group III, clefts of primary and secondary palates.

    1. **Unilateral,** right or left side ⎫ Total or
    2. **Median.**   ⎬ subtotal.
    3. **Bilateral.**   ⎭ (Fig. 12.)

THE INCIDENCE OF CLEFT LIP AND PALATE

Fogh-Anderson has made a very careful study of cleft lip and palate and has published his findings (1942). He quotes the incidence reported in many countries in the following table:—

			Number of births
1864	Frobelius	Russia	1—1525
1908	Rischbieth	England	1—1742
1924	Davis	U.S.A.	1—1170
1929	Peron	France	1— 942
1931	Schröder	Germany	1—1000
1934	Sanders	Holland	1— 954
1934	Grothkopp	Germany	1— 638
1939	Edberg	Sweden	1— 960
1939	Fogh-Anderson	Denmark	1— 665

These figures have been gained in differing ways, however, although most have been obtained from the records of maternity hospitals.

In Denmark surgical treatment for cleft palate is centralised in one hospital in Copenhagen so that an accurate estimate was possible. Fogh-Anderson found an incidence of 1.5 per 1,000 births, or 1 in every 665 live births. In 1942 he stated that 10% of these had other severe associated malformations, the majority of these being stillborn

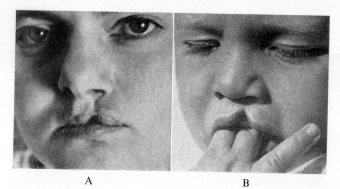

A.—Incomplete, single harelip. Notch in the prolabium with atrophic streak towards the nostril. B.—Incomplete single harelip involving about half of the height of the lip.

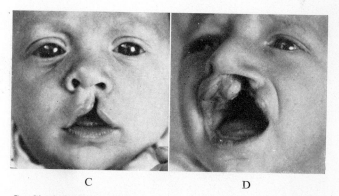

C.—Single, incomplete harelip involving most of the height of the lip.
D.—Single, complete harelip associated with alveolar cleft.

Fig. 11.—Group I clefts.
(Clefts of primary palate)

(Fogh-Anderson, P. (1942). *Inheritance of Harelip and Cleft Palate*. Copenhagen: Busck.)

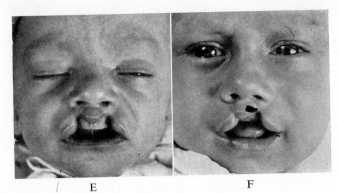

E.—Double, incomplete harelip, symmetrical. F.—Double, incomplete harelip, symmetrical.

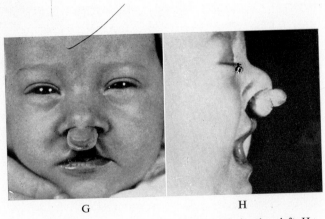

G.—Double, complete harelip with pronounced alveolar cleft. H.—The same, in profile, marked prominence of the premaxilla.

Fig. 11. (cont.)—Group I clefts.
(Clefts of primary palate)

(FOGH-ANDERSON, P. (1942). *Inheritance of Harelip and Cleft Palate*. Copenhagen: Busck.)

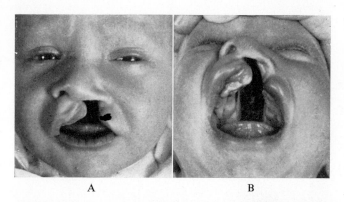

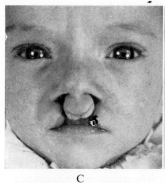

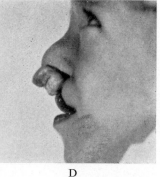

A

B

C

D

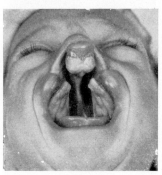

A. and B.—Single, complete
harelip with total alveolar cleft
and cleft palate. C., D. and E.
—Double, complete harelip with
total alveolar cleft and cleft
palate.

Fig. 12.—Group III clefts.
(Clefts of primary and
secondary palates)

(FOGH-ANDERSON, P. (1942). *Inheritance
of Hairlip and Cleft Palate*. Copenhagen: Busck.)

E

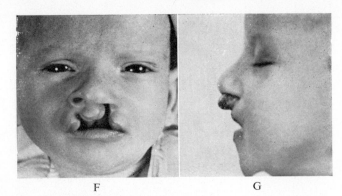

F   G

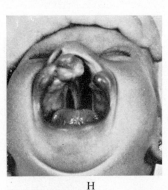

F. G. and H.—Bilateral harelip
+ cleft palate, asymmetrical.

Fig. 12. (cont.)—Group III clefts.
(Clefts of primary and
secondary palates)

H

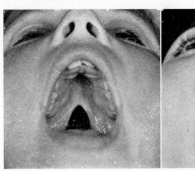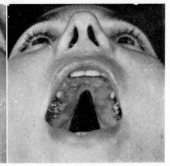

A   B

A.—Cleft in soft palate. B.—Cleft in soft and hard palate.

Fig. 13.—Group II clefts.
(Cleft of secondary palate)

(FOGH-ANDERSON, P. (1942). *Inheritance of Harelip and Cleft Palate*. Copenhagen:
Busck.)

or dying shortly after birth, and that a further 12% died within the first year of life. After one year the mortality rate was similar to that of the childhood population. The incidence of cleft palate in the surviving population would therefore be approximately one in 1,000. In a concensus of various studies of incidence it would appear to lie between 0.66 and 1.66 per 1,000 births.

Knox and Braithwaite (1963) studied malformations associated with cleft lip and palate and found these occurred in 2.8% of children with cleft lip, in 7.3% of those with cleft lip and palate, and in 12.2% of children with isolated cleft palate. The overall rate was 7.5%. The types of malformation included skeletal defects such as talipes, absence of thumb, bifid thumb, syndactyly and dislocated knees, and visceral malformations such as congenital heart disease, hydrocephalus, imperforate anus and pyloric stenosis.

Sex.—Most investigators agree that this condition is more common among boys than girls. Among 235 cleft palate patients Schwartz (1954) found 139 males and 96 females, or 59% and 41% respectively. Fogh-Anderson (1942), however, found among 625 patients that whereas harelip and cleft palate occurred most frequently among males, 347:151, or approximately 2:1, isolated cleft palate was found more frequently among females, 84:43, or again almost 2:1. This distribution was also found by Frazer and Baxter (1954) in a study of 102 patients. They found 37 males and 19 females with cleft lip and palate, and 18 females and 14 males with isolated cleft palate. They agree with Fogh-Anderson in thinking that there is probably no genetic connection between hare lip, with or without a cleft of the palate, and isolated cleft palate. Knox and Braithwaite found among 574 children that 329 (57.3%) were boys and 245 (42.7%) were girls.

B

Type of Cleft.—It has been noticed that unilateral clefts occur more frequently than bilateral clefts and that clefts on the left side are more common than on the right. Unilateral clefts of the lip were associated with clefts of the palate in 70% of Fogh-Anderson's patients, whilst in 86% of the bilateral clefts there was also a cleft of the palate. He gives the proportion of the three types of clefts among the patients seen by him as 50% having a cleft of the lip and cleft palate, 25% having a cleft of the lip only and 25% with a cleft of the palate only. In a consecutive series of 300 in Newcastle upon Tyne the proportions were 42% alveolar clefts involving lip and palate, 22% prealveolar and 36% postalveolar. Of the alveolar clefts (42%) 27% were unilateral and 15% bilateral. Knox and Braithwaite compared their figures with those of a large study in Birmingham by McMahon and McKeown (1953) and give the respective incidences for isolated cleft palate as 0.49 and 0.46 per 1,000; for cleft lip and palate as 0.51 and 0.51 per 1,000; and for isolated cleft lip 0.30 and 0.45 per 1,000.

ÆTIOLOGY

Various conditions have been investigated by many writers in an attempt to ascertain the cause of this malformation. It has been suggested that a "shock" received by the mother during pregnancy, or trauma due to an accident, may have affected the development of the child. The question of nutrition and the mother's health during pregnancy has been considered, but the incidence of clefts of the lip and palate has not been found to be higher in those social groups where such conditions might be expected to be a factor influencing development. It has also been suggested that amniotic bands might prevent union of the two parts of the palate, or that the position of the tongue, or even of a finger placed in the cleft in utero, might have obstructed growth.

Fogh-Anderson investigated the geographical distribution of cleft lip and palate in Denmark but found an even distribution corresponding to the density of the population without any geographical variation between country and town. He also found no significant difference between the social classes, nor any relationship to birth rank when the first born and the last born were considered, either for hare lip and cleft palate, or for isolated cleft palate. However, he demonstrated a familial history in 30% of the families of 903 patients seen by him.

Frazer and Baxter (1954) inquired into various prenatal conditions such as vaginal bleeding, febrile illnesses, loss of weight during pregnancy and menstrual irregularity within five years of the patient's birth. They concluded that "an analysis of the antenatal histories has not led to the identification of any relevant etiologic prenatal factors." They found, however, that in one third of the families of 102 patients more than one member was affected, and they showed that 11% of the patients with cleft lip and palate had close relatives, and 14% distant relatives affected, whilst in those with an isolated cleft palate 9% had close relatives who were affected and 13% distant relatives. They also failed to find any significant connection with birth rank, 41% being first born.

Schwartz (1954) found that in 35 of his 235 patients there were 51 incidents of cleft palate in the family history, 42 of these in relatives other than the immediate family. Twenty-four were paternally related to the patient, 15 maternally, and in three it could not be ascertained. Close relatives included three fathers, one mother and six siblings of the patient. He also found an incidence of clefts in 1 in 23 births in the families of the cleft palate patients, but only

1 in 256 births in a control group of 100 families with no known clefts of the lip or palate. He states therefore that "heredity plays an important role in the etiology of cleft palate. The exact mode of transmission is unknown," and that "Environmental factors, in particular maternal metabolism, endocrine balance and nutrition are also important. They may be etiological factors, *per se*, or they may be modifiers of heredity." It would seem, therefore, that most investigators believe that heredity plays an important part in the occurrence of clefts of the lip or palate.

Fogh-Anderson's work on "Inheritance of Hare Lip and Cleft Palate" involves a careful study of the inheritance factor in 703 patients and relatives numbering 25,000 persons. These were children, their parents, grandparents, siblings, siblings' children, parents' siblings, and children of parents' siblings. He considered various forms of inheritance such as sex-linked inheritance, simple dominance with failing or partial manifestation, simple recessivity, conditioned dominance and mutation. He summarised his findings as:—

"Hare lip (+cleft palate) and isolated cleft palate are two genetically quite independent malformations. Hare lip (+cleft palate) is, in the great majority of the cases an hereditary affection and the manner of inheritance is presumably that of conditioned dominance with sex limitation to males and but little manifestation in most genetic milieus, i.e. the gene occurs generally as a recessive gene and is independent of the other genes in the individual or family in question. Isolated cleft palate is only hereditary in a rather small number of cases, and the manner of inheritance is here in all likelihood that of simple dominance with failing manifestation and sex limitation to females. The possibility cannot be excluded that a number of 'solitary' cases may be due to mutation."

Frazer and Baxter (1954) have estimated the risk of inheritance and stated that for the unborn child the risk was 5% if a parent *or* sibling had a cleft of the lip or palate, and 15% if *both* were so affected. Whilst there may be a genetic influence in approximately 25% of cases, in the majority the cause would seem to be environmental factors influencing the developing embryo at the particular moment in time when fusion of the developing embryological parts is occurring.

Recent studies have suggested a multiplicity of causes. Braithwaite summarises these as maternal infection, toxicity, maternal dietary imbalance, maternal hormone activity and genetic influences. Cortisone, insulin and even aspirin have also been implicated. He describes how the foetus normally inherits an orderly pattern of development in which a series of active phases of cellular multiplication follow each other at different sites. The overall pattern of this sequence is laid down by inheritance, probably governed ultimately by chemical processes inherent in the genes. Such active phases of cellular division, which have high metabolic requirements and necessitate large demands on oxygen, are undoubtedly susceptible to environmental changes in the maternal metabolism. Interference with such processes at the appropriate time can undoubtedly lead to deformity of the corresponding site. It would seem to be wise that, in the early days of pregnancy, mothers should be kept as free from drugs as is practical.

Braithwaite and Watson (1950) have also suggested that failure of development of the vascular pattern, or absence of certain blood vessels, might play a major part in the formation of clefts due to limitation of supply to the internal maxillary artery prior to the formation of the carotid artery.

REFERENCES

BRAITHWAITE, F. (1964). Cleft Palate and Lip. In *Clinical Surgery*, ed. Rob, C. & Smith, R. London: Butterworths.

BRAITHWAITE, F. & WATSON, J. (1950). *Brit. J. Plast. Surg.* **11**, 38.

DAVIS, J. STAIGE & RITCHIE, H. P. (1922). Classification of Congenital Clefts of Lip and Palate. *J. Amer. Med. Ass.* **2**, 1323.

DORRANCE, G. M. & BRANSFIELD, J. W. (1946). The Push-Back Operation for Repair of Cleft Palate. *Plast. Reconstr. Surg.* **1**, 145-169.

FOGH-ANDERSON, P. (1942). *Inheritance of Harelip and Cleft Palate*. Copenhagen: Nyt Nordisk Forlag, Arnold Busck.

FRAZER, F. C. & BAXTER, H. (1954). Familial Distribution of Congenital Clefts of the Lip and Palate. *Amer. J. Surg.* **87**, 656.

FRAZER, J. E. (1940). *Manual of Embryology*. London: Baillière.

JONES, F. WOOD (1946). *Buchanan's Manual of Anatomy*, 7th ed. London: Baillière.

KEITH, Sir ARTHUR (1933). *Human Embryology and Morphology*. London: Arnold.

KERNAHAN, D. A. & STARK, R. B. (1958). A New Classification for Cleft Lip and Palate. *Plast. Reconstr. Surg.* **22**, 435.

KNOX, G. & BRAITHWAITE, F. (1963). Cleft Lips and Palates in Northumberland and Durham, *Arch. Dis. Childh.* **38**, 66.

McMAHON, B. & McKEOWN, T. (1953). The incidence of harelip and cleft palate related to birthrank and maternal age. *Amer. J. hum. Genet.* **5**, 176.

SCHWARTZ, R. (1954). Familial incidence of cleft palate. *J. Speech Hear. Dis.* **19**, 2, 228.

STARK, R. B. (1954). Pathogenesis of cleft lip and palate. *Plast. Reconstr. Surg.* **13**, 20.

VEAU, VICTOR (1931). *Division Palatine*. Paris: Masson et Cie.

CHAPTER II

THE NORMAL PALATE AND
THE PALATOPHARYNGEAL SPHINCTER

The hard palate

The soft palate

The oropharyngeal muscles concerned in speech:—

    (*a*) Palatal

    (*b*) Pharyngeal

    (*c*) The palatopharyngeal sphincter

The blood supply to the palate

Innervation of the palate

Function of the palatopharyngeal sphincter in:—

    Respiration

    Sucking and Swallowing

    Blowing

    Speech

THE NORMAL PALATE AND
THE PALATOPHARYNGEAL SPHINCTER

THE palate forms the roof of the mouth and separates the oral from the nasal cavities. It consists of two parts, the hard palate in front, and the soft palate behind.

THE HARD PALATE

The hard palate is a bony structure covered by a thick layer of soft tissues and is incapable of movement. It is

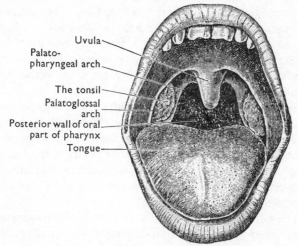

Fig. 14.—The cavity of the mouth.

bounded in front and at the sides by the alveolus, or teeth ridge, and its posterior edge is joined to the soft palate.

THE SOFT PALATE

The soft palate, or velum, is continuous with the posterior edge of the hard palate. Laterally, it is attached to the wall of the pharynx, and ends posteriorly in a free margin. It is composed of muscular and fibrous tissues, nerves and blood vessels, covered on its upper and lower surface by mucous membrane. The oral surface is concave when in a resting position, whilst the upper, or nasal surface, is convex and is continuous with the floor of the nasal cavities. The greatest range of movement of the soft palate occurs in the middle third where there is considerable bunching of the mucosa on the nasal surface when the soft palate is raised by the action of the levatores and other muscles to occlude the nasopharyngeal airway. The anterior segment just posterior to the hard palate consists chiefly of the palatal aponeurosis to which the muscles of the palate are attached. The posterior segment of the palate consists mainly of the uvula and plays a less active part in nasopharyngeal closure.

The uvula projects from the middle of the posterior free margin of the palate, and, arching downwards and outwards from it on each side are two curved folds of mucous membrane, the anterior and posterior pillars of the fauces, or palatoglossal and palatopharyngeal arches respectively. Between these arches on either side is a space which is occupied by the tonsils (Fig. 14).

The soft palate is capable of the fine and rapid movements essential to good speech. It separates the nasal cavities from the pharynx and mouth during the act of swallowing, and during speech, except for the production of nasal resonants, when the oral exit is closed by the lips or tongue, and the sound vibrations pass behind the soft palate and out through the nasopharynx and nostrils.

THE OROPHARYNGEAL MUSCLES CONCERNED IN SPEECH

These can be divided into two groups: (*a*) **palatal,** and (*b*) **pharyngeal.**

The palatal muscles.—These muscles are arranged in pairs, one on each side, and act symmetrically, being attached to the palatal aponeurosis.

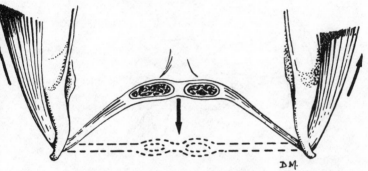

Fig. 15.—The tensor palati and the hamular processes. This muscle lowers the soft palate and may be concerned chiefly with swallowing rather than with speech.

The Tensor Palati.—This muscle arises from the base of the skull and enters the palate on each side from the pharynx after passing round a bony, hook-like process, the pterygoid hamulus. The tendon of the tensor palati passes round the hamulus as round a pulley and is surrounded at that point by a synovial sheath, a lubricating device to prevent damage due to friction (Figs. 15, 16 and 17). As it enters the palate it spreads out to meet and join with the tensor from the opposite side, and forms the palatal aponeurosis to which the other muscles are attached. Acting singly this muscle would draw the soft palate to one side; acting together the two muscles tighten and lower the soft palate (Figs. 15 and 16).

The Palato-glossus arises in the oral surface of the palatal aponeurosis and passes into the posterior part of the side of the tongue by way of the palato-glossal arch. Its fibres are not continuous across the surface of the soft palate. On contraction it depresses the sides of the soft palate and

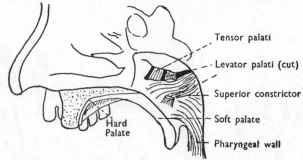

Fig. 16.—Dissection of the normal nasopharynx (Wardill).

draws the tongue upwards and backwards, at the same time narrowing the opening between the mouth and pharynx during the act of swallowing (Fig. 14). It acts in opposition to the levator palati and with the tensor palati in swallowing.

The Palatopharyngeus arises in the upper surface of the aponeurosis of the soft palate and passes into the lateral and posterior walls of the pharynx through the palato-pharyngeal arch on each side of the oropharyngeal isthmus. It acts in co-operation with the palatoglossus in swallowing, and probably with the levator and superior constrictor muscles during speech (Figs. 14 and 17). Oldfield (1941) suggests that on contraction it may "obliterate the sides of the nasopharynx" and therefore assist in nasopharyngeal closure.

The Levator Palati (Figs. 16 and 17) arises from the temporal bone at the base of the skull, and enters the upper surface of the aponeurosis of the soft palate on each side of the central line, where it spreads across to meet and

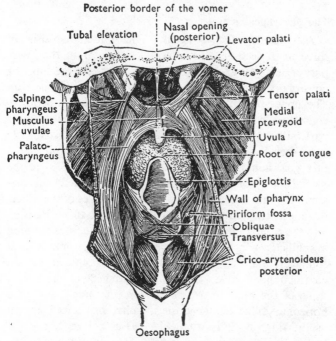

Posterior border of the vomer

Tubal elevation
Nasal opening (posterior)
Levator palati

Salpingo-pharyngeus
Musculus uvulae
Palato-pharyngeus

Tensor palati
Medial pterygoid
Uvula
Root of tongue
Epiglottis
Wall of pharynx
Piriform fossa
Obliquae
Transversus
Crico-arytenoideus posterior

Oesophagus

Fig. 17.—The pharynx open from behind.

blend with the muscle entering on the opposite side. The position on the oral, or lower, surface of the soft palate corresponding to the points of insertion of this muscle can be seen if one opens the mouth and says "ah." Two dimples appear on the oral surface as the muscle contracts. This muscle acts as a sling, and, on contraction, raises the soft palate upward and backward until its upper surface is drawn into contact with the posterior pharyngeal wall, thus acting in opposition to the tensor palati and palatoglossus.

The Musculus Uvulæ, on contraction elevates and shortens the uvula.

The pharyngeal muscles

The constrictor pharyngeus.—This muscle consists of three main sections, the inferior constrictor in the lower part of the pharynx, the medial constrictor, and the superior constrictor in the upper part of the pharynx (Fig. 16). The upper part of the constrictor pharyngeus superior is concerned with both speech and swallowing, the lower part with swallowing only. Certain fibres of this muscle have been found to have their origin in the region of the pterygoid hamulus or hamular process, or attached to the medial pterygoid plate. Whillis (1930) carried out dissection in this area and found that upper fibres of the superior constrictor passed around the pharynx to be inserted into the palatal aponeurosis of the soft palate, thus forming a sphincter which he described as the palatopharyngeal sphincter. Its function is important for speech as, on contraction, it causes an inward movement of the lateral walls of the pharynx with elevation, in some cases, of a horizontal ridge on the posterior pharyngeal wall known as the ridge of Passavant (Fig. 18) at a level above the lower margin of the soft palate. It cannot therefore be seen through the open mouth except in cases of cleft palate.

From time to time the existence of this ridge on the posterior pharyngeal wall has been queried. Calnan (1955) stated that from his observations he thought it was doubtful if such a ridge existed in the normal individual. He considered that it might represent hypertrophy of the pharyngeal muscles especially in some patients with cleft palates, and might even be related to swallowing rather than to speech.

Harlan Bloomer (1953) carried out observations on two patients with facial defects and also stated that he found no appreciable forward displacement of the posterior pharyngeal wall during blowing, whistling and speech, and suggested that in addition to the levator sling action and the sphincter action of the superior constrictor, the downward pull of the palato-pharyngeus muscle might also be involved

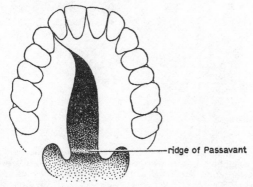

Fig. 18.—Ridge of Passavant seen in a case of cleft palate.

in nasopharyngeal occlusion. However, Ardran and Kemp (1955) have demonstrated through radiographic studies that in certain individuals with normal palatal and pharyngeal conditions a ridge of Passavant is evident during speech.

Townshend (1940) described the ridge of Passavant as being formed by the contraction of muscle fibres which run round the pharynx from the palate in a horizontal direction and considered that these fibres were part of the palatopharyngeus muscle which blend posteriorly with the superior constrictor very soon after leaving the palate. He observed the formation of a Passavant's ridge in a patient with an unrepaired cleft of the palate who had worn an obturator for thirty years. Nasopharyngeal occlusion was adequate and he considered that the ridge here was not essential for closure and therefore did not

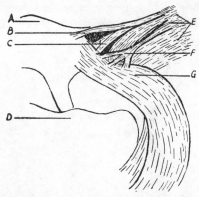

Fig. 19.—Schematic drawing of a posterior view of the right side of the nasopharynx to show the muscular relationships between the superior constrictor and palato-pharyngeus muscles. A.—Soft Palate. B.—M. pterygopharyngeus, palatal division. C.—M. pterygopharyngeus, hamular division. D.—Root of the tongue. E.—M. superior constrictor. F.—Muscle fibres connecting M. pterygopharyngeus and M. palatopharyngeus. G.—M. palatopharyngeus.

(HARRINGTON, R. (1945). *Laryngoscope,* 55, 499.)

represent hypertrophy. There has therefore been a difference of opinion as to whether the upper fibres of the superior constrictor forming the palatopharyngeal sphincter have their origin in the palate or in the region of the medial pterygoid plate, and also as to the relationship of this muscle to the palatopharyngeus and the levatores.

Harrington (1945) carried out a careful study of the

muscular relationships in the upper part of the normal pharynx. His findings indicated firstly, that there were individual variations both in the total muscular development and in the dispersion of the specific muscle fibres. Secondly, he found that in each of ten dissections certain fibres of the superior constrictor, the pterygopharyngeus, had their origin at the pterygoid hamulus (Fig. 19). In eight of the ten he also found a palatal insertion of the superior constrictor, described by Whillis (1930) as the palatopharyngeal sphincter. He considers that the palatal insertion of these fibres of the superior constrictor is therefore typical rather than the exception. He also found consistent connections between these muscle fibres and those of the palatopharyngeus.

He therefore suggests that the pterygopharyngeus muscle has two divisions, one being inserted into the palate and one at the hamulus, and that there are consistent connections between the pterygopharyngeus and the palatopharyngeus muscles, which he found to be so closely involved that it was almost impossible to separate them (Fig. 19). Townshend (1940) also observed these fibres and described them as being so hopelessly entangled in the human subject that it was almost impossible to say where one muscle began and the other ended. It is probable that these muscles contribute to the inward movement of the lateral pharyngeal walls and closure in the nasopharynx.

Whether or not the ridge of Passavant is concerned in nasopharyngeal closure it is apparent that complete closure of the nasopharyngeal airways is a normal function, and that such closure does not occur at only one level in the pharynx, but that there is extensive contact between the heaped up mucosa of the nasal surface of the soft palate and the posterior pharyngeal wall.

C

The palatopharyngeal sphincter

Air passing from the lungs, through the larynx to the oropharynx, has two means of exit. During quiet breathing with the mouth closed the muscles of the soft palate and pharynx are relaxed, and air passes into the nasopharynx (that part of the pharynx above and behind the soft palate) through the posterior nares and out by way of the nose (Fig. 20). Whilst speaking, singing, blowing or mouth-

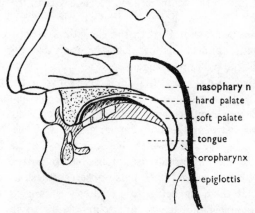

Fig. 20.—Soft palate in a resting condition. Air passing through the nose.

breathing the air which is being expelled is directed, after reaching the oropharynx, through the mouth and out between the lips, little or none passing into the nostrils. To prevent the air stream passing into the nose it is essential that there should be in the nasopharynx some means of completely shutting off the nasal cavities, thus ensuring the maximum of efficiency with the minimum expenditure of breath during speech and blowing (Fig. 21).

This closure is achieved by the synchronous action of the following muscles:—

1. **The superior constrictor pharyngeus**

   the pterygopharyngeus palatal division, or palatopharyngeal sphincter.

2. **The levator palati**

3. **The palatopharyngeus**

These muscles act together to close the nasopharyngeal airway, preventing the passage of air from the mouth and pharynx into the nostrils.

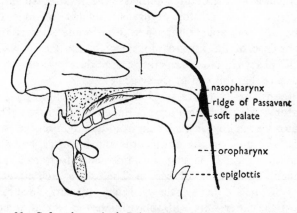

Fig. 21.—Soft palate raised. Palatopharyngeal sphincter closed. Air is passing through the mouth.

That the action of this sphincter produces complete separation of the oropharynx from the nasopharynx can be demonstrated (Wardill, 1933) if one allows a little normal saline to run into one nostril with the head tilted backwards, and whilst the soft palate is raised as when saying "ah." The head can be inclined to one side, and the fluid allowed to run into the other nostril, but, so long as the sphincter remains in a state of contraction the fluid will not run into the throat.

Negus (1929) quotes Hartmann as showing "that a pressure of 30 to 100 mm. of mercury was necessary to overcome the resistance of the soft palate when sounding a pure or non-nasal vowel, so complete is the physiological occlusion between the oropharynx and the nasopharynx."

Fenton Braithwaite (1958) pointed out that, from observations of muscle movements and attachments during and subsequent to surgical operations, closure of the nasopharyngeal air-way was probably achieved by the resultant interaction of these three muscles, the levator, superior constrictor and palatopharyngeus, whether a ridge of Passavant was apparent or not. Braithwaite stresses the importance of the inward movement of the lateral walls of the pharynx, and his operative procedures are designed to ensure that this can be freely achieved.

Braithwaite (1963) also describes the action of the levator and palatopharyngeal slings as follows: "The levator descending on each side from its origin on the petrous bone and passing downwards and forwards, and the palatopharyngeus passing upwards and forwards, are probably concerned with speech. The former arch elevates the soft palate in a backward and upward direction, whilst the latter sling will approximate the palatal arches and narrow the pharynx. Acting together they have a common palatal insertion for the incidence of their activity. The levator loop convex downwards and the palatopharyngeal loop convex upwards, by their point of common insertion in the palate become also an X-shaped muscle (Figs. 22-24). When acting together each loop will afford counter purchase for the other, and the interposed palate, steadied by the counter pull of the other, will convert each loop into a V. In effect, during contraction, it is as though

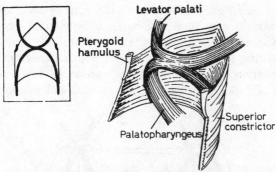

Fig. 22.—The levator palati and the palatopharyngeus muscles illustrated as an "x" shaped muscle.

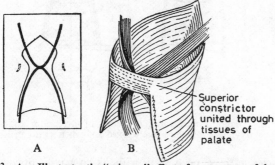

Fig. 23. A.—Illustrates the "scissors" effect of contracture of the "x" shaped muscle. B.—Shows the sphincter effect produced when the superior constrictor is freed from the medial pterygoid lamella and the hamulus, with the palate united.

Fig. 24.—The effect of the contracting arms of the two levator palati muscles.

From *Modern Trends in Plastic Surgery I.*, Butterworth 1963.

two muscles, each arising from the petrous bone of its own side, crossed within the palate to be inserted into the pharyngeal wall of the opposite side." (Fig. 25.)

Podvinec (1952) has also suggested that closure in the nasopharynx results from the interaction of two muscle slings. He describes each of the palatal and pharyngeal

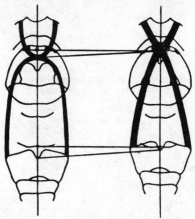

Fig. 25.—Diagram representing the slings of the levator and palato-pharyngeus muscles when relaxed and when contracted.

muscles as forming a sling with its concavity upwards or downwards. These are:—

    (*a*) with concavity upwards—the tensor palati, levator and the superior constrictor muscle slings.

    (*b*) with concavity downwards—the palatoglossus and the palatopharyngeus.

Podvinec found that when the soft palate was raised, as when the patient inflated his cheeks, the palatopharyngeus was stretched, converging steeply upwards to a point marked by a dimple on the oral surface of the palate. Both folds of the posterior pillars of the fauces were then in firm apposition to the posterior walls of the nasopharynx.

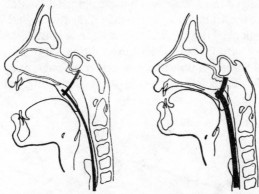

Fig. 26.—Lateral view showing the effect of interaction of the levator and palatopharyngeus muscles on the movement of the soft palate.

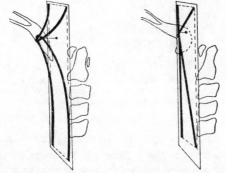

Fig. 27.—Diagrammatic view of the muscle action in Fig. 26.

From these observations he suggested that the action of the soft palate could be explained as being the result of simultaneous contraction of two muscle slings, those of the levator and the palatopharyngeus muscles. These muscles

in relaxation and on contraction are represented diagrammatically in Fig. 25. A lateral view showing the effect of
the interaction of these two muscle slings on palatal movement is shown in Fig. 26, and diagrammatically in Fig. 27.
The action of the superior constrictor is considered to be
synergic with that of the levator in lifting the palate and in
approximating it towards the posterior pharyngeal wall.
Two forces therefore operate at an angle (Fig. 28), and

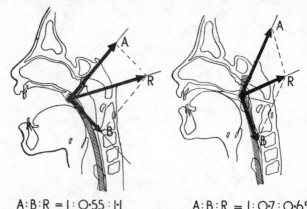

A:B:R = 1 : 0·55 : 1·1   A:B:R = 1 : 0·7 : 0·65

Fig. 28.—Diagram illustrating the resultant force and its direction
    on the soft palate of the two forces occurring on conttracture of
    the levator and palatopharyngeus muscles.

Podvinec considers that the decisive factor in raising the
soft palate may be the resultant component of these two
forces. The sling of the palatoglossus acts as a depressor
of the palate in opposition to this force, and is relaxed
during the elevation of the palate.

McCollum, Richardson and Swanson (1956), in describing
results of surgical treatment in children, state that non-
nasal speech was closely correlated with inward movement
of the lateral pharyngeal walls, and my personal observations

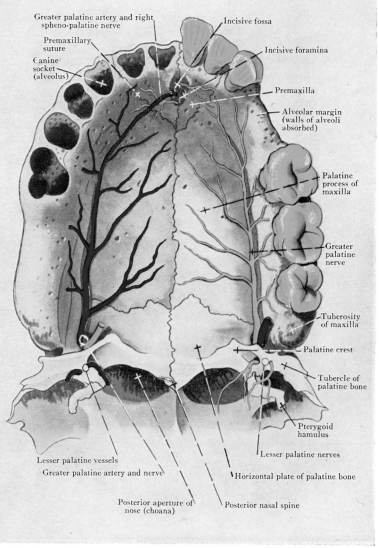

Greater palatine artery and right
spheno-palatine nerve

Premaxillary
suture

Canine
socket
(alveolus)

Incisive fossa

Incisive foramina

Premaxilla

Alveolar margin
(walls of alveoli
absorbed)

Palatine
process of
maxilla

Greater
palatine
nerve

Tuberosity
of maxilla

Palatine crest

Tubercle of
palatine bone

Pterygoid
hamulus

Lesser palatine nerves

Lesser palatine vessels

Greater palatine artery and nerve

Horizontal plate of palatine bone

Posterior aperture of
nose (choana)

Posterior nasal spine

Fig. 29.—The Bony Palate.

when assessing post-operative speech results amply confirm this. It is probable, therefore, that free mobility of the pharyngeal walls, and of the whole of the superior constrictor, is at least as important, if not more so, than a mobile soft palate. Closure in the nasopharynx then occurs through sphincteric action, comparable to that of the orbicularis oris for whistling, and is not accomplished only in an antero-posterior direction.

A recent study of the activity of the velopharyngeal muscles during speech has been made by Fritzell (1969) using electromyography and cineradiography. He states that his results indicate that overall E.M.G. activity recorded from the soft palate is closely related to the production of oral speech sounds and to velopharyngeal (palatopharyngeal) closure, but that information on the activity in individual muscles is limited and must be interpreted with great caution. The use of needle electrodes in the muscles of the palate and pharynx by the oral approach must interfere with the production and study of speech. He therefore used techniques to make intra-muscular recordings through a nasal approach. The electrodes were inserted into the levator, tensor and superior constrictor muscles in the walls of the epipharynx, so avoiding interference with articulation as much as possible. It is stated that the speech produced by the subjects during the experiments did not differ noticeably from their normal speech.

Fritzell demonstrated that the levator muscle showed a close relationship to the production of velopharyngeal closure and oral speech, whilst the production of nasal sounds within a sentence was preceded by decrease and disappearance of levator activity. An E.M.G. activity pattern of exactly the same type was shown by the superior constrictor muscle. This confirms the close association of the levators and certain fibres of the superior constrictor in the sphincter closure of the nasopharynx as described by Whillis (1930).

The palatoglossus muscle was active during speech but showed the opposite function, being closely related to the production of nasal sounds with active lowering of the soft palate.

Palatopharyngeus activity varied between subjects and sometimes showed very little relationship to speech, and Fritzell, therefore, could not confirm the hypothesis postulated by Podvinec that nasopharyngeal closure was associated with the combined activity of the levatores and the palatopharyngeus. Some activity was demonstrated during the production of oral speech sounds but with less consistency than the levator. The pattern of activity deviated from that of the levator, and he could find no simple synergisms between the activity of these two muscles. The palatopharyngeus, however, showed much greater activity during swallowing than for any other activity, and also appeared to assist in the narrowing of the pharynx.

Similarly, the tensor showed greater activity during swallowing and was often completely silent during speech. It is therefore of minor importance for speech, and fracture of the hamular processes during cleft palate surgery would not, therefore, have any detrimental effect on speech. These findings concerning the activity of the levator and tensor muscles agrees with that described by Wardill and Whillis (1936). Fritzell also describes a mean latency period from the onset of levator activity to the onset of velar movement of 40 to 64 msec. and from the onset of levator activity to the onset of sound as 334 to 336 msec., also noted by Wardill and Whillis and described by them as the "ready" position in preparation for speech.

This contribution by Fritzell to our greater understanding of muscle activity during speech, on which only a few brief comments are possible here, should be studied in detail by all those interested and concerned with these problems. In conclusion he states that "velar movements follow the levator activity very closely. The levator muscle appears to have the primary control of the position of the soft palate. The other muscles seem only to assist the levator or to modify slightly the gross pattern of velar movements as determined by the levator."

THE BLOOD SUPPLY TO THE PALATE

The blood supply to the palate is obtained from the *descending palatine artery*, which is a branch of the internal maxillary artery (Fig. 29). The descending palatine artery gives off two or three small arteries which supply the tonsillar regions and enter the soft palate posteriorly. It then passes forwards, emerging on to the oral surface of the hard palate through the posterior palatine foramen and continues forwards over the bony surface of the palate, close to the alveolar margin on each side, as far as the incisive fossa, situated just behind the incisor teeth. Here its terminal branch passes upwards through the incisive foramina to join with the terminal descending branch of the *sphenopalatine artery*.

The sphenopalatine artery is also a branch from the internal maxillary artery. It supplies the nose, the maxillary, frontal, ethmoid and sphenoid sinuses, and the nasal septum. One branch descends to the incisive canal and anastamoses with the terminal ascending branch of the posterior palatine artery, thus forming an anterior blood supply to the palate.

It is of importance in surgery that the blood supply to the palate enters through the bone and not, as in other parts of the body, through the periosteum (the fibrous membrane covering the bone). It is therefore possible at operation to strip the periosteum from its bony attachments without interfering with the blood supply.

The fact that there is an anterior blood supply is also important in cases of accident to, or destruction of, the posterior palatine artery during operation. In some methods of operation, to be described later, it is found to be advisable

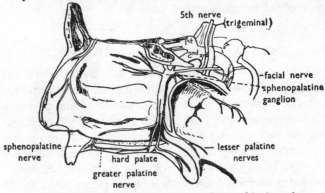

Fig. 30.—The right sphenopalatine ganglion and its branches.

to destroy the posterior palatine artery; the palate is then dependent for its blood supply on the smaller posterior group of vessels and on the sphenopalatine artery anteriorly.

INNERVATION OF THE PALATE

The sensory nerve supply.—The maxillary nerve, or second division of the trigeminal nerve, is a sensory nerve. It passes through the sphenopalatine ganglion (Fig. 29 and 30), where it is joined by secretory and sympathetic fibres from the facial nerve. This composite nerve then divides into three and is distributed to the nasal cavities, nasopharynx and palate. One of these branches is the sphenopalatine nerve

(Figs. 29 and 30). It passes across the nasal septum to the incisive foramen through which it passes to supply the anterior part of the hard palate. Another branch from the sphenopalatine ganglion is the greater palatine nerve, which descends to the under surface of the hard palate through the posterior palatine foramen and run forwards near the alveolar margin on each side, supplying the remainder of the hard palate. Two lesser palatine nerves are given off posteriorly and supply the soft palate and tonsilar region.

The motor supply.—The vagus and accessory nerves supply motor fibres to the muscles of the pharynx and to those of the soft palate, with the exception of the tensor palati. The greater superficial petrosal nerve, which arises from the facial nerve (Fig. 29), also carries motor fibres to the sphenopalatine ganglion and thence to the palatine nerves and the soft palate.

The tensor palati is supplied by the internal pterygoid nerve, a branch of the mandibular nerve which is the third and largest division of the trigeminal nerve.

Podvinec (1952) also thinks that the levator may have a double innervation, from the facial nerve and from the pharyngeal branches of the vagus, whilst the superior constrictor is innervated from the glossopharyngeus and the pharyngeal branches of the vagus. He therefore suggests that the co-ordinations for swallowing may differ from those of speech. For swallowing co-ordination of the muscles of the pharynx, palate and œsophagus is ensured by the glossopharyngeus and the vagus. For speech, however, he thinks the facial nerve may take the lead in co-ordinating the movements of the palatal, pharyngeal and facial muscles.

These nerves carry the motor impulses which are responsible for the movements of the muscles of the soft palate and of the palatopharyngeal sphincter.

THE FUNCTION OF THE PALATOPHARYNGEAL SPHINCTER

The entry of the expiratory air from the lungs into the pharynx, oral and nasal cavities is controlled by the laryngeal sphincteric muscles, and its exit by (*a*) the palatopharyngeal sphincter in the nasopharynx, and (*b*) at the lips by the orbicularis oris. The co-ordinated use of the muscles involved in the action of these three sphincters is essential for the control of respiratory air for voice and articulation, and for other activities such as sucking, swallowing and blowing. Such co-ordinations normally develop at birth for the physiological processes involved in respiration, sucking and swallowing, whilst phonation occurs with the first cry. This usually has a nasal quality and may not be associated with nasopharyngeal closure during the first few days of life.

Respiration.—Respiration may take place through the nostrils with the palatopharyngeal sphincter open, or through the mouth with the soft palate raised and the palatopharyngeal sphincter closed. It rarely occurs through both airways simultaneously, although this can be easily accomplished with conscious control.

Sucking.—In the normal adult method of sucking, fluids are drawn into the mouth by the movements of the tongue whilst the lips seal the opening to the mouth around the tube, straw or cup margin. The dorsum of the tongue is at first elevated against the soft palate, which is lowered, so closing the oropharyngeal isthmus. The palatopharyngeal sphincter is then at least partially open. The floor of the mouth, mandible and tongue are then lowered, creating negative pressure anteriorly in the mouth. The fluid is drawn into this space assisted by the action of the muscles of the lips and cheeks and the movements of the tongue.

When large quantities of fluid are drawn up by inspiratory effort from the chest, the palatopharyngeal sphincter is normally closed, but may at times be open to allow air to be drawn through the nasal air-ways simultaneously with fluid through the lips. This is the usual method employed by the child with inability to control the nasopharyngeal air-way.

The palatopharyngeal sphincter also remains open when the infant sucks and continues to breathe through the nose, alternately, or simultaneously whilst sucking. The soft palate is depressed somewhat and rests on the dorsum of the tongue, thus closing the oropharyngeal isthmus. The lips enclose the nipple and seal the entrance to the mouth, the nipple being held and compressed between the tongue tip and alveolus. A lowering of the floor of the mouth now creates negative pressure, and fluids are drawn into the mouth.

Where the alveolus and lip are cleft, the tongue tip will fail to experience normal contacts and resistance, as when attempting to compress the nipple. Compensatory adjustments are developed, and sensori-motor experience must necessarily differ from that of the child with a normal palate. These compensations may later affect the use and development of certain articulatory movements for consonant sounds post-operatively.

Swallowing.—Fluids are at first held in the mouth, resting in a depression upon the upper surface of the forepart of the tongue, which is then raised to direct the fluid to the back of the mouth and through the oropharyngeal isthmus, the posterior part of the tongue being lowered and the soft palate raised to receive it. At this stage the palatopharyngeal sphincter is normally closed to prevent regurgitation through the nasopharynx. However, as the fluids, or bolus, pass into the pharynx and into the involuntary phase of swallowing, the nasopharyngeal air-way again opens. The sensation of attempting to swallow with the palatopharyngeal sphincter closed can be experienced during a severe cold in the head, when the nasopharyngeal air-ways are occluded, or simply by attempting to swallow whilst the anterior nares are compressed firmly by the fingers.

In the child with a cleft palate such basic reflex movements and co-ordinations differ from those of the normal child from birth, and probably pre-natally in utero. Compensatory movements and adjustments are therefore developed to maintain the functions essential for existence. For example, to achieve the negative intra-oral pressure for sucking, the blade of the tongue may be raised in an attempt to close the cleft, whilst fluids are then directed in swallowing between the lateral margins of the tongue and cheeks, rather than centrally over the tongue.

Blowing.—Blowing usually requires that the breath should be directed at or into some object, as when blowing out a flame or inflating a balloon. Although blowing may be sustained simultaneously through the mouth and nose, greater and more effective pressure is obtained if the nasopharyngeal air-way is closed for the normal act of blowing through the mouth, and if the mouth is closed when blowing through the nose, as when clearing mucus from the nasal air-ways.

When the cheeks are distended with air, against the resistance of the muscles of the cheeks and closed lips, considerable pressure can be maintained in the mouth if the palatopharyngeal sphincter is closed. Alternatively, the air would leak through the nasal air-ways and the maintenance of pressure be impossible. Air so held in the mouth under pressure may be released at will through the lips or through the palatopharyngeal sphincter.

If closure in the nasopharynx is not possible, air may still be held in the mouth under some degree of pressure if the oropharyngeal isthmus is closed by depression of the palate and elevation of the dorsum of the tongue. This method is sometimes used by the child with an incompetent sphincter. Under such conditions the release of air through the mouth is not supported by the pressure of expiratory air from the lungs as occurs normally when the palato-pharyngeal sphincter prevents the outlet of air through the nasopharynx and the oropharyngeal isthmus remains open. The child with an incompetent nasopharyngeal sphincter therefore finds that blowing is ineffective rather than impossible, and can be assisted by closure of the nasal air-ways at the anterior nares.

During blowing, especially when much pressure is required as on inflating a balloon, the palate rises to its maximum height, the degree of closure being sufficient to balance the orally emitted air pressure. Harlan Bloomer (1953) also reported that blowing produced maximum upward movements of the soft palate, and Moll (1965) noted that the elevation of the soft palate was 2 to 3 mm. greater than was observed in speech. Bloomer described palatal and pharyngeal movements in blowing and whistling as being similar to those observed for speech, but found that they varied considerably from those for swallowing.

However, there is not only a difference of height but also a difference in type of closure. During blowing static closure is required over a period of time, whilst for articulation the soft palate is raised to the required position and from that position small, rapid movements occur controlling the emission of air through the palatopharyngeal sphincter. It is essential for articulation that there should be not only closure but also mobility.

D

THE ACTION OF THE PALATAL AND PHARYNGEAL MUSCLES DURING SPEECH

Muscle movements in the pharynx and of the soft palate during speech have been studied and described by various people. Wardill and Whillis (1936) observed nasopharyngeal closure in a patient with a normal palate. The orbit and part of the face had been removed and palatal movements could be viewed from the upper surface. They described the action of these muscles as follows:—

(a) The superior constrictor contracts and remains in a state of contraction so long as speech continues, thus causing narrowing of the nasopharynx from side to side.

(b) The soft palate is raised in preparation for speech by the contraction of the levatores palati into a position almost in contact with the posterior wall of the pharynx, the muscles of which have also contracted, causing bunching of the mucosa in the lateral walls and in a forward direction. In most cases the mobility and inward movement of the posterior and lateral walls of the pharynx is as important for pharyngeal closure as the upward and backward movement of the soft palate. From this position the muscles of the pharynx and palate are capable of small and rapid movements, the sphincter alternately opening and closing at an extraordinarily high speed.

The soft palate takes up the raised position, which may be described as the "ready position," in preparation for speech, and also during the production of the nasal resonants m, n and ng [ŋ] so that the actual movement of the palate whilst plosive consonants, necessitating complete closure, are alternated with nasal resonants, is very slight. During a sustained hum there appears to be only a very small opening through the palatopharyngeal sphincter, the palate remaining in the raised position.

Speech.—The sounds used in speaking are, essentially dependant upon expiratory air, and may be divided into two groups: *vocal tone*, produced in the larynx and modified in the nasal and oral cavities; and *articulation*, produced mainly in the oral cavity. Normal articulation of most consonant sounds requires a degree of pressure in the mouth which cannot be maintained if air escapes through an incompetent palatopharyngeal sphincter.

Articulation may be defined as the process by which sounds are produced in the mouth through movements, adjustments and contacts of the lips, tongue, mandible and soft palate associated with respiration and phonation.

An expiratory air stream directed through the mouth is as essential for the production of articulate sounds as is the air stream which is required to produce sounds in a wind instrument. This air stream for articulation may be voiceless, or in a state of vibration as for vowel and voiced consonant sounds, the air being set into vibration as it passes through the larynx, producing phonation. Resonance, modified by the contours of the pharyngeal, nasopharyngeal and oral cavities causes variations in the acoustics of the basic vocal tone and assists in the differentiation of the various vowels sounds used in speech.

During the process of articulation as used in speech this issuing air stream, voiceless or voiced, is subjected to changes and modifications due to alterations in the shape of the oral and pharyngeal cavities, narrowing of the aperture in various positions through which it passes or by complete momentary interruptions at differing points of contact in the oral cavity.

Articulation is an acquired motor skill developed gradually in childhood and dependent on the normal functioning of the motor system for the muscle movements and co-ordinations required, with normal sensory feed-back and monitoring processes through the auditory and other sensory pathways. It requires ability to imitate sounds heard and is established through repeated sensori-motor experience at conscious and sub-conscious levels, controlled by complex cerebral and neuro-muscular changes.

For this purpose human beings have adapted and developed certain reflex functions, primarily designed for the maintenance of life, such as those for respiration, sucking, chewing and swallowing. In a child with a cleft palate these movements and co-ordinations differ from those of the normal child from birth, and even in utero. Compensatory movement patterns are therefore developed to maintain the functions essential for existence. For example, to achieve negative oral pressure for sucking the posterior part of the blade of the tongue may be raised in an attempt to close the cleft. Where the alveolus and lip are cleft, the tongue tip will fail to experience normal contacts and resistance, as when attempting to compress the nipple in suckling. Compensatory adjustments are developed, and sensori-motor experience through sensory feed-back must necessarily differ from that of the child with no cleft of the palate.

The development of such abnormal, compensatory adjustments must, at a later date, influence the use of the tongue and lips for babbling and other sounds made in the mouth, and later still for the articulation of the sounds as used in speech. The chief difficulty experienced is inability to obtain sufficient intra-oral air pressure for the production of such sounds due to the absence of a competent palatopharyngeal sphincter in the child born with a cleft of the palate, or post-operative inability to control the closure of this sphincter. There may be either an anatomical insufficiency or failure to co-ordinate such closure in time and degree at the speed required for normal articulation in conversational speech. Such defects are the chief cause of the development of abnormal articulation in these children. However, the effect on the sounds used in speech varies.

Vocal tone and vowel sounds.—Vocal tone is produced in the larynx by the vibration of expiratory air at the level of the vocal folds, and is subsequently modified and amplified through resonance in the pharyngeal, nasopharyngeal and oral cavities. The vowels used in speech are dependent upon this basic vocal tone and are differentiated one from the other through acoustic modifications as the result of changes in the size and shape of these cavities, particularly the oral cavity, through movements of the jaw, tongue, lips, soft palate and palatopharyngeal sphincter.

Vowel sounds.—The position of the tongue for most vowel sounds offers little resistance to the passage of air through the mouth. The vowel [i:(ee)] being produced with the blade of the tongue raised towards the palate causes more resistance than a vowel sound such as [ɑ:(ah)], but very much less than is caused by the position of the articulatory organs for the plosive and fricative consonant sounds. However, although much less oral pressure is required for vowel sounds, a balance must be achieved between oral and nasal resonance which to the ear approaches normal, and this may be grossly distorted if the palatopharyngeal sphincter is incompetent or pharyngeal movements are abnormal and limited. The intelligibility of vowel sounds in cleft palate is rarely affected, although opinions differ as to what variations in resonance are acceptable.

Consonants.—The expiratory air is either held momentarily under pressure and released to produce a plosive consonant, or is allowed to escape through a small orifice under pressure, producing a fricative sound. The expiratory air may, or may not be set into vibration at the laryngeal level, producing voiced or voiceless consonants respectively.

The intra-oral and oropharyngeal air pressure for articulation is normally built up, with closure of the palatopharyngeal sphincter, in the cavity between the palate and the upper surface of the tongue, the lateral margins of which occlude spaces between the upper and lower alveoli, or lateral teeth, thus preventing the escape of air except at the required point of articulation.

The consonants (m), (n) and (ŋ) are differentiated one from the other by the point in the oral cavity at which the resonating air column terminates, at the lips for (m), at the teeth ridge for (n) and in the mid-palatal region for (ŋ). The sound is emitted through the nasal air-ways, but the palate is raised into the "ready" position for speech, although the palatopharyngeal sphincter is not completely closed. Actual movement of the palate whilst plosive consonants, requiring complete closure, alternate with nasal resonants, is very slight. During a sustained hum there appears to be only a very small opening through the palatopharyngeal sphincter, the palate remaining in the raised position. Thus these consonants rarely present difficulty to the child with a cleft palate, and can be acoustically recognisable when there is a much larger opening than is normal through the nasopharynx.

The difficulty a cleft palate patient will experience in the articulation of other consonant sounds will depend upon the degree of oral pressure required for each sound which must be balanced by the degree of closure of the palatopharyngeal sphincter. The consonants (l) and (r) and the semi-vowels (w) and (y) offer little resistance to the issuing air stream and are frequently normal, or at least recognisable, when the palatopharyngeal sphincter is incompetent.

The palatopharyngeal sphincter is closed just prior to and at the moment of articulation for the plosive consonants. The fricative consonants, produced by air passing through an opening which must of necessity be small, cause considerable back pressure and require firm closure of the palatopharyngeal sphincter. Adequate oral pressure, therefore, for these sounds cannot be maintained if the palatopharyngeal sphincter is incompetent.

It has been noted that the soft palate is raised more for some sounds than for others. For example, it is raised more for (k) than for (t), and higher for voiced than for voiceless consonants. The consonant (s) would appear to require the maximum degree of closure for articulate sounds. If closure of the palatopharyngeal sphincter is inadequate, the resulting articulation lacks normal force, consonan⸀s may be omitted, or sounds more easily produced substituted; the intelligibility of speech is then affected in varying degrees.

At one time it was suggested that the importance of nasopharyngeal closure had been overstressed, and that complete separation of the oral from the nasal air-ways might not be necessary for speech. However, it is now generally accepted that closure of the palatopharyngeal sphincter is required as described.

Taub (1966) has devised and described an oral panendoscope which provides a method for direct observation of palatopharyngeal areas during speech, and which facilitates the audio-visual recording of the function of the mechanisms for speech in the nasopharynx. X-ray studies are not always adequate, as they fail to show the multi-dimensional facets of the structures involved in speech production, and the surface anatomy with its muscular movements and sphincter-like action. By this method nasopharyngeal closure, occurring during speech, is confirmed. It is possible for the lips to close around the part of the instrument which is inserted into the mouth and pharynx, permitting the necessary intra-oral air pressure, nor does it essentially interfere with tongue movements for consonant articulation. Direct clinical and photographic laryngoscopy is also greatly facilitated by the use of this instrument.

Although the soft palate remains in the raised or "ready" position during speech, the palatopharyngeal sphincter does not remain tightly closed throughout. It may be slightly open on vowel sounds thus allowing some degree of nasal resonance, particularly as on the French nasalised vowels, and in countries, or dialects where there is increased nasal resonance associated with vocal tone. However, closure in the nasopharynx is required to provide sufficient oral air pressure for clear articulation, particularly for the sustained fricative consonant sounds, and momentary complete closure to give sufficient oral pressure for the plosive consonants. **Palatopharyngeal closure is therefore required, but more important still is the ability to control the timing and degree of closure in co-ordination with the movements of the tongue and lips for articulation.**

It is true that some patients achieve good speech when complete closure is impossible, or even with an open, unrepaired cleft, but such speech, although possibly clear and intelligible, has obvious defects to the trained ear. Without nasopharyngeal closure, as described, the requisite air pressure in the mouth for the articulation of plosive or fricative consonant sounds is normally unobtainable. However, many patients with cleft palates compensate for their defect by learning various tricks which may help to make speech more or less intelligible, but which may eventually become the cause of much trouble to the speech therapist. This will be discussed later.

TREATMENT FOR CLEFT PALATE

To make it in any way possible for a cleft palate patient to acquire normal speech he must first of all be provided with the means to separate the oral and nasal air-ways Treatment may require surgery, the fitting of an obturator, orthodontic treatment or speech therapy, and frequently the combined efforts of a team consisting of a surgeon, orthodontist, prosthetist and speech therapist.

Modern cleft palate surgery, however, is now so successful and able to produce a palate which is indistinguishable functionally from the normal that this is the method of choice except in rare cases, and the restoration of the physiological mechanism required for normal speech is the criterion by which the success of any treatment for cleft palate is judged. The surgeon is no longer satisfied with simply closing the cleft, but operation must produce a long soft palate which, with the help of the muscles concerned, is capable of forming a competent palatopharyngeal sphincter. It is also important that the soft palate should be mobile and capable of the rapid movement, previously described, which is essential for normal speech. A palate may be long and capable of reaching the pharyngeal wall, the sphincter may even be competent during sustained blowing, but if the soft palate is tense and rigid or the lateral and posterior pharyngeal walls immobile, the patient will have difficulty in achieving normal speech. (See case histories 23 and 24, Chapter VIII.) These factors are all considered in modern cleft palate surgery, and how such aims have been fulfilled will be described in the following chapter.

REFERENCES

ARDRAN, G. M. & KEMP, F. H. (1955). (Personal Communication.)
BLOOMER, H. (1953). Observations on Palatopharygneal Movements in Speech and Deglutition. *J. Speech Hear.* **18,** 230.

BRAITHWAITE, FENTON (1958). (Personal Communication.)

BRAITHWAITE, F. (1963). *Modern Trends in Plastic Surgery*. I. ed. Gibson, T. London: Butterworths.

CALNAN, J. S. (1955). Movements of the soft palate. *Brit. J. plast. Surg.* 5, 4.

CUNNINGHAM (1935). *Manual of Practical Anatomy*. London: Oxford University Press.

FRITZELL, B. (1969). *The Velopharyngeal Muscles in Speech*. Göteborg: Aktiebolag. See also *Acta oto-lar*. Suppl. 250.

HARRINGTON, R. (1945). M. Pterygopharyngeus and its relation to M. palatopharyngeus. *Laryngoscope, St. Louis*, 55, 499.

McCOLLUM, D. W., RICHARDSON, S. O. & SWANSON, L. T. (1956). Habilitation of the Cleft Palate Patient. *New Engl. J. Med.*, 254, 299.

MOLL, K. L. (1965). Cinefluorographic study of Velopharyngeal function in normals during various activities. *Cleft Pal. J.* 2, 112.

NEGUS, V. E. (1929). *Mechanism of the Larynx*, p. 414. London: Heinemann.

OLDFIELD, M. C. (1941). Cleft Palate and the Mechanism of Speech. *Brit. J. Surg.*, 29, 197.

PODVINEC, S. (1952). The Physiology and Pathology of the Soft Palate. *J. Laryng.*, 66, 452.

TAUB, S. (1966). The Taub Oral Panendoscope. *Cleft Pal. J.* 3, 328.

TOWNSHEND, R. H. (1940). The formation of Passavant's bar. *J. Laryng.*, 55, 154.

WARDILL, W. E. M. (1928). Cleft Palate. *Brit. J. Surg.*, 16, No. 61, 127.

WARDILL, W. E. M. (1933.) Cleft Palate. *Brit. J. Surg.*, 21, 82.

WARDILL, W. E. M. & WHILLIS, J. (1936). Movements of the Soft Palate. *Surg. Gynec. Obstet.*, 62, 836-839.

WHILLIS, J. (1930). *J. Anat., Llond.*, 65, Part 1.

CHAPTER III

AN OUTLINE STORY OF THE DEVELOPMENT OF CLEFT PALATE SURGERY

Median suture

Flap methods of closure

Closure by compression

Operative procedures to improve the speech result

Operation for Clefts of Primary Palate

Secondary Surgical Procedures

Further Results of Surgery

AN OUTLINE STORY OF THE DEVELOPMENT OF CLEFT PALATE SURGERY

IT is not proposed to give here details of operative technique. This is of use mainly to the surgeon and has been described fully in surgical books and papers. The aim is rather to describe the principles upon which the various methods of operation are based, and to show how, by an interesting process of development, modern cleft palate surgery has been evolved to meet the requirements necessary for normal speech.

The condition of cleft palate has been known to occur since earliest times, certainly since the first century. Smith and Dawson, in their work entitled *Egyptian Mummies*, have noted the discovery of one case of cleft palate, but the history of operative procedures is scanty until the beginning of the nineteenth century. From this time until the present day there has been continuous progress both in methods and technique.

At first surgeons operated upon clefts only of the soft palate, but as new instruments were devised and technique improved, procedures were soon extended to include operations on clefts involving the hard as well as the soft palate. Operative methods developed along three principal lines, which differ fundamentally from each other. They are:—

Closure of the cleft by median suture;

Flap methods, in which a flap of tissue, from the palate or from some more remote part of the body, is used to close the cleft; and

Methods involving compression of the upper jaw by mechanical means until the two halves of the palate are forced together.

Towards the end of the nineteenth century, when successful anatomical results were being obtained, it was noticed that good closure of the cleft did not necessarily produce any improvement in speech. Passavant, in 1862, was one of the first to introduce procedures with the definite aim of improving the speech result, and from this date the physiological function of the repaired palate became of more and more importance, until now it is the criterion by which any operative procedure is judged.

CLOSURE OF THE CLEFT BY MEDIAN SUTURE: THE "VON LANGENBECK" OPERATION

In 1817 von Graefe, one of the first to place on record his methods of operation, described the closure of a cleft of the soft palate. He caused inflammation of the edges of the cleft, drew them together, and sutured them in the middle line. In 1819, Roux, in Paris, described a method by which he sutured together the edges of the cleft after first cutting away a thin strip of tissue along each edge in order to produce a raw area, and allowed the two halves of the palate to unite. Other surgeons experimented along similar lines, but such methods were usually found to be unsatisfactory, as the tension required to draw the two halves of the palate together against the lateral pull of the palatal muscles caused the sutures to tear out, and the newly repaired palate to break down, resulting in partial or complete failure to obtain closure of the cleft.

Attention was therefore directed to relieving the tension under which the palate was sutured. Two methods were used. In one case the muscles of the palate, such as the palato-glossus, palato-pharyngeus and the tensor palati, were cut, these being the muscles which tended to pull the two halves of the palate apart; by the other method, after suture, incisions were made in the tissues of the palate. These incisions were in the form of longitudinal slits which gaped when the edges of the cleft were drawn together, thus relieving some of the tension. The raw areas eventually healed by granulation.

Dieffenbach, in 1828, first suggested the separation of the

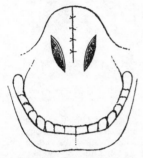 

Fig. 31.—Diagram to show suture of soft palate and lateral incisions of Dieffenbach.

Fig. 32.—Diagram to show Mettauer's incisions to relieve tension in the palate.

soft parts of the palate from the underlying bone before suturing the edges of the cleft, and he then used lateral incisions to relieve the tension after the sutures had been inserted and tied (Fig. 31). In 1837, small incisions in several parts of the palate were used by Mettauer in America. These incisions penetrated through the soft tissues, and allowed the edges of the cleft to come together with less tension (Fig. 32).

Procedures, so far, had been confined to closure of clefts of the soft palate only, but as instruments and technique improved attempts were made to close clefts involving both the hard and soft palates. About 1844, Fergusson, in England, and many others, were experimenting with various methods for obtaining a satisfactory anatomical closure, but it was left to von Langenbeck, in 1862, to describe in

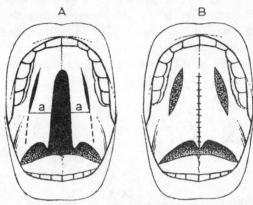

Fig. 33.—A.—Diagram to indicate the extent of the incisions in Langenbeck's operation. The thick black lines show the primary incisions; the thick dotted lines the extension backwards of these to relieve any lateral tension (made after the insertion of the sutures); the thin black lines (*a—a*) indicate approximately the position of the free posterior border of the bony palate.
B.—Shows the position of the sutures and the condition of the parts at the close of the operation.—William Rose (modified).

detail the operation of median suture which has since borne his name.

For this operation von Langenbeck used anæsthesia obtained by applying ice to the palate. The operation included:—

1. Removal of a narrow strip of tissue from the edges of the cleft.

2. Lateral relaxation incisions made parallel to the alveolar ridge.

3. The dissection of the tissues of the hard palate, including the mucoperiosteum (the fibrous membrane covering the bone) from the bony part of the hard palate, and the division of the tissues of the soft palate.

When the flaps of the palatal tissues so obtained were loose enough to meet in the mid-line, the sutures were inserted and tied (Fig. 33). These flaps, having been dissected from the bone and drawn together in the mid-line, were necessarily lowered away from the bony arch of the hard palate. Large raw areas were thus left on the nasal aspect, with consequent formation of scar tissue and resulting contracture. It is for this reason that the palate produced by the Langenbeck operation tends to be short and incapable of normal function. With varying modifications, and additions, the principle of this operation is, however, still in use at the present day.

FLAP METHODS OF CLOSURE

Many surgeons have devised operations in which a flap of tissue, obtained from some part of the body, is used to bridge and close the cleft. Briefly, the method is as follows. A flap of tissue is cut and partially removed from its position, although remaining attached at one end. Part of this flap is then sutured in the mouth to cover the cleft in the palate, the remote end remaining attached at its original situation for some days, and dependent on its former blood supply. When the flap has united with the halves of the palate, and the new blood circulation is established, the flap is cut across. Any part of it not required to cover the defect in the palate is then returned to its original position.

In this way surgeons have used flaps obtained from the

E

inside of the cheek and from the upper lip. Flaps taken
from the tongue were tried, but found to be unsatisfactory.
Von Eiselberg implanted the whole of a little finger into a
cleft, afterwards detaching the finger from the hand. He
also reported an operation where a flap was taken from the
forearm, the arm being fixed in plaster bandages to hold it
close to the head until the blood supply was established.
This was in 1901. Ten years later Blair, in America,

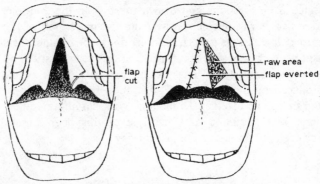

Fig. 34.—Krimer flap operation.

used a flap taken from the neck, and Rosenthal, in 1917,
employed a similar flap from the upper arm. Flaps cut
from the forehead and turned down into the mouth have
also been used.

Another method based on the use of a flap was described
by Sir Arbuthnot Lane in 1897. Since 1827 attempts had
been made to close the cleft by means of a flap dissected
from one side of the palate and turned over to cover the
cleft, this flap being then sutured to the opposite half of
the palate (Fig. 34). From operations of this type, the
"Lane operation" was eventually evolved. The principle
of this operation is shown in Fig. 35. A large flap is raised

by dissection from the hard and soft palate on one side, and is turned over as one turns the page of a book and sutured to the other side, but remains attached along the edge of the cleft. The raw surface of the flap then faces towards the mouth. (Lane 1908.)

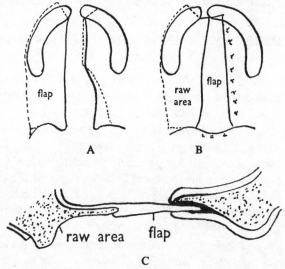

Fig. 35.—The Lane operation. A.—Flap cut, incisions along dotted line on left; palatal tissues separated on right. B.—Flap everted and sutured in position to opposite side of palate. C.—Section showing method of joining the flap to the opposite side.

Lane advised very early operation, during the first week of life or even on the day of birth. By closing the cleft so early, he hoped to obtain subsequent normal development of the palate, nose and nasopharynx by means of normal respiration. As the mouth was very small at this early age, Lane repaired the cleft in the palate before the lip in the case of a complete cleft, and in other cases often divided a normal lip in order to gain better access to the mouth.

The chief disadvantage of a "flap operation" is that no attempt is made to reconstruct the normal musculature of the soft palate, and that a "tense and fibromuscular septum between the mouth and nasal cavity" remains following this operation. Some results obtained by the use of this method are quoted later (p. 87).

CLOSURE BY COMPRESSION — THE "BROPHY" METHOD

Closure of a cleft by compression is an old method, though this procedure is usually attributed to Brophy, and is known by his name. It has been carried out in three ways.

1. Continuous pressure is applied on the cheeks over the upper jaw bone by some form of mechanical device until the edges of the cleft are gradually forced together. When sufficient pressure has been applied, the edges of the cleft are freshened and sutured, and, as the wound heals, the edges of the two halves of the palate, now lying in contact along the mid-line, are joined together.

2. A palatal bar is applied to the teeth, exerting pressure on each side of the upper jaw. This bar can be shortened from time to time by means of a screw device, as the two halves of the palate are gradually approximated. Eventually, sutures are inserted after freshing the edges, as in the previous method.

3. In the third method, strong pressure is applied to force the two halves of the palate together, where they are held in position by means of wires passed through the bone of the palate or alveolus.

In Brophy's work on "Cleft Lip and Palate," published in 1923, he advised closing the cleft by compression as early after birth as possible, as so much less pressure is required at an early age than later, when the bones are more completely ossified, the operation then being more difficult, and the result less satisfactory.

This operation presupposes that a cleft palate consists merely of a separation of two well-developed halves of an otherwise normal palate. This is known to be untrue; a cleft palate being due to arrested development, there is a consequent deficiency of tissues. Thus closure by compression must result in abnormal narrowing of the upper jaw, and though such methods may still have their use, other operative procedures produce results which approximate more closely to the normal.

OPERATIVE PROCEDURES DEVISED TO IMPROVE THE FUNCTIONAL RESULT

In 1862, Passavant drew attention to the lack of improvement in speech following operation for cleft palate, and ascribed the nasal intonation, so noticeable in cleft palate patients, to inability of the soft palate to reach the posterior pharyngeal wall. The Langenbeck operation, in general use at that time, so often produced a shortened, though fairly mobile soft palate. To obviate this disadvantage, he tried various methods, all designed to assist the soft palate to make contact with the posterior pharyngeal wall. Many of his ideas are ingenious, but not all proved to be successful.

Firstly, he attempted to lengthen a palate, already closed by the Langenbeck operation, by uniting the upper parts of the palatopharyngeal muscles in the mid-line, in order to produce an extension to the soft palate. Union is reported in three cases, but speech remained nasal (Fig. 36).

Secondly, he sutured the soft palate itself to the posterior pharyngeal wall. At least the soft palate had no option in

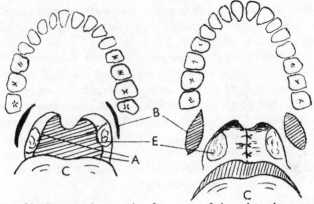

Fig. 36.—Passavant's operation for suture of the palato-pharyngeus muscles, A. B.—Lateral incisions. C.—Tongue. E.—Tonsil.

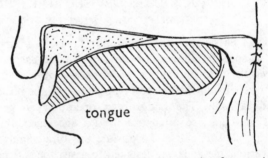

Fig. 37.—Diagram to show Passavant's operation for suturing the soft palate to the posterior pharyngeal wall.

this case! This was said to give better speech results than the first method (Fig. 37).

Thirdly, incisions were made in the palate as in the diagram (Fig. 38), and the whole of the soft palate was displaced backwards. Later, the defect in the hard palate was closed by means of a flap. Passavant reported good results from this method.

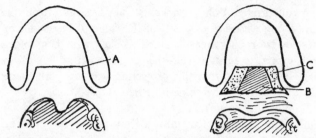

Fig. 38.—Passavant's operation for backward displacement of the soft palate. A.—Line of incision. B.—Nasal cavity. C.—Bone.

In 1863, he described the contraction of the superior constrictor muscle on the posterior pharyngeal wall, producing the cushion, or ridge, which has since borne his name (Fig. 18). Basing his ideas on the function of this ridge in speech, he later condemned all his previous methods, and described an operation for securing forward displacement of the posterior pharyngeal wall.

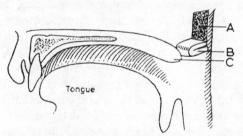

Fig. 39.—Passavant's operation for forward displacement of the posterior pharyngeal wall. A.—Raw area from which the flap was removed. B.—Flap sutured to form projection. C.—Soft palate.

Fig. 40.—Passavant's stud-shaped obturator.

A quadrilateral flap was cut and dissected from the underlying tissues at the level of the ridge of Passavant on the posterior pharyngeal wall. This flap was then folded and sutured to form a shelf-like projection (Fig. 39). However, it was found that this projection was not permanent, and disappeared after some time had elapsed.

Finally, Passavant made an obturator resembling a collar stud. This he inserted into a buttonhole-like incision running transversely across the middle of the soft palate through its entire thickness, by this means hoping to secure backward displacement of the palate and nasopharyngeal closure (Fig. 40).

But Passavant was not the only one to draw attention to the functional results. Sir William Fergusson (1864), describing the speech results after operation by the Langenbeck method, says: "Immediately after operation the modification in the voice can be at once detected. In eight or ten days the tone of the voice is at once found to be changed for the better. Improved articulation, however, comes more slowly. Years, many years, are required for distinct articulation when the whole organs are to all appearances in perfection; and after the most successful operation for cleft palate, months and years are required to alter defective sounds. With some the change comes sluggishly, but with others they are so rapid and perfect that in a few years the original defect cannot be detected except by a practised ear." This extract is quoted in full, as it describes, without need for further comment, the functional results obtained at that time, and is an indication of the increasing interest which was being taken in the speech of the patient.

About the same time, a suggestion was put forward by Simon that, after operation, patients should wear a form of pince-nez to prevent nasal escape. Whether this was intended as a temporary procedure until articulation improved and new habits were acquired, or whether it was to be a permanent appliance is not clear, but it again illustrates the recognised need for the prevention of nasal escape.

It has been described previously (p. 27) how the tensor palati muscles, before entering the soft palate, pass around hook-like bony processes, the hamuli, situated one on each side of the mouth close to the posterior part of the alveolus (see Figs. 15, 48, 50 and 51). In 1889, Billroth advocated

Fig. 41.—Schlitsky's obturator.

Fig. 42.—Wolff-Schlitsky pharyngeal obturators.

division of the hamular processes during repair of the palate, in order to lessen the tension in the tensor palati muscles and allow the palatal halves to approximate more easily. He supplemented the operation with the wearing of obturators (Figs. 41 and 42), designed to prevent nasality and improve speech.

Rutenberg, like Passavant, turned his attention to bringing forward the pharyngeal wall. In 1876, he described how he produced a scarred semi-circular area on the posterior pharyngeal wall at the level of the ridge of Passavant. By this means he hoped to produce a thickening, or bulge, at that site, and so assist a shortened soft palate to reach the pharyngeal wall. As this method proved inadequate, he suggested suturing the scarred area longitudinally. However, there appears to be no available evidence that this method was actually carried out by Rutenberg (1876) or produced any improvement in speech.

Further evidence of the interest being taken in speech is seen in an article by J. C. Bond, published in the *Lancet* (1893). This appears to be the first detailed account of the speech defects associated with cleft palate, and emphasis is now laid on the need for some speech training subsequent to operation. He mentions the "nasal element in speech," and explains that the "real test is whether power is restored of completely shutting off the nasal cavity at will, and this can readily be ascertained by noting whether the patient can forcibly blow out a lighted taper through the mouth without any air escaping through the nose." He ascribes the speech defects remaining after the Langenbeck operation to two causes, namely: (1) a soft palate which is too short; and (2) rigidity of the soft palate due to contraction produced by scar tissue. The defect, he says, is not due to any deficiency in the muscular action of the levator palati, but to the fact that these muscles can only raise the palate to an extent permitted by its length and mobility.

Mention is made of the device, so often observed in cleft palate patients, whereby the anterior nares are contracted to prevent air escaping through the nose; and Bond also describes "a marked transverse ridge on the posterior pharyngeal wall, which comes forward, as it were, to meet the palate," the ridge of Passavant.

Several practical suggestions are put forward to improve speech after operation. These include:—

1. Massage of the soft palate, "which is a mechanical gentle stretching of the velum by the finger, pressing it upwards and backwards, and thus moulding it into shape to shut off the nasal cavity."

2. "Forcible expulsion of air through the nasal cavity at the same time trying to stop it by raising the velum." The mouth remains closed during this exercise.

3. "A succession of quick, deep inspirations with the mouth open, as this is associated with marked raising of the palate."

4. Whistling and blowing games.

Very few surgeons, up to that time, had published detailed accounts of the speech results of their operative procedures. This is perhaps not surprising when one realises that the practical difficulties associated with obtaining these results are by no means few. As speech may continue to improve for several years after operation, cases must be kept under observation and results periodically reviewed. This requires much time and patience, and only those with a desire for scientific truth, and an interest and enthusiasm for this work, have devoted the time required to obtain the necessary information. Sir James Berry, in 1905, was the forerunner of these. He published a detailed account of all cases operated upon by him, 67 in number, and followed this by a similar account of a further 81 cases in 1911.

Berry used the Langenbeck operation, and, writing in 1905, thought that the best age for operation was three to four years. He never operated on a child under twenty-two months, though many of his cases, 43 out of 67, were over four years of age at the time of operation, most of these having previously been operated upon by other surgeons. Of the 67 cases published in 1905, Berry says of the speech result that "no case was absolutely normal," at the same time drawing attention to the fact that the results were "possibly not final as speech steadily improves for years after a cleft palate operation," this, of course, depending on the success of the operation.

In 1915, in a Hunterian lecture delivered before the Royal College of Surgeons, Blakeway summarised the speech results of the above cases operated upon by Berry as follows:—

Speech result	Good			Fair			Bad		
Age at operation -	under 2	2-8	over 8	under 2	2-8	over 8	under 2	2-8	over 8
Complete cleft -	5	12*	7	—	12†	2	—	5†	—
Cleft of soft and part of hard palate ◦	1	10	11	2	15	5	—	2	2
Cleft of soft palate only - -	3	6	—	—	6†	2	1	3†	—

* Three of these cases received some training.
† Includes several mentally defective children.

Speech results naturally depend to a large extent on the ambition and acuity of hearing of the patient, and not on the operative results alone, and when classifying such results the ear of the examiner, and the standards he uses in judging, are also factors of importance. The above results will, therefore, be of more value if it is noted that a case described as "speech good" has, in Berry's own words, "slight trouble with s, sk, st and initial j." This case was eighteen years of age, and had been operated upon at twelve years.

"Speech fair"—"cannot say initials s, t, z, sh, st." Age was then nine years, the operation having been carried out at three and a half years. "Speech fair"—"can pronounce all consonants but still has slight nasalisation." Age twenty-one years, operated upon at sixteen years. "Speech bad"—"practically unintelligible." Many of these cases were from very poor homes or suffered from some mental defect.

Out of 148 cases submitted to operation, the results in 112 cases are shown in the above table. The remaining 36 included cases still too young to be speaking, cases operated upon too recently for improvement to have taken place and those not seen recently or not traced.

It is interesting to note that of the 12 cases operated upon under two years of age, 9 (75 %) obtained a "good" speech result. Of those operated upon between two and eight years the result was "good" in only 39.5%, and of those over eight years, in 62%.

But good speech is not normal speech, and still further suggestions were being put forward by surgeons to improve the speech result.

In 1920 Ganzer, in Germany, described a method designed to produce a longer soft palate than that obtained with the von Langenbeck operation. He carried the lateral incisions further forward to form a V-shaped incision behind the incisor teeth (Fig. 43). After dissection, the loose tissues of the entire palate were displaced backwards, thus producing a lengthening of the soft palate. Halle and Ernst and others also obtained a longer soft palate by a similar method, the forerunner of the "push back" operation.

By this time it was generally recognised that the post-operative condition of the soft palate was all important in

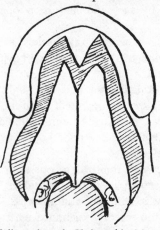

Fig. 43.—From Halle to show the V-shaped incisions of Ganzer placed behind the incisiors for backward displacement of the soft palate.

speech, but it was pointed out by Sir Harold Gillies, in 1921, that closure of the hard palate often produced malocclusion of the teeth and narrowed nasal passages, with resultant nasal intonation. Working with Kelsey Fry, he advocated closure of the soft palate at the expense of the hard palate, the resulting deficiency in the latter to be closed by a dental plate. This operation owed its origin to the bad functional results which were being obtained with the Langenbeck operation, and the authors' arguments for it are stated as follows:—

"1   In unoperated cases involving the hard palate the occlusion of the non-involved teeth is normal.

"2. After operation on the hard palate nearly all patients have abnormal occlusion of the non-involved teeth.

"3. As a result of operation on the hard palate most patients have narrowed features and nasal passages with resultant nasal intonation in speech.

"4. In any case most patients require to wear a dental plate whether operated upon or not."

Gillies recommended that:—

"1. The soft palate should be detached from the hard palate and sutured as far back as possible in the pharynx, thus making the hard palate defect greater.

"2. The hard palate defect should be closed by an appliance from earliest infancy, and

"3. The operation on the lip should be carried out as soon after birth as possible, and the operation on the palate before the development of speech.

The aims put forward for the dental treatment are:—

"1. To assist in the feeding of the child before operation is advisable.

"2. That the appliance made should maintain the soft palate in its correct position, preventing any tendency for it to be drawn forward by contraction, and, if necessary, to stretch it backwards to enable it to make contact with the posterior pharyngeal wall.

"3. To construct a permanent prosthetic appliance to compensate for the deficiency in the hard palate, and, if necessary, the anterior part of the soft palate."

A few years later, in 1925, Dorrance, in America, published details of a procedure resembling in principle the method of Ganzer, which he described as the "push-back" operation. In this operation a semicircular incision is carried round the palate, parallel to, and just within, the alveolus. The tissues of the palate are then raised and

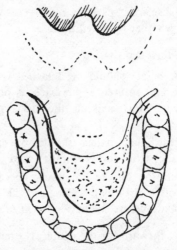

Fig. 44.—Case of congenital shortening of the palate after performance of the Dorrance "push-back" operation. The dotted line shows position of the palate before operation. Can also be used when operation for cleft palate has resulted in a short soft palate, or as second stage in repair of a cleft, combined with suture of the edges of the cleft.

freely dissected from the underlying bone. The flap thus raised is sutured loosely in position again until the blood supply is well established. At a second operation, the flap is again raised and displaced backwards until the edges of the cleft come together. They are then freshened and sutured (Fig. 44). In the case of a complete cleft, involving the alveolus and lip, the anterior part of the palate must first be closed before the "push-back" operation can be carried out. Dorrance describes the method in great detail, but gives no results as to speech.

"The main, indeed almost the only object of operating upon a cleft palate, is to enable the patient to speak intelligibly," said Sir James Berry, addressing a meeting of the Royal Society of Medicine in 1927.

At this meeting George Grey Turner discussed the surgery of cleft palate, and described the results obtained by himself, using the Langenbeck-Fergusson operation. He avoided lateral incisions wherever possible, but sometimes used relaxation scratches on the surface of the palate.

Of 155 operated cases, 90 were available for an investigation of the functional results. Owing to the absence of any standard, the classification of speech results was difficult, but Grey Turner grouped them as follows:—

"1. *Normal*—No one would ordinarily detect that the patient had ever suffered from cleft palate - - - - - - - - 10

"2. *Good*—Can say all words intelligibly, though there may be difficulty with some combinations of words - - - - - 35

"3. *Fair*—Patient has considerable difficulty in pronouncing some words, and though these patients may be readily understood by those who are accustomed to the disability, they are not ordinarily understood without close attention on the part of the listener - - - - - - - 25

"4. *Bad*—The patients have great difficulty in saying some words - - - - - 17

"5. *Unintelligible*—These patients seem to have only one sound for everything - - - 3"

F

Very few of the above cases had had the advantage of speech training, and the series included some in which the palate had not been completely restored. In 44 cases where the operation had been entirely successful in closing the cleft the speech results were:—

Normal	-	-	-	7
Good	-	-	-	20
Fair	-	-	-	14
Bad	-	-	-	3

Grey Turner found that although the cleft was easily closed in children under one or two years of age, there was little improvement in speech. In fact he found that older children obtained a better speech result as they "recognised their limitations and improved their defect."

These results are typical of the Langenbeck-Fergusson operation, which, for reasons previously described (p. 65) does not usually succeed in producing the physiological mechanism necessary for normal speech. "Evidently," says Grey Turner, "it is not sufficient merely to have a complete and movable velum, but the whole of the palate must be of normal length, must be mobile and sensitive, and must suffice either by itself or together with the pharyngeal muscles to close completely the route between the mouth and the nose."

Speaking at this same meeting, Victor Veau (1926), of Paris, compared the results obtained by him when using the Langenbeck procedure, and when using the "Veau operation," details of which were later published in his book, "Division Palatine," 1931. Eighty-nine cases were operated upon by Veau using the Langenbeck operation; some years later he was able to trace 40 of these patients, and found the speech results to be as follows:—

"25% spoke well with little or no training, but not one normally.

"15% improved with training over a long period.

"60% showed no improvement in speech."

In contrast to these results, using the "Veau" technique in 100 cases, the following results were obtained:—

Type of cleft	Soft palate only	Soft palate and part of hard	Unilateral complete	Bilateral complete
Normal Speech 40	12	12	16	—
Defective Speech 60	8	19	27	6
Total—100	20	31	43	6

Divided according to age at operation the results were:—

Age	—1 year	1-2 yrs.	2-4 yrs.	4-6 yrs.	6-9 yrs.	over 9
Normal Speech 40	14 (70%)	9 (70%)	6 (26%)	5 (33%)	3 (23%)	3 (18%)
Defective Speech 60	6 (30%)	4 (30%)	17 (74%)	10 (67%)	10 (77%)	13 (82%)

From this table it can be seen that Veau obtained his best speech results when he operated at an early age. Although the percentage of normal speech results obtained is the same in patients operated upon under one year as it is for those between one and two years, this percentage trends to decrease rapidly as the age at operation increases. If the speech result were the only consideration, it is obvious that the earlier operation is preformed the better, but there is another factor of importance, and that is the rate of mortality. In 334 cases operated upon under the age of four years, Veau states that he had a total mortality of 19, being 3.8%. The following figures show how this rate varied with the age at operation:—

| | Mortality | |
Age	(a) 1929	(b) 1933
Under one year -	- 9.4%	5.2%
One to two years -	- 5.7%	1.4%
Two to three years	- 2.7%	—
Two to four years -	- —	0.9%
Three to four years	- 1.8%	—

Although the 1933 figures showed a considerable reduction in the mortality rate since 1929, it was still very much higher under one year than when operation was performed later. For this reason Veau preferred to operate at about two years of age (1931), the mortality rate being a factor which must be taken into account when deciding the optimum age for operation.

The Veau operation included at least two important modifications of the Langenbeck type of operation. Veau contended that much shortening of the soft palate, occurring after the latter operation, was due to contraction of scar tissue formed from the large raw area left on the upper, or nasal, surface of the soft palate. To obviate this he:—

1. Sutured the mucous membrane of the nasal surface of the palate separately.

2. Followed this by his "suture musculaire," or separate suture of the muscles and tissues of the palate—this being the most important part of the procedure.

3. Completed the operation by suture of the oral mucous
   membrane.

Veau used lateral incisions, meeting in the form of a V
behind the incisor teeth, as used by Ganzer, Ernst and
others (Fig. 45). The two flaps of palatal tissue, having
been thoroughly dissected from the underlying bone, were
displaced medially and backwards, and were then sutured as

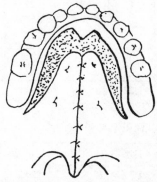

Fig. 45.—Incisions and flaps as used by Veau.

described above. In the case of unilateral and bilateral
complete clefts, Veau operated on the lips as early in life as
was advisable, at the same time uniting the alveolus and
anterior part of the hard palate. The cleft of the soft palate
and remainder of the hard palate was then closed later,
usually between one and two years of age.

In 1933 Veau published the speech results in a further
100 cases of cleft palate. He divided his cases into three
classes as follows:—

1. Those who had normal speech, not only to the
   untrained ear, but to the phonetic expert.

2. Those who could pronounce all the phonetic sounds, but associated with them additional noises such as nasal escape or nasal tone.

3. Those who could not pronounce certain sounds, notably p, t, k or ch [tʃ] s, j [dʒ] and z.

Type of cleft	Soft palate only	Soft pal. and part of hard	Uni-lateral complete	Bi-lateral complete	Total
1. Normal	15	21	22	4	62
2. Nasal escape or nasal tone	6	5	10	2	23
3. Deficient consonants	1	5	7	2	15
Total	22	31	39	8	100

According to age at operation:—

Age	—1 yr.	1-2 yrs.	2-4 yrs.	4-6 yrs.	6-9 yrs.	over 9
Normal Speech	15	18	12	8	4	4
Defective Speech	5	8	8	4	3	10
Total	20	27	20	12	7	14
Percentage of normal results	75%	70%	60%	66.6%	57%	28%

Comparing these results with those previously quoted, it will now be noticed that Veau had obtained normal speech in four out of eight bilateral complete alveolar clefts.

A comparison of the results obtained with the "Lane operation" and with the Langenbeck operation was made at the same meeting of the Royal Society of Medicine in 1927 by C. A. R. Nitch. He stated that he had operated upon 23 cases, using the Lane flap operation: of these he had traced six. In all the soft palate was short and rigid, and the speech results were, in three cases poor, and in three bad. Using the Langenbeck operation he had operated upon 12 cases, but only one had been traced. The speech in this case was poor. Fifty-one cases were treated by a modified Langenbeck technique, but of these he had been able to trace 35.

Speech good (perfect, or nearly so) - - 13—37.1%
Speech poor (typical cleft palate) - - 17—48.6%
Speech bad (practically unintelligible) - 5—14.3%

W. E. M. Wardill, speaking at this meeting, emphasised the inconsistency in the speech results which were being obtained using the standard methods of operation. "Perfect anatomical results show gross defects in speech; others, with apparently poor anatomical results, speak very well indeed," and he contended that the type of speech obtained was proportional to the competence of the palatopharyngeal sphincter. "Perfect function can never be attained unless a perfect anatomical and physiological valve be first formed. The converse of this is not equally true," as all speech therapists would agree. Bad habits acquired before operation persist in spite of a competent palatopharyngeal sphincter, and the factors of mentality and acuity of hearing in the patient also play a definite part.

By a series of measurements on normal and cleft palate skulls, Wardill demonstrated that the dimensions of the pharynx were increased in the latter in the antero-posterior direction and from side to side, the increase in width of the pharynx from side to side being greater than in the antero-posterior direction. The bony deformity was small, but from a knowledge of the anatomy of speech production, it can be seen that a defect in closure even as small as 2 mm. will produce the well-known cleft palate type of speech. Here, then, is another important factor which the surgeon must consider.

To obviate this, and ensure more reliable functional results, Wardill (1933) devised the operation of pharyngo-plasty, an operation designed to reduce the increased dimensions of the nasopharynx and to produce a more prominent forward bulge at the level of the ridge of Passavant (Fig. 46). This operation could be used in conjunction with any type of operation for closure of the cleft. Wardill himself combined it, at this time, with the Langenbeck-Fergusson, Gillies-Fry and Veau operations. He also included fracture of the hamular processes in order to relieve tension in the tensor palati muscles.

In 1933 he published details of the speech results obtained in 55 cases, operated upon as above. These cases were divided into four groups:—

"1. Those who possess the prime factor of importance, namely, a competent palatopharyngeal valve, and who therefore have the functional physiological mechanism for the production of normal speech— 19 cases.

"2. Those who speak without any cleft palate stigma, and are, therefore, apart from their dialect and other peculiarities, perfect speakers—13 cases.

"3. Those who have neither normal speech nor a physiologically competent valve—6 cases.

"4. Those who are too young to apply the various tests or to make certain of the condition by their speech, also cases in which the operation is of recent date —17 cases."

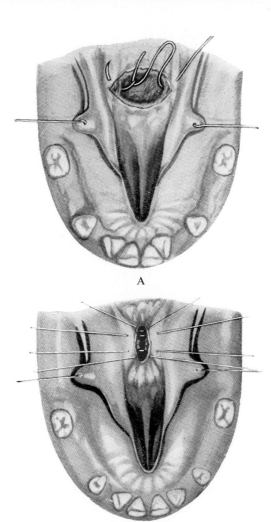

Fig. 46.—Wardill's pharyngoplasty.

A.—Shows incision in posterior pharyngeal wall and area undermined. The needle is shown passing through the left salpingopharyngeal fold.

B.—Four sutures inserted ready for tying. Shows the effect of traction upon the sutures, and how they tend to narrow the nasopharynx, the salpingopharyngeal folds being dragged together.

According to age at operation these cases were classified as follows:—

Age at operation	—1 year	1-2 years	2-4 years	4-6 years	6-12 years	12-20 years	Over 20
Competent valve	—	—	3		6	5	4
Normal speech	3	—	7	—	1	—	2
Defective speech	—	—	1	—	1	2	2
Too young to be sure or operation too recent	3	7	5	—	1	1	—

According to type of cleft:—

Type of cleft	Soft palate only	Soft and part of hard pal.	Uni-lateral alveolar	Bi-lateral alveolar
Competent valve	1	6	10	2
Normal speech	4	5	4	—
Defective speech	—	4	—	2
Too young to be sure. or operation too recent	3	8	6	—

It will be noticed that the average age at operation is high in these cases. Wardill himself chose to operate before speech was established, usually from six months to two years of age, but in the series under consideration many older patients had presented themselves for operation.

In these 55 cases the operative result is ascertainable in 38, the remainder being too young, or the operation of too recent date, to allow of classification. Of these 38, 6 were surgical failures both as regards physiological function and speech, and 32 were successful operative results, being 84%.

In any surgical procedure on the palate the blood supply must always be considered (p. 43). Were this completely destroyed, healing would be prevented as the certainty and speed of this process in any part of the body depends on the abundance of the blood supply. The long flaps used by Veau depend for their blood supply on the posterior palatine artery and on those smaller vessels supplying the soft palate and tonsillar region, the sphenopalatine artery having been cut across by the incisions behind the incisor teeth. Many surgeons, however, agree that the posterior palatine artery, if left intact, tends to anchor the flaps and prevent that freedom and absence of tension which is so essential in the production of a mobile soft palate.

For this reason Denis Browne performed a two-stage modification of the Langenbeck operation, which he described in 1932. At the first operation incisions were made, in the palate at each side, and the posterior palatine artery was cut. The palate then depended for its blood supply anteriorly on the sphenopalatine artery, and the smaller posterior group of vessels. When the new blood circulation had become thoroughly established, usually after an interval of about three months, the second stage was undertaken. This included long lateral incisions (Fig. 47), which ran from the canine tooth in front backwards, close to the alveolar margin, and ended in the tonsillar region. The muscles of the palate were liberated from their lateral attachments and were displaced towards the middle line, the hamular processes being fractured. The edges of the cleft were pared, the mucoperiosteum was detached from the hard

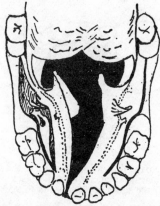

Fig. 47.—Diagrammatic drawing of a complete single cleft. On the right side the line of incision is marked out: the hamulus, the tendons of the tensor and the posterior palatine artery are shown as though the mucosa were transparent. On the left side the palate, both hard and soft, has been freed for suturing. In the bare palate bone left by its inward shifting can be seen the stump of the artery which has been cut at a previous operation, while the hamulus is broken off its base and has fallen inwards, and of course the tendons of the tensor palati should not be exposed as it is in the drawing.

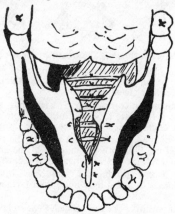

Fig. 48.—Diagrammatic drawing of the stitching of a cleft of the soft and hard palate.

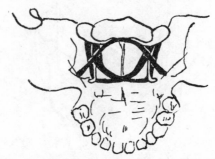

Fig. 49.—Diagrammatic drawing of the base of the skull, showing the muscles forming the sphincter (in solid black). This figure is the foundation for the series of drawings in Fig. 50.

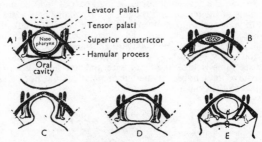

Fig. 50.—Diagram showing the treatment of the soft palate.

A. Normal sphincter in relaxation. The constrictor and the levatores are relaxed, and the tensor is contracted, pulling the soft palate away from the posterior pharyngeal wall.

B. Normal sphincter in contraction. The tensor is relaxed, allowing the middle of the soft palate to go up into a dimple. The constrictor and levatores are contracted, shutting the nasopharyngeal passage.

C. Formation of the cleft of the soft palate. The bony framework is the same as before, but both the muscles of the anterior sling are shortened, and end not far from the hamular process.

D. The result usually produced by suturing without shifting the muscles. The palate is thin and tight and rather farther away from the posterior pharyngeal wall than normal.

E. Method of suturing recommended. The relaxation incisions have been made and the hamulus has been snapped off inwards. This allows the ends of the muscles to meet without stretching.

palate, and the muscular and fibrous attachments of the soft palate from the posterior edge of the hard palate. The nasal mucosa was sutured separately, as in the "Veau" operation; the edges of the cleft were then drawn together and firmly sutured (Fig. 48).

Browne described the nasopharyngeal sphincter as consisting of two interacting slings (Fig. 49). The diagrams (Fig. 50) show the action of these muscles in closing the sphincter, the deficiency when the palate is cleft, and the relaxation obtained in the tensores when the hamular processes are fractured. Describing this, Browne, said "The hamular process can be snapped off at its base without interfering with the synovial sheath of the pulley (see p. 27), and so allowed to be displaced inwards and upwards to a position which will not interfere with the joining of the two tensores. In this new position it must finally become fixed by the healing process so as to afford once more a fulcrum to the tendon that curls round it."

In 1934 Browne described a method for narrowing the nasopharynx in order to ensure improved functional results. After dissection, he passed a purse-string suture round the entire nasopharyngeal sphincter, just beneath the mucosa. This suture ran behind the superior constrictor, exactly in the line of the ridge of Passavant and emerged through the raw edges of the soft palate (Figs. 51 and 52). It was tied after the nasal mucosa had been sutured and caused narrowing of the nasopharynx (Fig. 52B). No speech results of this procedure have as yet been published; but Browne obtained a very high percentage of primary unions with good speech results.

By a gradual process of experiment, Wardill eventually evolved the "4-flap" method of operation, which he described in 1937. This was based on the Veau flap operation,

but the two long Veau flaps were replaced by four short
ones. Though described as a "flap" operation, this term is
not used here to denote an operation such as the "Lane"
operation, where a flap is everted, but is an operation of
median suture, based on a knowledge of the anatomy and

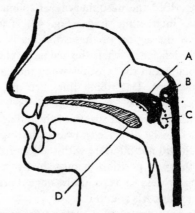

Fig. 51.—Closure of the nasopharynx.

A. The soft palate in the position of closure, showing a depression
in its centre opposite the level of closure, and the uvula well away
from the posterior wall. A white dot shows the position of the ring
suture when finally tied. B. Passavant's ridge, with a white dot
showing position of the ring suture. C. The position of the soft
palate when closing the nasopharynx, as given in textbooks. It
corresponds to the general notion of its action as that of a flap-valve,
rather like a cardiac one. D. The position of the palate after a classic
Langenbeck operation. The mucoperiosteum of the hard palate has
been swung downwards to meet in the mid-line, and the soft palate is
shortened by being stretched from side to side.

function of the palate. Wardill did not claim that by
this operation finality had yet been reached, but that this
method had been proved to produce the physiological
mechanism necessary for satisfactory speech results, and
when practised on infants before about two years of age,
enabled them to learn to speak naturally and correctly

without any speech training. This procedure combined the advantages of the Veau, Gillies and Dorrance operation. Wardill emphasised the necessity for lack of tension on the suture line if a mobile velum was to be attained, and whilst continuing to include fracture of the hamular processes, carried this further and sacrificed all bony attachments of the soft palate and divided the posterior palatine artery. This operation was always combined with pharyngoplasty.

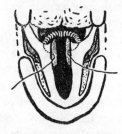 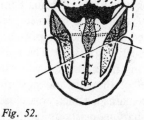

Fig. 52.

A. Diagram of the insertion of the circular suture in the line of the sphincter which is recommended. It can be seen entering the raw surface of the soft palate, passing completely round the pharynx under the mucosa, and emerging through the raw surface of the opposite side.

B. Diagram of the suturing of the ends of the tensors of the palate. The circular suture has been drawn tight and knotted, and its ends passed round the tendinous expansion of the tensors on either side. It will be drawn tight and knotted, taking all strain off the other sutures.

Briefly, incisions were made in the palate as in diagram (Fig. 53), the hamular processes were divided, and four flaps were freely dissected and raised from their underlying bed, the nasal mucosa on the upper surface of the palate was also separated from the bone. These flaps, when entirely free (Fig. 54), were displaced medially and posteriorly until they came together without tension. They were then sutured in position, the nasal mucosa being first sutured separately as in the Veau operation (Figs. 55, 56 and 57). The method used in the dissection and displacement of the flaps possessed a great advantage in that no raw areas were left after suture in any mobile part of the palate, such as are found in the typical Langenbeck operation, the raw areas which remained being over bone. Again the V-Y advancement obtained by this method (Fig. 58) produced the greatest possible length of velum.

This operation had the advantage of being applicable to all types of cleft and produced a long, mobile soft palate with a competent palatopharyngeal sphincter. It had the further advantage of being completed in one stage. In the case of an alveolar complete cleft Wardill, following Veau, repaired the lip and anterior part of the hard palate as soon after birth as possible. The repaired lip was then useful in moulding the upper jaw while the bone was still malleable. A cleft of the soft and posterior part of the hard palate then remained, which was closed by the "4-flap" method with pharyngoplasty at about one to two years of age.

In his work in cleft palate surgery, T. Pomfret Kilner (1937) combined the surgical procedures he had observed and found most useful. He formerly used pharynoplasty (Wardill), but with the continued development of surgical technique, he found it possible in most cases to obtain satisfactory function of the palatopharyngeal sphincter without performing a pharyngoplasty. Though this operation on the posterior pharyngeal wall narrowed the pharyngeal isthmus, as previously described, the resultant scarring may lessen the mobility of the pharyngeal muscles in that region. Veau flaps were used, with extensive freeing of the soft palate tissues from the posterior borders of the palatal processes, and flaps from the vomer were also used when available, to assist in closing the nasal surface of the palate. Fracture of the hamular processes was used and Kilner stated that he had no doubts about the relaxation given by this means. He had seen no disability produced by this

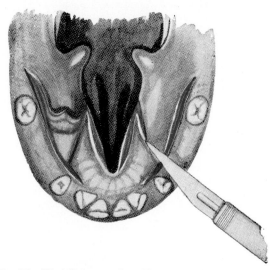

Fig. 53.—Wardill 4-flap operation. The mucoperiosteum of the hard
palate is completely severed by an oblique incision.

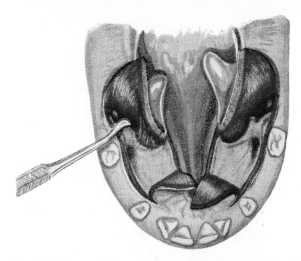

Fig. 54.—The greatest care is taken to get free separation of the soft palate from the bony surface of the hard palate. Note position of the pterygoideus internus muscle and the fact that the nasal mucosa remains intact.

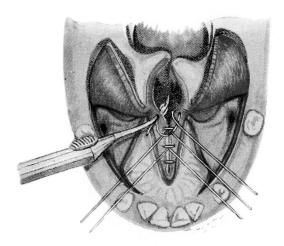

Fig. 55.—The nasal mucosa is sutured according to the method of Veau. Note that two of the sutures have been left long to anchor the flaps.

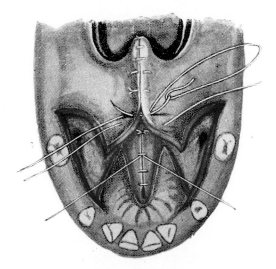

Fig. 56.—Insertion of the sutures into what was formerly the muco-periosteum of the hard palate.

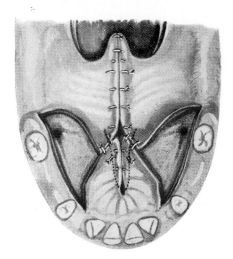

Fig. 57.—Repair completed. The dotted line shows the approximate situation of the united nasal mucosa.

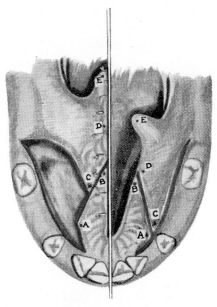

Fig. 58.—Diagram to illustrate V-Y advancement of the velum obtained with the Wardill 4-flap technique. The letters indicate the corresponding positions before and after operation.

procedure, and thought that the function of the tensor palati muscle might be changed when it was released, and that it might, under these circumstances, become an additional elevator of the palate. Further freedom of the tissues was obtained by free separation of the lateral pharyngeal wall from the internal pterygoid plate as practised by Ernst and Axhausen. The Wardill 4-flap operation with longer anterior flaps based on the anterior palatine arteries was found useful for closing wide clefts which extended far forward.

In the case of a submucous cleft, an operation similar to the above is often necessary to obtain normal speech. The nasopharynx may be more capacious than the normal, and speech will then be of cleft palate type due to incomplete nasopharyngeal closure. Though these cases are rare, and it is therefore impossible to give a definite opinion, it is probable that speech therapy without operative treatment will be insufficient for the achievement of normal speech.

A bifid uvula alone may have no effect on speech, but if associated with an enlarged nasopharynx, as in the case of the submucous cleft, it may be sufficient to prevent naso-pharyngeal closure. These conditions have been described by Dorrance as "congenital insufficiency of the palate," and for which the push-back operation was primarily designed. Whether operative treatment is required will depend on whether or not the patient possesses normal function of the palatopharyngeal sphincter.

From the foregoing it will be seen how with an increased knowledge of the anatomy of the palate and the physiological mechanism necessary for speech, operative procedures have developed. The chief points included in most modern cleft palate operations are:—

(1) The two halves of the palate are sutured in such a way that the muscles are united as in the normal palate,

G

and the length of the soft palate increased so far as is possible.

(2) The suturing of the soft palate must be done without tension, and for this purpose structures such as the hamular processes and the posterior palatine artery may be destroyed, care being taken that the blood supply to the palate is maintained or the tissues will not survive.

(3) Suturing is carried out so as to avoid as far as possible the formation of scar tissue on both the nasal and oral surfaces. This would otherwise cause thickening and lack of flexibility in the soft palate.

(4) If there is a scarcity of tissues the hard palate is sacrificed for the benefit of the soft palate, the hard palate defect being closed later by a dental plate.

It is interesting that in recent years, chiefly in the United States of America, there has been an attempt to use some of the methods first suggested by Passavant in the nineteenth century. McCutcheon (1954) appreciated that an intimate relationship existed between the insertion into the palate of the palatopharyngeus and the superior constrictor of the pharynx. He therefore attempted to produce a longer soft palate by suturing the palatopharyngeus muscles in the mid-line, thus producing a posterior extension to the soft palate as did Passavant (Fig. 36). Passavant's operation of dissecting a flap from the posterior pharyngeal wall and suturing this to the soft palate has also been revived, a combination and modification of the two methods illustrated (pp. 70, 71).

This operation, known as the pharyngeal flap procedure, has become increasingly common in recent years, particularly in the United States where it is used both as a primary and a secondary procedure.

Briefly, a piece of tissue from the posterior pharyngeal

wall is dissected and one end is sutured to the upper surface of the soft palate whilst the other end remains attached in its original position (Fig. 59), thus forming a bridge of tissue across the nasopharynx.

The type of flap varies. It may be inferiorly based, that is remaining attached to the posterior pharyngeal wall at its lower end, by means of which the blood supply to the flap is maintained. Or the lower end of the flap may be detached,

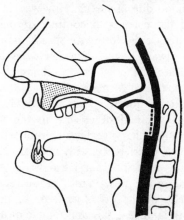

Fig. 59.—Diagram showing a high superiorly based pharyngeal flap. The dotted line indicates the area from which the flap was removed.

as in the superiorly based flap, the blood supply being maintained through the attached upper end. Whilst both may cause narrowing of the nasopharynx and help to occlude the nasopharyngeal airway, neither contributes towards normal anatomical conditions and the usual functional nasopharyngeal closure.

Whilst the superiorly based flap may assist the action of the levatores in raising the soft palate, the inferiorly based flap may even interfere with, limit, or even prevent the lifting action of the levatores of the soft palate. Owsley

(1968) has used a superiorly based flap at a higher level in in the nasopharynx than is usual, and reports improved results from this modification.

It has also been thought that muscle fibres of the superior constrictor from the posterior pharyngeal wall, now in the transverse flap, may sometimes continue to show muscle activity and assist in nasopharyngeal closure. To some extent, also, a short soft palate is maintained in a more posterior position during speech. However, in some cases, the bridge of tissue tends to contract during subsequent years and a satisfactory closure for speech soon after operation may not always be maintained. Owsley has lined the raw lower surface of the flap in an attempt to lessen such contraction due to scar formation.

Such operations, however, aim to provide a substitute for the normal method of closure in the nasopharynx. Operations on the pharyngeal wall produce scarring and frequently some interference with normal movements of the lateral and posterior pharyngeal walls. Alteration in the positioning of the muscles may produce undue tension in such muscles as the thyrohyoid, or of other muscles associated with laryngeal, jaw and tongue movements, and may sometimes cause alteration in the pitch of the voice. Such procedures may also cause abnormal and peculiar types of resonance due to obstruction in the nasopharynx, as when a pharyngeal flap is sutured to the soft palate.

Braithwaite (1958) has utilised the proposition that when the medial pterygoid plate is dissected free from fascial and muscular attachments, certain beneficial muscular re-organisations may take place. He operates on the cleft lip and anterior palate when the child is 10 lb. in weight, is thriving and free from any infection. The palate is repaired as near the age of one year as is possible.

Whillis (1930) described the upper fibres of the superior

constrictor and called this portion the "palatopharyngeal, sphincter." As previously described (pp. 30-33) the upper portion of the superior constrictor appears to consist of two lamellae, one passing medially into the soft palate and the other gaining attachment to the hamulus laterally. In the operation used by Braithwaite the attachments of this lateral lamella are freely dissected, the hamulus is completely detached, the tensor may be divided, and the upper pharyngeal walls are freely dissected laterally from outside the pharynx. The upper end of the pterygo-mandibular raphe with its attached fibres of the superior constrictor, and the freely dissected lateral muscular fibres of Whillis (the palatopharyngeal sphincter muscle fibres), are then displaced medially to become attached to the soft palate. These are the initial stages in the formation of an adequate sphincter the completion of which is the mid-line suture of the palatal muscles. The medial and lateral muscular lamellae and the adjacent fibres of the superior constrictor all become inserted into the soft palate forming a complete sphincter whose natural tone appears to narrow the pharynx especially in its lateral regions. There is no doubt that complete freeing of the soft palate at operation, associated with the above dissection, allows good nasopharyngeal closure to be obtained, and it is felt that the narrowing of the nasopharynx in its lateral zones is not the least of its attributes.

Such free dissection of tissues to permit apposition of muscles and their more normal positioning will lead to subsequent gradual development towards normality. This is better seen in the surgery of cleft lips. Here free dissection is continued until the nose can be correctly positioned and the two sides balanced. Simple suture of the muscles on each side of the cleft is then completed. It is important to realise the essential part played by the activity of the united muscles of the lip. It is usual for the development of the two sides of the cleft lip to be unequal and for development to be also limited. This method of repair, therefore, usually produces at first a more or less marked notch of the lip margin, or even puckering of the suture line, which is accepted at that time. However, once the muscles are united in good position and able to exert normally balanced forces, there is rapid growth of the sutured elements. Because the lip is sutured without tension, the normal daily muscular activity of the lip and the circumoral muscles produces growth and development until the lip margin becomes normal for the age of the child. The alveolar arch is also improved by the muscular activity and the adequate balance between lip and tongue tip pressures. Attempts to produce a long, adult lip in a child of six months can only result in future deformity during subsequent growth. It is the mature surgeon who can accept temporarily what may appear to be a fault, knowing through experience that given the right conditions of mobility and freedom nature can be stimulated to improve the condition as would normally have occurred in utero.

Similarly, following such surgical treatment of the cleft palate, post-operative observations suggest that the diameters of the nasopharynx are reduced and approach the normal. Although articulatory defects may persist for some years following such operation at between one and two years of age it is rare to find a child who has any nasal escape of air, except in a few cases where insufficient development of the palatal plates forming the hard palate has caused a residual fistula in the anterior part of the palate. The tone of the voice is also normal following this operative procedure. This is a consistent finding and is probably due to the resulting mobility of the lateral and posterior pharyngeal walls which is obvious on post-operative examination, in addition to a freely mobile soft palate.

McCollum, Richardson and Swanson have also found that a successful repair of the palate has depended largely on wide and extensive mobilisation of tissues, and that, on post-operative clinical examination, "activity of the lateral pharyngeal walls appeared to be the most important single factor in the physical production of good speech." Especially have they found that absence of nasal tone is correlated with marked inward movement of the lateral pharyngeal walls.

STAGES IN THE OPERATION AS PERFORMED BY BRAITHWAITE (1966)

Lip and anterior palate.—The aim of this operation is to establish the condition of the child's lip as it should have been at the embryonic stage of development between the thirty-fifth and forty-first day and to repair the anterior palate.

In the alveolar complete cleft the anterior palate is first closed using incisions as shown in Fig. 60. The septal mucosa is dissected and the margins inserted under the palatal mucosa (Fig. 61) and sutured.

The incisions in the lip are based on Veau's description and are shown in Fig. 62. Free dissection of the tissues between the cheek and maxilla, laterally, permits the central positioning of the columella and of the lip elements without tension. The lip is sutured in three layers, the internal mucosal layer, the muscles on each side of the cleft and finally the skin (Fig. 63). Results of surgery for cleft lip are shown in Figures 64-67.

Following repair of the lip and anterior palate there is an intact alveolus and the palatal cleft is reduced to a cleft of the soft palate and a partial cleft of the hard palate (Fig. 68).

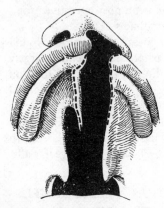

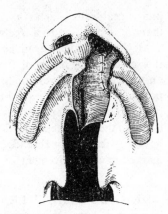

Fig. 60.—The incisons for the repair of the anterior palate.

Fig. 61.—The sutured nasal floor and anterior palate.

Fig. 62.—(A) Diagrammatic representation of Veau operation; (B) a further stage of the operation with the skin and mucosa discarded.

Fig. 63.—Further stages in the suture of the cleft lip according to Veau.

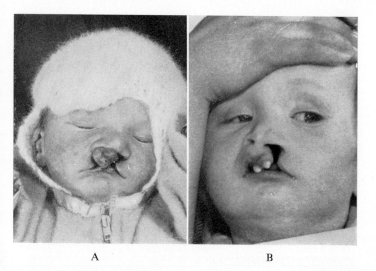

A   B

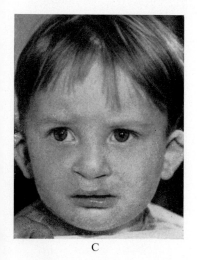

Fig. 64.—Repaired cleft lips
showing subsequent growth.

C

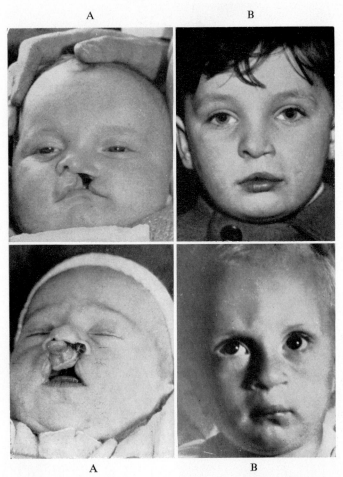

Figs. 65 and 66.—Repaired cleft lips showing subsequent growth.

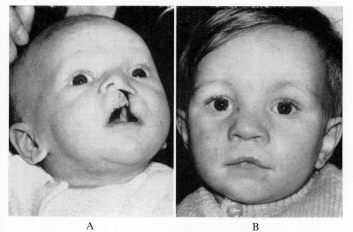

A   B

Fig. 67.—Repaired cleft lips showing subsequent growth.

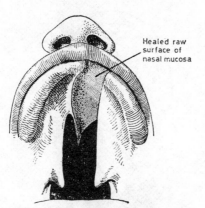

Fig. 68.—The healed anterior palate.

Operation on the palate, in infancy.—The incisions used are shown in Fig. 69A. They are taken from the angle of the mandible and continued forward to about the level of the canine tooth. The palatal flaps are raised from the bone of the hard palate using an elevator (Fig. 69B) and the palatine artery exposed (Fig. 70 and 71). If the fibrous processes

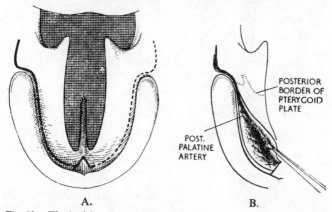

A.   B.

Fig. 69.—The incisions to be followed in the repair of the cleft palate.

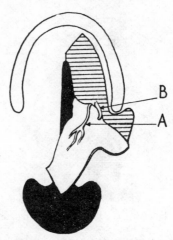

Fig. 70.—Flap dissected up left side of displaying (A) Palatine artery (B) Hamulus.

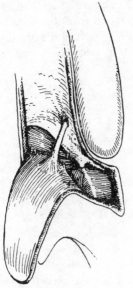

Fig. 71.—Incisions continued laterally and posteriorly to medial pterygoid lamella.

surrounding the artery are carefully dissected a backward
displacement of the palatal flaps by about 0.25 in. is possible.

The incisions are then continued posteriorly to the medial
pterygoid lamina (Fig. 71), the hamulus is dissected, fractured and displaced medially, and all muscular and mucosal
attachments are dissected from the medial side and posterior
edge of the medial pterygoid lamina (Fig. 72).

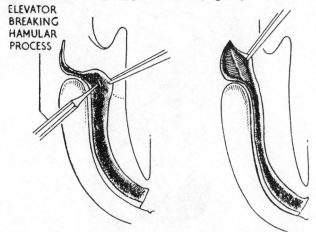

Fig. 72.—Dissection and fracture of hamular process and from
medial pterygoid lamina.

Incisions then continue around the pharynx, the lateral
walls of which are freed from the underlying neck fascia as
far as, and into, the space of Ernst. The lateral fibres of the
superior constrictor are then displaced medially with the
soft palate, eventually to be sutured with the levatores in
the soft palate. This allows the two halves of the palate to
meet easily in the mid-line (Fig. 73).

Fibres attaching the raised palatal flaps to the posterior
border of the hard palate are then dissected. The medial
edge of the soft palate is divided longitudinally and

dissected until the muscle fibres are exposed and the levator muscle endings identified in the tissues of the soft palate (Fig. 74). The whole procedure is then repeated on the opposite side.

Finally the mucosa of the lower edge of the nasal septum is divided and sutured to the nasal mucosa of the palatal flaps using catgut sutures (Fig. 75).

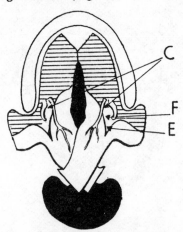

Fig. 73.—Both flaps now dissected. Both medial pterygoid plates (C) dissected free from superior constrictor (F). Space (E) widely opened and packed separating pharynx not only from bone attachments but from deep cervical fascial attachments.

The palatal mucosa and muscles of the soft palate (the levator and fibres of the superior constrictor) are sutured in one layer using wide mattress sutures of silk, alternating with simple stitches. Suturing commences with the uvula and is continued until the anterior apices of the palatal flaps are reached. An anterior triangle of tissue, lying just behind the central alveolus, is raised, using an elevator, to facilitate the suturing of the palatal flaps (Figs. 76, 77 and 78).

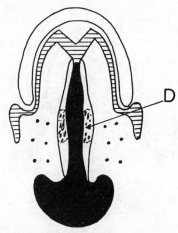

Fig. 74.—Flaps replaced: soft palate dissected to show levator palati (D). Dots show site of mattress sutures.

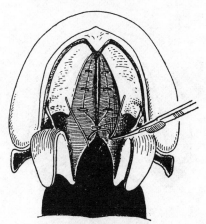

Fig. 75.—Suture of nasal mucosa to mucosa of lower edge of nasal septum.

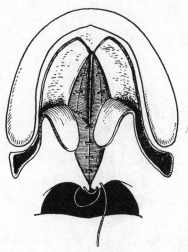

Fig. 76.—Suture of palatal muscles and mucosa.

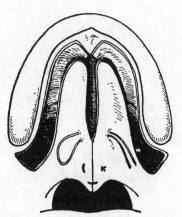

Fig. 77.—Suture of palate continued.

The posterior lateral spaces of the pharynx are packed
with gauze soaked in Whitehead's varnish and these packs
afford support to the sutured palate during healing. They

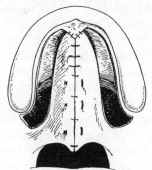

Fig. 78.—The repaired cleft palate.

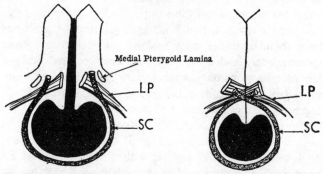

Fig. 79.—Levatores overlapped (LP). Superior Constrictors (SC) joined
by mattress sutures.

are removed on the tenth day after surgery and within
twenty-four hours the neck fascia, muscles and integument,
fall in to close the gap and support the lateral pharyngeal
walls in their new, medially displaced position. The narrowing of the pharynx and inward positioning of the lateral

pharyngeal walls is shown in Fig. 79. It should be noted that no incisions are made in the pharyngeal walls so that there is no scarring or loss of mobility of what is normal tissue.

By these procedures the palate is displaced posteriorly by the sutured superior constrictor fibres which were transposed into the soft palate, and upwards by the sutured levator. Gain in length is obtained by suture of the medial edges of the anterior portions of the palatal flaps.

Should there be a shortage of tissue anteriorly, inadequate for complete closure, which can occur when embryonic development is arrested at an early stage in the development of the palatal plates, a fistula, or aperture may be left just posteriorly to the central alveolus. It is better to permit this rather than to narrow the maxilla in attempts to obtain complete closure. If necessary a fistula in this position may be closed later by a dental appliance which will in no way affect the movement of the soft palate and nasopharyngeal closure. However, although no bone grafting is used it has been found that the great majority of such fistulæ close spontaneously and completely, the time required being a few months to perhaps several years and dependant upon the degree of adequacy of the palatal tissues. Further details are given later of the results of this operation.

However, whilst the fistula persists speech cannot be normal even if palatopharyngeal closure is adequate. Ability to produce [k] and [g] with normal intra-oral air pressure will indicate that nasopharyngeal closure is adequate, although production of more anterior sounds, that is anterior to the fistula, [t], [d] and [s] will lack adequate air pressure for normal articulation.

Much depends in such an operation upon the personal skill of the surgeon. The time usually required is 20 to 30 minutes and results have been helped by modern methods of anaesthesia and the use of antibiotics.

A

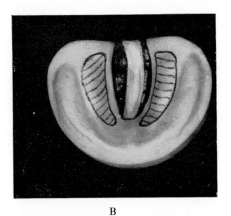

B

Fig. 80.—Stimulating appliance for use in primary cases; model showing pressure areas.

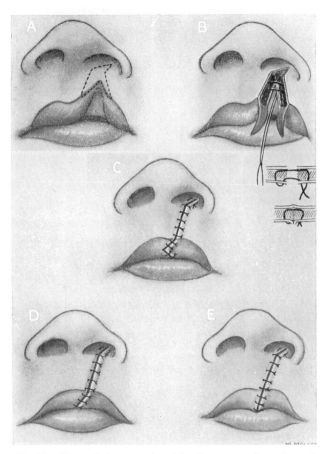

Fig. 81.—The technique employed in the repair of a unilateral pre-alveolar cleft.

A. Incisions indicated by dotted lines.

B. The first muco-muscular suture passed.

Inset.—The muco-muscular mattress suture tied, giving full apposition of muscle, everting mucosal edges and bringing skin edges together ready for suturing without tension.

C., D. and E. Suturing completed. Alternative ways of treating vermilion border: (C) by imbricating flaps, (D) by flap from outer element of lip, and (E) by equal flaps from both elements.

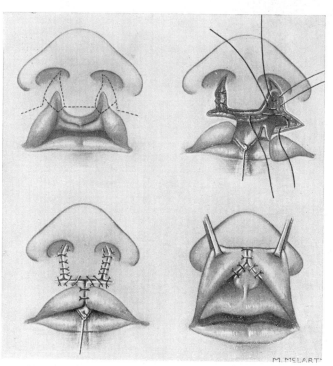

Fig. 82.—The technique employed in the repair of a bilateral pre-alveolar cleft. This follows in all material respects to the procedure advocated by Veau for secondary repair of bilateral complete alveolar clefts.

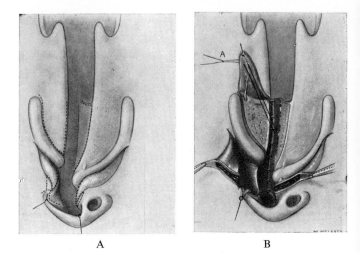

A   B

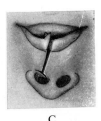

C

Fig. 83.—First operation on complete unilateral cleft of lip, alveolus
and palate.

    A. Incisions.

    B. Floor of nose reconstructed by approximation of muco-
       periosteal flaps from vomer and upper surface of left
       palatal process. Buccal muco-periosteal flap ready to be
       drawn into position over suture line by silkworm gut
       suture "A".

    C. Position of parts in lip repair: sutures omitted.

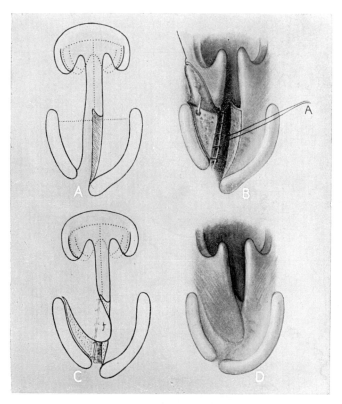

Fig. 84.—Hard palate part of repair at first operation on a unilateral complete cleft of lip, alveolus and palate. (Group III Left. Complete.)

A. The cleft.
B. Reconstruction of floor of nose.
C. Buccal flap overlying nasal suture line.
D. Late result of operation.

Following such surgery in early life it has been observed that there is stimulation of growth of muscle tissue and increase in activity. Observations on such growth and the speech results have been continued now for 18 years and are reported in outline on page 108 and in greater detail, page 121.

Bone grafting.—This has been used since 1954 in attempts to obviate the defect in the hard palate. Thin bone inlays, taken from various sites, have been implanted to bridge the anterior part of the cleft and, as the result of further bone development, prevent inward displacement of the maxilla and give support to the alveolar arch.

In 1955 at the British Dental Congress, McNeil (1956) claimed that by taking advantage of normal growth factors—periods when there is acceleration of growth, periods when the osteogenic potential is high—it has been possible to assist closure of congenital clefts of the hard palate by mechanical stimulation of the growth impulse during the periods mentioned. It is known that forces which are within the limits of tolerance will act to stimulate bone opposition if they are applied to particular regions and in such directions that they can be regarded as intensified *normal* forces.

McNeil has used such stimulation to treat patients in which a breakdown of tissue in the hard palate has followed surgical treatment or where the hard palate, or part of it, has intentionally been left unclosed by the surgeon. The appliance is designed to exert gentle pressure over a considerable area of the hard palate, but care is taken that no pressure is applied to the free edges of the palatal defect. He also found that in infants the use of appliances designed for other purposes than bone stimulation brought about growth changes of the palatal region. He has therefore attempted to bring about narrowing of the hard palate by the

H

age of 15 to 18 months by osteogenesis so that surgery will then be confined to repair of the soft palate and only a small defect of the hard palate. This figure (Fig. 80) shows the areas over which pressure is applied and the stimulating appliance.

This work is still developing and it remains to be seen how much it can contribute to the treatment of cleft lip and palate. However, McNeil stresses that surgery is an important factor in the treatment of cleft palate and the need for the closest co-operation from the outset between the surgeon and the dental specialist.

OPERATION FOR CLEFTS OF THE PRIMARY PALATE (Group I and Group III)

Though a functional palatopharyngeal sphincter is the first essential in obtaining normal speech, defective articulation may persist under these conditions when there has been a cleft of the lip and adequate function has not been achieved by operation The main essentials for good speech are an upper lip which is mobile and which can make good apposition with the lower lip for the bilabial consonants p, b, and m. Again, it must be possible for the patient to raise the lip margin above the level of the lower edge of the upper incisor teeth. If this is not possible difficulty will be experienced in the articulation of the consonants f, s and th. There may also be some distortion of consonant sounds where the alveolus is irregular, where the premaxilla is too prominent or where there are no upper incisor teeth. The operative result obtained is, therefore, not only of cosmetic value—but is also important in the development of normal speech.

Figs. 81 and 82, (Kilner, 1937), illustrate a method used in the closure of unilateral and bilateral Group I clefts.

In Group III cases, where there is a cleft of the lip and the alveolus with a complete cleft of the palate, the anterior part of the hard palate is closed prior to closure of the lip and at the same operation, as shown in Figs. 82-84. See also the method described p. 103 and Figs. 60-67.

SECONDARY OPERATIONS

Operative procedures fall mainly into two main groups, namely those which attempt to lengthen the palate and those which aim to bring forward the pharyngeal wall to meet, and compensate for, the short soft palate.

In the past many surgical procedures were inadequate, and as the production of a normal functional palato-pharyngeal sphincter was not always considered, it is not surprising that in some post-operative cases normal speech was never possible.

In the child with a cleft palate there are varying degrees of development of the bone and muscles. Frequently the palatal processes are small and undeveloped or asymmetrical. There is also poor development of muscle tissues on one or both sides, and in such cases the production of a palate of normal size by means of surgery is not possible. Although surgical union may stimulate growth, this may still be uneven, with greater development of muscle tissue on one side than on the other. Patients will therefore be found from time to time in whom one operation has failed to produce the requisite conditions for normal speech.

The Dorrance push-back operation, previously described, may be used as a secondary procedure to lengthen a short soft palate, or the pharyngeal wall may be brought forward and the pharynx narrowed by a pharyngoplasty.

Mr W. Hynes (1950) has developed and described a pharyngeal operation involving a muscle transplant which has proved useful in the adult where previous surgery has been insufficient, and especially in those cases where the pharynx is abnormally large and there is lack of mobility in the pharyngeal walls. By means of the Hynes pharyngoplasty the size of the pharynx is reduced and an actively contractile muscle sphincter is produced.

Briefly, the operation consists in raising two flaps, detached at their lower ends, from the lateral walls of the pharynx (Fig. 85), each flap containing muscle tissue. A transverse incision is made across the posterior wall of the pharynx above the level of the ridge of Passavant (Fig. 86) and the two flaps are raised, turned inwards and sutured in this transverse incision (Fig. 87). The defects in the lateral walls are then sutured and a prominent ridge remains on the posterior pharyngeal wall. This produces narrowing of the pharynx (Fig. 88) and is capable of contraction simultaneously with that of the levatores palati. Following this pharyngoplasty, repair of the palate is carried out by the technique which seems most appropriate, or in the case of a very short soft palate a push-back operation may also be performed. Fig. 89 shows a static posterior pharyngeal ridge produced by the pharyngoplasty, and Fig. 90 another case showing the sphincter closed. Fig. 91 demonstrates the reduction in size which may be obtained by this type of pharyngoplasty.

At first Hynes used this method as a secondary procedure, as already described, in cases where a good functional result had not been achieved by previous operations on the palate. More recently he has suggested (1954) that even in children, if a sufficiently effective pharyngoplasty is first carried out, the posterior and lateral walls of the pharynx can be advanced to such an extent that only a simple primary repair of the palate is required. He uses the soft tissues of the palate to close the cleft without any

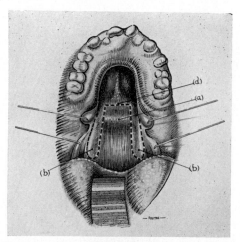

Fig. 85.—Pharyngoplasty by Muscle Transplantation. Incisions used: (b) raises the mucomuscular flap and (d) is the transverse incision lying above the level of Passavant's ridge.

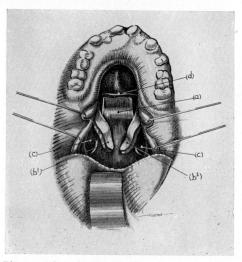

Fig. 86.—Pharyngoplasty by Muscle Transplantation. Mucomuscular flaps raised.

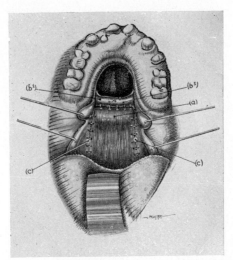

Fig. 87.—Pharyngoplasty by Muscle Transplantation. Mucomuscular flaps transposed and secondary defects in lateral pharyngeal walls closed by direct suture.

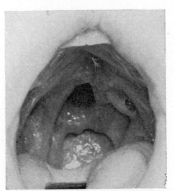

Fig. 88.—The treatment of a "failed cleft palate." A static posterior pharyngeal ridge made by pharyngoplasty.

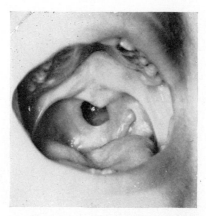

Fig. 89.— Palato-pharyngeal sphincter made by pharyngoplasty—Sphincter open.

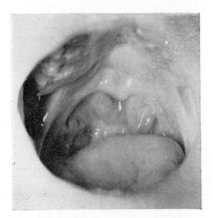

Fig. 90.—Palato-pharyngeal sphincter made by pharyngoplasty—Sphincter closed when patient said "Ah."

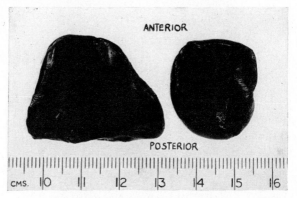

Fig. 91.—Reduction of the cross-section of the oropharynx
after pharyngoplasty. The figure on the left is the cross-
section of a stent mould of the pharynx before operation;
that on the right is a cross-section of a pharyngeal mould
at the same level at the end of the operation.

attempt to lengthen the soft palate and claims that surgical damage to the palate is minimised. The soft palate is also thought by this method to possess a high degree of movement. The pharyngoplasty reduces the diameters of the pharynx in the region of the palatopharyngeal sphincter by the transference of tissue from the lateral to the posterior pharyngeal wall to compensate for the inadequate soft palate. Such operative procedures can be carried out in children aged 15 to 18 months.

The Rosenthal pharyngeal flap operation already described (p. 98) has been stated to improve speech in some patients. This method does not assist the normal muscular control of the nasopharyngeal air-way by improving the action of the palatopharyngeal sphincter. It may, however, cause narrowing of the pharynx laterally and help to occluded the air-way when previous surgery has not been successful.

FURTHER RESULTS OF CLEFT PALATE SURGERY

When this book was first published it was stated that very few surgeons had published their results. Some have since done so, and the following figures indicate what could be expected from surgery at that time. Unfortunately, the methods of describing the speech results vary and not all have been assessed by a speech therapist. Some mention nasal tone whilst others ignore this defect and assess their results on the degree of palatopharyngeal efficiency and the ability to articulate certain consonant sounds. These are sometimes assessed only in single words and their use in spontaneous conversation is not always mentioned.

In 1941 Oldfield described his results in 113 of his patients with repaired clefts of the palate. Closure of the hard palate resulted in 96; 12 had only partial closure and had a dental plate to cover a defect in the hard palate; whilst in five there was a breakdown resulting in non-union. Eighty-six patients had soft palates which were long and mobile whilst in 22 the soft palate was stiff and short. A "good anatomical result" was therefore said to have been obtained in 86 out of 108 patients, or 80%.

Eighty-seven patients were tested for nasopharyngeal closure. Fifty-nine of these, or 68%, had a competent sphincter, whilst 28 had only partial or inadequate closure in the nasopharynx for articulation.

Speech was assessed as "excellent" if it was impossible to detect that a cleft palate had ever been present—32 patients. It was "good" if "greatly improved and they could speak so clearly that even strangers could understand them"—31 patients. Some of these could pronounce all individual consonants correctly but had nasal intonation or huskiness when talking quickly. Oldfield does not state whether this huskiness was due to a nasal escape of air or to some other cause. Others had "perfect sibilant sounds." Ten were assessed as "bad" having "typical cleft palate defects and being difficult to understand." Oldfield therefore assessed a "favourable" speech result in 86.3% of his patients, and unfavourable in 13.7%.

In 1947, Bentley assessed the results on 90 patients operated upon by the Wardill technique. Three of these were found to be mentally defective. He states that pharyngoplasty was carried out in 41 cases, all of whom subsequently had palatopharyngeal closure. In 46 a pharyngoplasty was not used and 44 of these had a competent nasopharyngeal sphincter. Bentley does not state definitely, however, if nasopharyngeal closure was adequate for conversational speech, nor if there were any defects in the hard palate, but that 85 of 87 patients, 95%, had a competent sphincter. The speech results were classified as follows:—

Type of cleft	Total	Speech perfect	Speech perfect except for minor hard palate or lip faults	Imperfect	Imbecile
Post alveolar	41	27	8	4	2
Complete	49	19	18	11	1
Total	90	46	26	15	3

According to these figures, normal speech had developed in only 46 of these 90 patients, that is 51%, yet it is stated that only two had an incompetent palatopharyngeal sphincter. Bentley states that in the group with minor defects [k] and [g] were used normally but there was faulty articulation of [s] [t] [th] and [d] due to "defective alveolar contours," and that [f] [v] [m] [p] and [b] were defective when the upper lip was tight. In the group described as "imperfect" there were gross defects of the jaw in six patients, defective speech sense in five, stammering in two and an incompetent sphincter in two patients. It is apparent, therefore, that a competent sphincter is not the only requirement for normal speech, but that operative techniques should be designed to prevent abnormal development of the lip, jaw or alveolus which may hinder the normal development of speech as in 32 of the patients in this series. These patients were assessed some years after operation when the possibility of further spontaneous improvement was unlikely.

Battle gives the speech results in a small series of 37 patients operated upon by himself, the lip being repaired at three months and the palate at one year. In those who were old enough to talk speech was normal in 31 and bad in six. That is 84% had normal speech. The standard of defect is, however, not defined.

Battle also gives his findings when carrying out an examination in 1939 of cleft palate patients operated upon by different surgeons at different ages. He found 88 perfect speakers, 54 of whom had been operated upon before three years of age. Only three of these had required speech therapy for very short periods. Twenty-three had had surgical treatment between three and eight years of age, and ten had required speech therapy averaging over a year each. There were eleven perfect speakers operated upon after the age of eight years, and eight of these had received speech therapy for at least one year. These figures at this date (1939) emphasise the importance of early operation if speech therapy is to be rendered unnecessary in these patients.

McCollum, Richardson and Swanson (1956) have pointed out how much modern methods of anæsthesia and of treatment by antibiotics have contributed to the improved results of cleft palate surgery. The risk to life associated with early operation has been minimised, and in a series of 1,034 cases of primary repair of the palate, mostly under two years of age (the lip when the child was 6 lbs. and the palate at 20 lbs. weight), the mortality was nil. They studied the speech results in two groups of patients. In a selected group of 108 children, the ages at the time of assessment ranging from three to seventeen years, the mean age being seven and a half years. They were operated upon between 1942 and 1952, and were selected because they lived within a 300 mile radius of Boston and could attend for assessment. The second group of 56 was drawn from a consecutive series of 75 patients operated upon in 1946 and 1947 and

who were available for study. They assessed the speech
on the degree of nasality as follows:—

	Selected group (108)	Consecutive series (56)
Normal, non-nasal - - -	70%	50%
Non-nasal with faulty articulation - - - - -	13%	21%
Slight nasality - - - -	11%	11%
Moderate nasality - - -	4%	2%
Hyponasal - - - -	2%	2%
"Cleft palate speech" - -	0%	14%
Total non-nasal cases - -	83%	71%

One hundred and sixty-four of these children also had
a thorough dental examination and it was found that
although facial patterns as determined by cephalometric
evaluation differed from the *ideal* normal pattern they did
not differ appreciably from those of a random sample of
the normal population. Early operation had not in these
children, therefore, contributed towards deformity of the
maxilla or seriously affected dental occlusion.

The speech of the patients operated upon by Braithwaite
in Newcastle upon Tyne has been assessed entirely by
speech therapists. Details of the method of assessment
are given in Chapter V. Between 1949 and 1961, 360 children
were submitted to primary repair of the palate in infancy.
Of these, 193 (53.5%) were boys and 167 (46.5%) were
girls. Of these 360 children, 177 (49%) had clefts of the
primary and secondary palates, 16% being bilateral and
33% unilateral; 183 (51%) had clefts of the secondary palate
only, 13% being total, 34% subtotal and 4% submucous.

Their ages at the time of operation ranged from eight
months to 11 years, 237 (65%) being operated upon between
one and two years of age. Forty-four children (12%), of

whom 11 (4%) had submucous clefts of the palate, were operated upon after their third birthday. Therefore 88% had primary surgery on the palate before three years of age.

It should be noted that these figures exclude operations upon clefts of the primary palate only, that is clefts of the lip, or of lip and alveolus where the secondary palate (hard and soft palates) were intact. Also, in this series, there was no selection of cases. All those referred were treated by the method described.

These children were seen regularly at the follow-up clinic, usually at one month after operation on the palate, and thereafter at intervals of six months. Thus their progress was observed continuously. A detailed assessment of their progress was summarised in 1961 and again in 1968. At the final survey in 1968 the average age of this group of patients was 11 years, the age range being seven to 21 years.

The assessment was based on three factors (a) the efficiency of the nasopharyngeal closure during speech, (b) resonance, and (c) articulation during conversational speech. The general observations may be summarised as follows:—

1. *Anatomical.*—The majority had adequate nasopharyngeal closure when first seen one month after surgery. In a few closure was not complete at first, or was not used by the child, but palatal movement improved with time and growth through stimulation due to muscular activity. In the majority the alveolar arch was adequate for normal articulation and in this respect corresponded to arch deformity found in the normal child population.

z. *Vocal resonance.*—In general, vocal tone was that of the young child with a normal palate as judged on the early vocalisations and speech as it developed. There were variations throughout the period of observation when the child had a cold or sinusitis at the time of the visit, and with growth of the pharynx and larynx at puberty.

Removal of tonsils and/or adenoids, when essential for medical reasons or to preserve hearing, usually affected resonance temporarily and in a few there was, for a period, some nasal emission through the palatopharyngeal sphincter.

3. *Articulation.*—As the children began to speak increasingly, it was noticed that most had a period of varying length when defective articulation of consonant sounds was used. This was thought to be due to faulty patterns of articulation, developed during the babbling stages of speech development, around six to eight months of age. However there was no nasal emission of air, intra-oral air pressure was adequate and vocal tone and resonance on vowel sounds were normal.

The most important observation was the gradual, spontaneous improvement of articulation towards the normal, noted at successive visits. Some children required six months, others two to three years, to change their consonant substitutions and develop normal articulation. This they achieved with no speech therapy and probably with little or no correction at home. Parents were especially requested not to correct the child's articulation but to allow it to develop normally without any self-consciousness.

Articulation was assessed during conversational speech and compared with what could be described as "normal" for the age of the child. For example many children of two and a half years of age do not use [s] blends. Some children used a defective [r]. This is common amongst many adults and one child used the same defective [r] as his older sister who had a normal palate.

The sound [s] usually presents the greatest difficulty and may be variable, normal in one position in a word and defective in another. Other children used an [s] which could not be described as a substitution sound, but there was some distortion which did not affect intelligibility.

Children tended to use posterior substitutions for anterior consonant sounds, e.g. [k] and [g] for [t] and [d] with [s] being palatal and produced in the [k] rather than in the [t] position.

Temporary changes of articulation sometimes occurred during second dentition, and an orthodontic appliance usually caused distortion of some consonant sounds, at least temporarily.

Where an anterior fistula had been left by design, due to a shortage of tissue at the time of operation as previously described, there was lack of intra-oral air pressure for anterior consonants, although [k] and [g] could be normal if palatopharyngeal closure was adequate. These fistulas tend to close spontaneously with growth but affect articulation until closure is complete. A dental plate may be fitted to occlude the fistula temporarily, or worn permanently if the fistula should persist.

DETAILS OF RESULTS

1. *Efficiency of the palatopharyngeal sphincter.*—It was found, in 1961, that 95.8% of the 360 children had adequate nasopharyngeal competence for speech. In 2.5% there was closure but some inco-ordination during speech. For example, two children had good closure on blowing but some nasal leak of air during speech. Two had a similar inco-ordination, but only at times when they were nervous, whilst one had adequate intra-oral air pressure for single words but this was not completely maintained in continuous speech. Seven children, 1.8%, had an incompetent palatopharyngeal sphincter with nasal escape of air during speech.

In 1968, 97% had adequate closure, whilst some degree of nasal emission was present in 3% of the patients.

	1961	1968
Adequate palatopharyngeal closure for speech	95.8%	97%
Incompetent palatopharyngeal sphincter	1.8%	3%
Inco-ordination during speech	2.5%	

2. *Resonance.*—Resonance and vocal tone was assessed on a five-point scale. On this scale 1, 2 and 3 represented variations in the normal range of resonance for English speech; four represented excessive nasal resonance but little or no nasal escape of air; five represented excessive nasal resonance with nasal escape of air. In 1961, an assessment of the 360 children was not possible in 19 who were too young and not speaking, seven of these being mentally defective. Of the remainder, 94% had vocal tone which was within the normal range. Seven children had abnormal resonance associated with enlarged adenoids or inco-ordination in the use of the palatopharyngeal sphincter, and eleven children had increased nasality due to inco-ordinaor an incompetent nasopharyngeal sphincter during speech.

In 1968, 94% had vocal tone within the normal range. Increased nasal resonance without nasal emission of air was present in 3% and in 3% there was some degree of nasal emission with inadequate intra-oral air pressure for consonants.

3. *Articulation.*—In 1961, 31 of the 360 children had insufficient speech for assessment of the articulation used, 23 being under four years of age, seven were mentally defective and one had a severe congenital hearing defect.

Of the remainder, 197 (58%) had normal conversational speech the majority having passed through varying degrees of defective articulation, whilst 82 still had resolving defects yet with adequate intra-oral air pressure for the articulation used. Fifty of these were still under six years of age at the time of assessment.

Sixteen children under the age of six years, seven being under two years, had small residual fistulas in the anterior part of the hard palate at that time. As previously described seven children had inadequate nasopharyngeal closure and eight other children had some degree of inco-ordination in the use of the palatopharyngeal sphincter at the time of assessment. Nine per cent of the children therefore had defective articulation attributable to inadequate intra-oral air pressure at the time of assessment. By 1968 spontaneous development of articulation had occurred in 71% of the children, whilst 29% required some speech therapy.

Speech Therapy.—Of these 29%, 19% required minimal speech therapy or guidance to the mother, whilst 10% (36 children) required more intensive therapy. In 11% the articulatory defects were minimal, usually of s only, whilst 14% had more extensive consonant substitutions, 4% responding rapidly to very little therapy. Among these children were also those who had a submucous cleft and others who had been operated upon later in life after defects of articulation had become firmly established. Speech therapy is not arranged until the child is at least four years of age, although if speech is not developing well the mother may be advised at an earlier stage as to how she may carry out simple exercises with her child at home.

It has been noticed that defects of articulation tend to be more persistent in children with the more severe type of cleft. Although this is not the only factor involved, for example, operation on the palate in a child with a bilateral cleft may be at a later age following two operations on the lip, we found that 43 per cent of children with bilateral complete clefts, 23 per cent of those with unilateral complete clefts and 18 per cent of those with post-alveolar clefts had required speech therapy.

Hearing.—The majority of these 360 children had hearing within the normal range. Four children had a sensori-neural loss, very severe in one child. He required special education and developed only minimal communication through speech. Thirty-six children, (31%) had at some period, conditions of the middle ear such as otalgia or otorrhœa and of these 28 had intermittent middle ear or conductive hearing loss at times. In only eight was there any true diminution of hearing.

Of the 40 children, 36 with middle ear conditions and four with a sensori neural loss, 31 developed normal articulation and of the remaining nine, three had a defective s only; three (including the child with the severe loss) had marked articulatory defects and three had some nasal emission It is apparent, therefore, that the hearing loss in most of these children in no way affected their hearing for speech.

Tonsils and adenoids —Removal of tonsils and/or adenoid was essential in nine children. Of these, six maintained naso-pharyngeal competence, two had a temporary inco-ordination and one had nasal emission of air due to naso-pharyngeal incompetence which persisted for several months.

REFERENCES

BATTLE, R. J. V. (1954). The Past, Present and Future in the Surgery of the Cleft Palate. *Brit. J. plast. Surg.*, 7, 217.

BENTLEY, F. H. AND WATKINS, I. (1947). Speech after repair of Cleft Palate. *Lancet*, 2, 862.

BERRY, J. (1905). *Brit. med. J.*, **2**, 853.

BERRY, J. (1911). *Brit. med. J.*, **2**, 1052.

BERRY, J. (1926). *Proc. R. Soc. Med.*, **10**, part 3, Sect. Surg. 127.

BLAKEWAY, H. (1915). The Operative Treatment of Cleft Palate. *Lancet*, **1**, 479.

BOND, J. C. (1893). On the ultimate condition of Cleft Palate case after operation. *Lancet*, **2**, 627.

BRAITHWAITE, F. (1958). Personal Communication.

BRAITHWAITE, F. (1964). *Cleft Lip and Palate*, Edit. Rob, C., and Smith, R. Chap. 5. London: Butterworth.

BROWNE, D. (1932). The operation for Cleft Palate. *Brit. J. Surg.*, **20**, 7.

DORRANCE, G. M. (1925). Lengthening the Soft Palate in Cleft Palate Operations. *Ann. Surg.*, **82**, 208.

DORRANCE, G. M. (1943). Cleft Palate. *Ann. Surg.*, **117**.

FERGUSSON, W. (1864). Harelip and Split Palate. *Lancet*, **1**, 177.

GANZER, HUGO (1917). *Berl. klin. Wschr.*, **54**, 209.

GILLIES, H. D. AND KELSEY FRY (1921). A New Principle in the Surgical Treatment of Congenital Cleft Palate and its Mechanical Counterpart. *Brit. med. J.*, **1**, 335.

HYNES, W. (1950). *Brit. J. Plast. Surg.*, **3**, 128.

HYNES, W. (1953). The Results of Pharyngoplasty by Muscle Transplantation in *Failed Cleft Palate* cases, with special reference to the influence of the pharynx on voice production. *Ann. R. Coll. Surg. Engl.*, **13**, 17.

HYNES, W. (1954). The Primary Repair of Clefts of the Palate. *Brit. J. Plast. Surg.*, **7**, 242.

KILNER, T. POMFRET (1937). *St. Thom. Hosp. Rep.*, Vol. II.

KILNER, T. POMFRET (1937). Cleft Lip and Palate. In Maingot, *Post-Graduate Surgery*, p. 3807.

LANE, W. A. (1908). *Hare Lip and Cleft Palate*. The modern treatment of cleft palate. *Lancet*, **1**, 6.

McCOLLUM, D. W., RICHARDSON, S. O. AND SWANSON, L. T. (1956). Habilitation of the Cleft Palate Patient. *New Engl. J. Med.*, **254**, 299.

McCUTCHEON, G. T. (1954). Modified Passavant Technique of Cleft Palate Repair. *Ann. Surg.*, **139**, 613.

McNEIL, C. KERR (1950). Thesis for Degree of Ph.D., University of Glasgow.

McNEIL, C. KERR (1956). Congenital Oral Deformities. *Brit. dent. J.*, **101**, 191.

McNEIL, C. KERR (1964). Early treatment of cleft lip and palate. In *International Symposium, University of Zurich*. Ed. Hoetz, R. Berne: Huber.

OLDFIELD, M. C. (1942). Cleft Palate and the Mechanism of Speech. *Brit. J. Surg.*, **29**, 197.

OWSLEY, J. AND BLACKFIELD, H. (1965). The Technique and Complications of Pharyngeal Flap Surgery. *Plastic Reconstr. Surg.*, **35**, 531.

OWSLEY, J. AND LAWSON, L. I. (1968). Reports of the high superiorly based flap. American Cleft Palate Association 1968 Congress, Miami.

RUTENBERG, D. (1876). Uber Gaumenspaltennaht und Erzielung einer reinen (nicht naselnden) Sprache durch Vorlagerung der hinteren Schlundwand. *Wien. med. Wschr.*, **26**, 815, 839, 862.

VEAU, VICTOR, (1926-27). *Proc. R. Soc. Med.*, **10**, part 3. Sect. Surg., 127.

VEAU, Victor (1931). *Division Palantine*. Paris: Masson et Cie.

VEAU, Victor (1933). *Bull. Soc. Nat. Chir.*, **59**, 1372-82

WARDILL, W. E. M. (1933). Cleft Palate. *Brit. J. Surg.*, **21**, 82

WARDILL. W. E. M. (1937). *Brit. J. Surg.*, **21**, 347.

WARDILL, W. E. M. (1938). *Speech*, pp. 9-16.

I

CHAPTER IV

PROBLEMS ASSOCIATED WITH CLEFT PALATE : FEEDING, GROWTH AND SPEECH

Some notes on feeding

Orofacial growth and development

Orthodontics Pre-operative
　　　　　　　Post-operative
　　　　　　　Obturators

Stages in the development of normal speech

Development of speech in a child with a cleft palate

Age for operation

Speech results and age at operation

PROBLEMS ASSOCIATED WITH CLEFT PALATE

TWO main difficulties face the child born with a cleft palate, and the first of these is that of obtaining food in order to maintain life ; the second is that of making himself understood through the use of speech. Basic to these is the abnormal condition of the palate and upper lip at birth and the subsequent growth and development of the palate, alveolus and facial contours, including dentition.

In addition, particular care is required in order that the child will be in a fit condition to withstand operation at an early age.

SOME NOTES ON FEEDING

Normally the child employs pressure, squeezing the nipple with the lips between the tongue and alveolar process, at the same time maintaining suction during the act of swallowing. In the infant this is achieved by the raising and lowering of the tongue and the floor of the mouth, so creating an intra-oral negative pressure which allows fluid to be drawn into the mouth in a rhythmical pumping and squirting activity. With a cleft palate this is rendered difficult as the negative pressure is not easy to maintain. However, human nature is adaptable, and this obstacle is not insurmountable unless the lip and alveolus are also cleft, when greater difficulty will be experienced. Adequate compression of the nipple then becomes impossible, and artificial means of feeding must be resorted to until such time as the lip and anterior part of the palate can be repaired. However, breast feeding is encouraged whenever possible.

There are various devices available, such as suction plates designed to make a temporary closure of the cleft, or special teats fitted with a flange to occlude the gap in the alveolus, but one of the most satisfactory methods is the use of a cup and teaspoon to which the baby readily adapts himself. Expressed breast milk should be provided for the infant where possible, and extra vitamins given in all cases. We ask the mother to make the baby familiar with a spoon before he comes into hospital so that there will be less difficulty after operation when spoon feeding is used. It is thought that this imposes less strain on the suture line. At the time of the operation on the palate the child will be weaned and will be accustomed to the use of a spoon. When the lip is well healed breast feeding can be resumed.

At the time of operation the child should have a haemoglobin level of over 75% and must be free from any infection of the nose and throat. Operation on the cleft lip is performed when the baby is over 10 lbs. in weight and is gaining weight, and on the cleft palate as soon after the age of eleven to twelve months as is possible. Preoperative feeding for the baby with a cleft lip consists of a half strength milky feed not less than three hours before operation. Another is given three hours afterwards.

Post-operative feeding for the baby with a cleft lip consists of a half-strength feed as soon as he is co-operative, followed by full strength feeds after the first twelve hours.

The suture line is kept clean by the application of a mild antiseptic solution and sterile liquid paraffin.

After operation on the cleft palate clear fluids are given for the first twenty-four hours, milky fluids for the next twenty-four hours, followed by a normal soft diet. Water is given to drink after each feed in order to keep the suture line free from debris. Post-operatively the child's arms are usually kept lightly splinted to prevent interference with the suture line, and sedation is given if necessary. Skin sutures in the cleft lip are removed on the 4th and 6th day and tension sutures on the 10th day. The lateral gauze packs in the palate are removed on the 10th day and the sutures in the central suture line on the 14th day under a light anaesthetic.

In some cases the mother is admitted with her child if she so desires, and attends to her own child, having been taught to adopt full aseptic measures.[1]

GROWTH AND DEVELOPMENT OF THE OROFACIAL STRUCTURES

For many years it was considered that the most successful functional results were obtained when operation for closure of the palate was carried out in infancy, the lip operation being performed about the end of the third month, and in two stages if the cleft was bilateral, the palate about the end of the first year.

From the study of certain surgical results it was suggested in 1949 (Graber) that operation in early life interfered with growth of the palate, and that post-operative malformations and deficiences were the direct result of early surgery which damaged the growing points of the maxilla. It was therefore considered that operation should be postponed until considerable growth had occurred, at the age of six or seven years.

There is some divergence of thought as to the principal

[1] For these notes on feeding and nursing care, I am indebted to Sister R. West, of the Plastic Unit, Hospital for Sick Children, Newcastle upon Tyne.

sites of maxillary growth. Some consider that this occurs mainly through proliferation of the basal bone at four sutures, namely the fronto-maxillary, the zygomaticus-temporal, the zygomaticus-maxillary and the pterygopalatine, whilst others consider that the main growth centre for the maxilla is situated in the cartilaginous nasal septum, the greatest increase occurring during the first six months.

It was pointed out that maxillary growth is active for the first twenty years of life, the palate growing anteroposteriorly with associated orofacial growth in the vertical and lateral directions. Brash (1924) and Todd (1931), from work on a large series of normal material, have shown that five-sixths of the total maxillary width has been completed by the fifth year and complete lateral development by the tenth year. The palate grows anteroposteriorly until its length is double that at birth, two-fifths of this growth being completed by the fourth year, the greatest increase occurring during the first and second years of life. A considerable amount of growth is, however, not the result of basal bone development but due to the formation of alveolar bone as the teeth develop and erupt. Kettle (1954) suggests that during the early stages of growth in the first two years, operative procedures would be less likely to cause disturbances of growth at that age than at five or six years of age when growth is more active, especially in the downward and forward directions. He describes a rapid increase in palatal length after eruption of the first permanent molars with proportional increase in both the palatal processes of the maxilla and the palatine bones, a further rapid increase in growth occurring between nine and twelve years of age.

It has been stated that in the adult with an unoperated cleft palate maxillary growth is normal, but measurements of the facio-oral proportions have shown increase in width in both the bony structures and in the pharynx in such patients.

Wardill (1928) demonstrated by measurements of normal and cleft palate skulls that there is a bony deformity in the latter, all the dimensions of the pharynx being increased, but more expecially from side to side.

CLEFT PALATE SKULLS COMPARED WITH NORMAL

	CLEFT PALATE (mm)			NORMAL (mm)		
	Nasion to occipital pt.	Trans. Diam.	Trans. Hamulii	Nasion to occipital pt.	Trans. Diam.	Trans. Hamulii
1	180	153	38·5	176	148	35
2	162	149	43	171	133	28
3	156	133·5	32	160	133	33
4	127	117	27	151	124·5	23
5	123	103	24	148	124	26
6	122	101	24·5	133·5	117	23·5
7	121	102	31	120	92	21·5
8	117	111	31	112	90	18
9	101	82	23	107	84	22
10	100	94	26	103	90	19
11	93·5	88	24·5	99	82·5	19.5
12	93	83	25	96	82	17·5
	Glabella to occipital pt.	Trans. Diam.	Trans. Hamulii	Glabella to occipital pt.	Trans. Diam.	Trans. Hamulii
13	175	128	41	178	179	34
14	187	150	42	190	147·5	36
15	187	145	43·5	195·5	141·5	32·5
16	169	125	39·5	180	141	30

Peyton (1931) carried out similar measurements on living skulls and also found a greater transverse diameter of jaw and maxilla. Subtelny (1955) investigated the dimensions of the nasopharynx in 142 children under three years of age. These included 91 unoperated cases of cleft palate and 51 children with normal palates. He again confirmed that the width of the nasopharynx was significantly greater in cleft palate patients than in the normal child, and that there was also increased width between the two hamular processes and the maxillary tuberosities associated with a greater inclination of the medial pterygoid plate in relation to the cranial bone. He found, however, that individual patients showed a wide range of variation, especially cleft palate children, some approaching closely the range of normal children and others showing marked deviation.

It is also often observed that in adults upon whom no surgery has been performed, or where surgery has failed, the pharynx is abnormally capacious, possibly the result of the absence of normal muscle action. If operation is postponed beyond infancy there will be increasing difficulty in reducing the deformity, whilst early closure will allow the palatal muscles to function, and by this means the size of the pharynx may be reduced.

Jolleys (1954) believed that the muscle fibres of the palate and pharynx fail to grow because they do not experience the normal pull of the muscles on the other side. He investigated Graber's suggestion that growth of the maxilla was hindered by damage to the growing points and by restricted blood supply following early operation, by studying clinical records of 254 patients, 165 of whom he examined. The palates of these patients had been operated upon by various surgeons with varying techniques some years previously. The measurements he carried out showed that although growth might be limited in some repaired clefts in the horizontal plane, there was continued full development in the vertical direction. He therefore considered that the interference with development was not the result of damage to the blood supply, nor to the growing points of the maxilla, but that growth was restricted by fibrous tissue and undue tension in the palatal muscles. The problem is therefore one of surgical technique which must be designed to unite the two halves of the palate without tension and with the formation of minimal scar tissue. The normal growth processes may then be stimulated by balanced muscle forces rather than hindered. Such stimulation of growth will be most effective in early infancy before the period of rapid development is passed.

McCollum, Richardson and Swanson (1956) substantiate

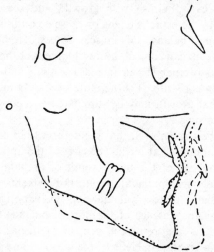

Fig. 92.—Summary of cephalometric findings. Solid line represents means for 111 cleft palate patients, broken line represents Downs ideal-normals, and the dotted line represents twenty-five un-selected controls.

(SWANSON, L. T., McCOLLUM, D. W. & RICHARDSON, S. O. (1956). *New England Journal of Medicine*, 254, 299.)

Jolley's findings from the study of 112 patients, submitted to operation in infancy, in that early operation does not necessarily interfere with maxillary growth. The cephalometric results in these patients, when analysed (Fig. 92), showed that although there was a marked difference from the *ideal* normal standards, there was no significant statistical difference between the patients with repaired cleft palates and the *average* normal.

Pruzansky (1955) also stated that the lateral constriction of the maxillary arch could not be attributed in all instances to arrest of growth due to surgical damage, and in 1964 "that it is clear that the damage to maxillary growth, lamented a decade ago, was largely the product of surgical practice no longer in vogue in this country (U.S.A.), that deficiences can diminish with growth, and the first consideration is the establishment of muscle continuity and a more normal balance of muscle forces." Such muscle forces in the lip can control the development of the alveolus, and in the soft palate can increase growth and mobility, especially in early life. It is therefore becoming increasingly accepted that growth may be stimulated and controlled by appropriate surgery.

It must be remembered that the deformity in cleft palate does not commence at birth. The cleft of the lip and palate exists at the end of the third month of prenatal life, and during subsequent prenatal growth the elements of the lip and maxillary plates will develop in varying degrees, hindered by the absence of the normal balance of muscle forces and as the result of genetic predisposition. The deformity is greatest in clefts of the alveolus and lip, where the two unequal lateral elements in a unilateral cleft, or the three alveolar elements in a bilateral cleft, may be separated widely due to the lack of restraint usually exercised by the normal lip. In the bilateral cleft the premaxilla is carried forward by the nasal septum. In the unilateral cleft the premaxilla, attached to one side, is usually unduly prominent or rotated outwards, while the lateral segment may be turned inwards, or at least fail to approach the alveolus of the opposite side. In defects of the soft palate only, or of the hard and soft palate, the maxilla may develop within normal limits or there may be only limited developments of the parts of the palate which are not cleft, with deficiency of maxillary growth. Where the lip only is cleft and the alveolus continuous, there is usually little or no deformity of the alveolar contours unless the cleft continues into the floor of the nose with a partial cleft of the alveolus, when there will usually be wider separation between the parts of the lip, and deficient development of tissues.

However, it cannot be overlooked that there is a high incidence of maxillary underdevelopment in cleft palate patients. Foster (1962) suggests that this may be related to genetic factors, the extent of development at the time of interference with growth and an agenesia of growth associated with the cleft palate deformity. This must be considered as a factor in post-surgical development.

The growth and development of the palate has been described briefly and the possibility of interference with such growth by early surgical treatment. Growth, however, may be stimulated by appropriate surgery if carried out in early life at a time when there is the possibility of rapid development. Early operation may also prevent, or at least restrain, the abnormal increase in width of the nasopharynx in unrepaired clefts of the palate described by Wardill, Peyton and Subtelny and considered to be the result of the absence of normal controlling muscle forces.

ORTHODONTIC TREATMENT

Until the last ten years orthodontic treatment was mainly post-operative and concerned with the abnormalities of alveolar and dental growth. More recently attention has been directed to the value of controlling and modifying the curvature of the maxilla and pre-maxilla in alveolar, or clefts of the primary palate.

To assist development of the normal curvature of the alveolar arch McNeil (1956) advocates that orthopædic treatment should commence before surgery in infants with such clefts.

Pre-operative.—He points out that at birth the parts of the maxilla are often in good alignment despite the alveolar cleft, but that malalignment may develop quite soon, or following some types of surgical closure of the lip. To control arch alignment he has suggested the fitting of a simple appliance even as early as a few hours after birth, or following surgical closure of the cleft lip. Such an appliance includes the means for controlling the dental arch either to improve the alignment of the two segments in a unilateral cleft, to assist the backward displacement of the premaxilla in a bilateral cleft, or to first widen the arch in order to accommodate the premaxilla prior to surgical repair. This appliance and its effect is illustrated in Fig. 93. The effect of the positioning of the premaxilla in the bilateral type of cleft is shown in Fig. 94.

Burston (1959) has also worked in this field and considers that in the absence of such orthopædic correction, surgery tends to perpetuate the malrelationship of the segments, with malocclusion when the teeth erupt.

Shiere and Fisher (1964) also mention the advantages resulting from the fitting of such an appliance and state that normal bottle feeding is established within 24 to 48 hours after birth when such an appliance has been inserted. Pruzansky (1964) states that such treatment facilitates repair of the lip, improves feeding, retards premaxillary growth and promotes growth of the maxillary segments. It also has psychological advantages for the parents and improves speech function.

Walther has described a splint to assist development of the arch. This is cemented in place when the lip has been repaired and before operation on the palate (Fig. 95). If there is deformity of the arch the splint may be divided and a palatal element fitted (Fig. 96) until the palate is operated upon at two and a half to three and a half years of age. Later the arch may be maintained with an upper removable appliance.

When it was considered advisable that operation should be postponed to a later age in order to avoid interference with growth, an obturator was fitted to assist articulation even in very young children. Harkins (1948) and others designed such obturators (Fig. 97). These were known as speech aids and were constructed for children as young as two and a half years of age. In such young children it was necessary to establish tolerance for the material within the oral cavity, and later a pharyngeal piece was added. Such obturators were refitted at frequent intervals as the child grew. This may still be a useful procedure if, for any valid reason, it is considered advisable to postpone surgery.

Post-operative.—Most orthodontists agree that alveolar arch development is influenced by the balanced action of stimulating forces exerted by the tongue and the restraining forces of the muscles of the lips and facial muscles, growth depending on both the skeletal pattern and the muscle pattern in any individual. Gwynne-Evans (1952) discusses development in relation to the skeletal, soft tissue and dento-alveolar structures. He makes a broad distinction between the growth of the skeletal framework and the growth of the alveolar portion of the jaws, stating that "the main factors governing the pattern of growth in skeletal bones in general are inherited." Stockard's experiments on the cross breeding of pure-bred dogs, he states, suggest "that one set of genes pre-determines the structural pattern of the upper jaw and another set of genes that of the lower jaw, the growth of the upper and lower jaws may therefore be independent of each other." He also thinks that environmental factors may effect growth or even "prevent fulfilment of the potential growth pattern," but that only surgery could alter the structural pattern of the jaws. Such growth is differentiated from that of alveolar bone which is dependant for its formation on the teeth and is built up as they erupt, also being absorbed if teeth are lost.

Post-operatively, deformities of the alveolar arch tend to occur and require the skill of the orthodontist in adjusting and controlling this development in order to obtain the best possible occlusion.

Kettle (1954) has summarised the causes of maldevelopment and failure of growth as:—

1. due to contracting scar tissue,
2. disproportionate elements of lip and tongue pressure,
3. lack of stimulation when the muscles are not united,
4. a tight lip, and
5. defective growth potentials due to the genetic build-up of the patient.

Where there is a residual fistula in the hard palate following operation, a dental plate may be necessary to cover the aperture and prevent the leakage of air from the mouth into the nasal cavities which will otherwise reduce air pressure for articulation. Even a small aperture may hinder or even prevent the normal development of speech. Such an appliance should be fitted as soon after operation as dentition permits so that the development of compensatory habits of articulation may be avoided. This is especially important in those children where nasopharyngeal closure is adequate (Fig. 98).

Where surgical failure has resulted in a short soft palate a "push back" operation may assist nasopharyngeal closure but leave a large aperture in the hard palate which will require a dental prosthesis to compensate for

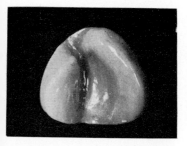 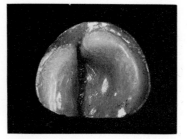

A. B.

A.—Condition before commencement of treatment. B.—Ten days after treatment had been commenced.

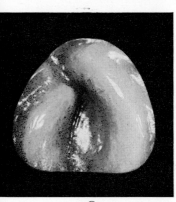 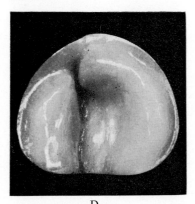

C. D.

C.—Condition before commencement of treatment. D.—Two weeks after treatment had been commenced.

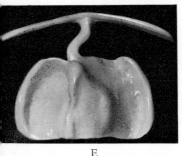 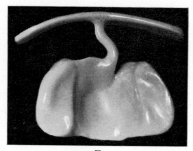

E. F.

E.—Fitting surface of appliance. F.—Lingual surface of appliance.

Fig. 93.—Appliance used to assist development of normal alveolar contours.

Facing page 144.

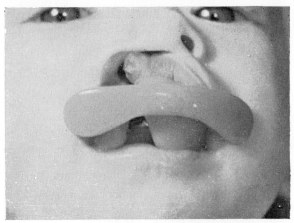

G.—Appliance in position.

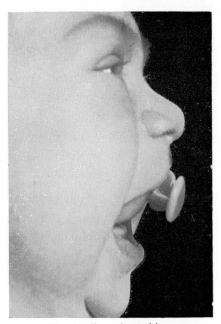

H.—Appliance in position.

Fig. 93. (Cont.).—Appliance used to assist development of normal alveolar contours.

(McNeil, C. Kerr (1954). *Oral and Facial Deformity*. London: Pitman).

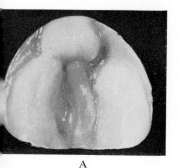

A   B

A.—Before treatment.   B.—After premaxillary correction.

Fig. 94.—The effect of the appliance where there is abnormal protrusion of the premaxilla.

(McNeil, C. Kerr (1954). *Oral and Facial Deformity.* London: Pitman.)

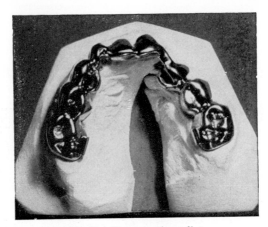

Fig. 95.—Pre-operative splint.

(WALTHER, D. P. (1954).   *Dental Practitioner*, 4, 385.)

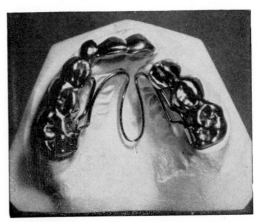

Fig. 96.—Pre-operative splint divided with palatal element.

(WALTHER, D. P. (1954).   *Dental Practitioner*, 44, 385.)

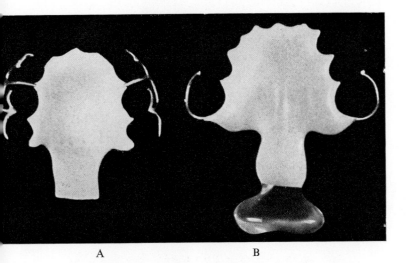

A   B

Fig. 97.—Incomplete and completed speech aids for small children.
A.—Palatal section extended to the divided uvula; B.—Completed
speech aid with pharyngeal section.

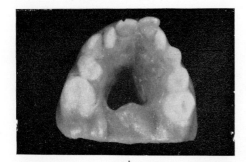

Fig. 98.—Dental plate used to cover a fistula in the palate.

A

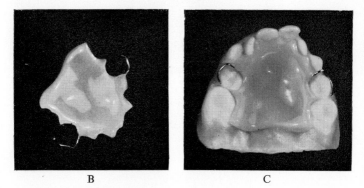

B   C

A.—The Unrepaired Defect. B.—The Appliance. C.—The Appliance *in situ.*

(McNeil, C. Kerr (1954). *Oral and Facial Deformity.* London: Pitman.)

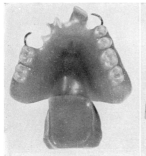

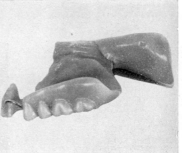

A

B

C

Fig. 99.—Illustrating various types of obturators.

Reproduced by kind permission of
Mr R. G. D. GAIN, Dental Departmen
Guy's Hospital, London.

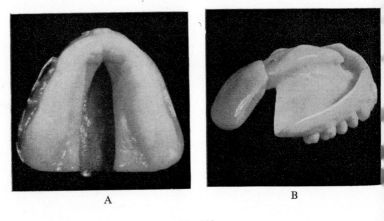

A   B

Fig. 100.
A.—The Extent of the Malformation.   B.—The Appliance.

(McNeil, C. Kerr (1954).   *Oral and Facial Deformity.*   London: Pitman.)

the partial absence of tissues in the region of the hard palate and which will assist in maintaining the backward displacement of the soft palate.

Where there is a deficiency of tissue in the anterior region of the hard palate many surgeons intentionally leave a fistula rather than attempt closure which must necessarily cause some narrowing of the alveolar arch. As previously described, a small dental plate may later be fitted to prevent the leakage of air from the mouth to the nose.

The obturator.—This is a prosthetic appliance similar to a dental plate which is worn by the patient to form a roof to the mouth and cover the cleft. It was first designed and used many years ago as an alternative to surgery. When the need for closure in the nasopharynx was first realised obturators were fitted with an extension or bulb which fitted into the nasopharynx and was designed to assist nasopharngeal closure. In modern times such prostheses have been modified. They are lighter in weight and in some the bulb is replaced by a broad extension into the pharynx around which the pharyngeal muscles can contract (Fig. 99).

Speech may be considerably improved by such appliances, and they may offer a better prognosis than surgery carried out by those unskilled in the special techniques required for the operative treatment of cleft palate.

In fitting such an obturator it must be designed so that the musculature of the palate and pharynx may be able to contract around it, yet it must not interfere with nasal breathing nor the pronunciation of the nasal consonants m, n and ng [ŋ]. It should, however, provide the requisite conditions for adequate intra-oral air pressure without nasal escape, and should prevent excessive nasality on the vowel sounds. The bulb should be situated where the greatest restriction in the nasopharynx occurs so that it may

K

be as small as possible. It is usually easier to fit such an obturator when there has been no previous surgery, and in some cases it may be necessary to redivide the sutured soft palate if function is inadequate in order that the obturator may be fitted more successfully. An improved cosmetic and functional result may be achieved by the addition of teeth to the denture, also assisting articulation.

Moolenaar Byl (1948) has had considerable experience of speech therapy with patients using obturators, especially during the years of the war, 1940-45, when little cleft palate surgery was possible in Holland. She states that the obturator aims at shaping the resonating cavities as favourably as possible for speech, not at imitating the function of the velum. It may be necessary to modify the bulb several times until the shape is found which gives the best speech results in any individual patient. When this is accomplished speech may improve immediately, or speech therapy may be required. Moolenaar Byl also found that muscular activity is sometimes increased around the bulb, the size of which may need to be decreased, or, in a growing child increased. The use of such an obturator may so improve habits of articulation that once these are established improved speech may be maintained when the obturator is not being used. McNeil (1954) also describes an obturator designed to close the cleft in a palate and with an extension posteriorly to act as an artificial soft palate (Fig. 100).

Blakeley (1960, 1964, 1969) has also used pharyngeal obturators to obtain nasopharyngeal closure and intra-oral pressure for consonant articulation. He also states that it is his clinical impression that in certain cases the presence of the obturator may stimulate additional palatal and/or pharyngeal muscle activity around the bulb.

Initially it may be necessary to use a large obturator which causes hyponasality and interferes with the normal resonance and production of [m], [n] and [ŋ]. Otherwise the patient may relax the muscles around the bulb to allow him to retain his accustomed nasal resonance. Even nasal breathing is temporarily impossible. (The obturator is removed at night to permit normal breathing during sleep.) The value of this procedure lies in the fact that all speech is denasalised completely until the patient accepts auditorily his own denasalised speech. Once this stage is reached the bulb may be gradually reduced in size allowing the palatal and pharyngeal muscles to function around the bulb to maintain the newly acquired resonance tone. Speech therapy is required to change any consonant substitutions and faulty patterns and when the patient has achieved good articulation and is progressing towards normal speech an obturator-reduction programme can be commenced. In some patients this reduction has been continued until nasopharyngeal closure can be maintained for speech without any obturator (Fig. 101).

This procedure has been found most useful in children aged three to four years of age although it may also be used in older patients. In children with whom such an obturator is used, improvement in speech may occur spontaneously when adequate air pressure is available. However, speech therapy is recommended to help the child to gain the maximum benefit from the use of the appliance.

The patient's resistance to changes in his speech is an important factor in all therapy and is especially demonstrated in these procedures. Children have been known to say, "Yes, I can hear the difference but I like mine better," when the therapist is attempting to change articulatory patterns. The treatment by these procedures therefore involves four stages: (1) Denasalisation of all speech sounds until auditorily acceptable to the patient, the obturator bulb being ufficiently large as to prevent any muscular adjustments

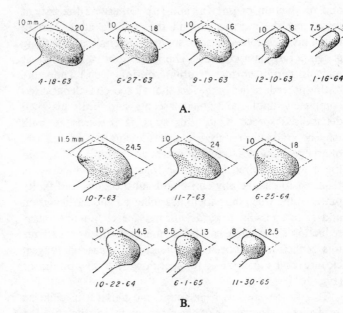

A.

B.

Fig. 101.—A. Stone models of a series of obturator reductions cul-
minating, after nine months, in removal of the appliance
with completely compensated palato-pharyngeal muscles
and normal voice and articulation. The child was five
years, four months of age when he obtained the obturator
and had a repaired unilateral cleft lip and palate.

B. Obturator reductions, 12 millimeters laterally and 3·5
millimeters anterio-posteriorly, occurring over a twenty-
five month period. Thereafter, no additional palatopharyngeal muscle compensation took place. Having
normal voice and articulation, the child then underwent
a pharyngeal flap procedure as a substitute for the
prosthesis. Normal speech was maintained. He had a
repaired unilateral cleft lip and palate and started wearing
the speech prosthesis at age three years, nine months.
The greatest muscle compensation invariably occurs in
the lateral pharyngeal walls.

by the patient to continue his nasalised speech; (2) reduction in size of the bulb to stimulate muscular activity to maintain the now acceptable change in resonance; (3) speech therapy to obtain normal patterns of articulation once adequate intra-oral air pressure is available; (4) further gradual reduction in size of the obturator bulb as muscular activity and articulation improves and as is clinically possible.

STAGES IN THE DEVELOPMENT OF SPEECH

The second difficulty is that associated with speech. The development of articulate speech is not an instinctive process. A child does not arrive in this world with an inborn predisposition to express himself in any particular language, and one born of English-speaking parents will readily learn to speak in a foreign tongue if surrounded by people using that language.

Again, there are no special organs designed primarily for speech; but, by a process of adaptation, man has learnt to make use of apparatus existing for other purposes, such as the respiratory apparatus, the jaws, lips, tongue and palate, used primarily for mastication and swallowing of food, and the facial muscles. Even the larynx, as pointed out by Negus (1929) had no primary function relating to speech, but was evolved to act as a valve to guard the entrance to the lungs and to regulate the inward and outward flow of air during respiration. Before a child can express his thoughts in language he must pass through many stages, during which process he gradually acquires the ability to co-ordinate the movements of the various muscle groups, and, eventually, articulate speech.

The growth of speech is dependent on the neurological development of the child, and both the sensory impresssion received and the neuromuscular control of the speech organs are concerned in this process. The nervous system of the human being is the mechanism by which one is enabled to react to the external stimuli of the environment, and which controls the activity of the other systems of the body so that the whole may act in harmony. As this development proceeds the child is able to make increasing use of the spoken sounds he hears around him, and imitation both of the sounds he hears from others and of those he makes himself becomes important in the process of speech development. Impulses arising in the sense organs such as the eye or ear reach the brain by means of afferent or sensory nerve fibres, the most important afferent pathway for speech development in the normal child being the *auditory* nerve. *Visual* impressions, though of less importance in normal speech development, also play a part; and in the case of a child born deaf, or becoming deaf before speech has developed, the visual afferent pathway may take the place of the auditory one, as when a child learns to understand speech through lip reading. *Tactual* sensations result from contacts between various parts of the speech mechanism, tongue, teeth and lips, and *kinæthetic* sensations, or impressions of movement, enable the child to distinguish the positions and movements of the particular parts of the speech mechanism being used in articulation. If any of these afferent impressions are hindered in their passage from the point of origin to the brain, the process of learning to speak will be hindered because the child does not receive adequate stimuli. The most important defect is that of a lesion in the auditory pathway, causing deafness.

Efferent or motor nerve fibres innervate the muscles concerned in speech and control the movements of articulation. These nerves supply motor fibres to the muscles of respiration and to those of the larynx, pharynx, soft palate, tongue, jaw and lips, which are concerned in the process of respiration, phonation and articulation.

Afferent fibres carry the sensory impulses to the cerebral cortex and a feed-back or monitoring system is established associated with the sensory impressions of the movements and sounds produced during the process of articulation.

Through this system of sensory and motor nerve fibres, with the association areas of the cerebrum, speech patterns are gradually built up, and co-ordination of the muscles concerned in articulation is developed, largely based on the primitive reflex patterns for respiration, crying, sucking, and swallowing and involving co-ordination with respiration and phonation.

Where abnormal reflex patterns develop in attempts to compensate for an abnormal anatomical condition such as cleft palate, the sensory feed-back will tend to perpetuate these with the establishment of abnormal patterns of movement and co-ordination which are basic for articulation, and which may eventually interfere with the development of normal articulation. These patterns form very definite speech habits, and any alteration in such habits in a child or adult will therefore necessitate the breaking down of such neuromuscular patterns and the building up of new ones in their place.

In the case of the cleft palate patient such faulty habits develop because of the child's inability to produce sounds normally owing to the cleft palate, due to insufficient oral air pressure, and are not necessarily the result of any central cortical inability to imitate the sounds of speech. Nevertheless these habits are the basis of the defective speech in cleft palate patients, and, as in any other form of speech defect, they must be eradicated and new and correct speech habits developed in their place.

Speech is usually not established at the earliest until

towards the end of the second year of life, but the actual sounds used in speech are acquired very much earlier. As the neurological development proceeds a normal child learns to make use of its vocal organs, using expressive variations all vowel sounds, primarily to procure satisfaction of its instinctive needs, and secondly, for the enjoyment experienced in hearing the sound of its own voice, speech being a natural outlet for the personality even in its earliest forms.

In the first days of life the child is able to use the vocal cords for the production of sounds such as crying, and very soon those in association with him can readily distinguish varying tones and expressions indicative of hunger, fatigue, pain, and comfort. As these cries produce the required satisfaction, so does the child learn their value in acquiring some control of his environment. Although at first confined to vowel sounds, before long, about the tenth week, lips and tongue begin to play their part, and consonant sounds make their appearance. Shinn (1893) has described an instance of this as early as the seventh week. These sounds arise as a modification of the laryngeal tone as the child indulges in oral play or babbling, and by this process gradually gains motor control over the varying muscles which are necessary to the co-ordinated functioning of the speech mechanism. It is thought that the sounds used in this babble stage develop spontaneously, and irrespective of anything heard in the child's environment. Even a child who is found to be too deaf to learn to speak may develop some form of babbling, which may possibly depend on the production of laryngeal sounds, perhaps accidentally and simultaneously with lip and tongue movements, or it may be confined to vowel sounds only.

Gradually there is a change from mere vowel sounds to the use of sounds which more nearly resemble language. Self imitation seems to play an important part at this stage, the child repeating the same sound over and over again, this process being the precursor to a later stage when the child begins to reproduce the sounds heard in his environment. Such syllables as mamama and mumumumum soon make their appearance, and it is noteworthy that in producing these sounds, the child is making good use of the soft palate, the alternate nasal resonants and vowel sounds forming an excellent exercise for the muscles concerned in the opening and closing of the palato-pharyngeal sphincter.

Towards the end of the fifth month the child is beginning to pay more attention to his surroundings, movements attract him, and he will show interest in watching the play of his mother's lips, often attempting to catch the lips with his hands, or subconsciously imitating their action. Consonant sounds become more frequent and varied, but there appears to be no definite order in which the sounds occur. A chance position of tongue or lips, a sound is produced, and is imitated and repeated again and again by the child. If imitation of other people were the chief factor, it would seem natural for the labial sounds, such as p, b, and m, to develop first, for, not only are the positions for these sounds easier to imitate, but the muscles of the lips have been well exercised in the act of sucking. However, k and g have been known to occur as early as p and b, though such sounds as s, z, sh [ʃ], f and v are usually later in making their appearance, and may not develop until after the necessary dentition or development of the alveolar arch.

It is possible that the earlier sounds produced by the child involves the activity and control of fewer muscle groups, or are those which require a less accurate adjustment of the organs of speech. West, Kennedy & Carr, (1937) basing their statement on information from several sources, give the order of development of consonant sounds as follows: m, b, p, w, h, n, t, d, k, g, ng [ŋ], j [dʒ], ch [tʃ], v, f, l, r, th [θ, ð], sh [ʃ], ʒ, z, s. However, there is found to be much variation among individuals, and probably the most that can be said is that, of this series, the first eleven sounds [m to ŋ] are simpler and develop earlier than the remaining twelve. As the use of these consonant sounds increases they become gradually linked to vowel sounds being used first initially, then finally, and at last medially.

A healthy, normal child will lie for long periods enjoying his own experiments, playing with various sounds, gurgling, and, at the same time, indulging in physical exercises with many combinations of arms and legs. All the while this constant repetition of sounds and syllables is producing auditory images in the mind of the child, and, owing to the neurological processes previously described, these become firmly established and linked with the kinæthetic and tactile sensations of the organs of speech, forming the basis of speech habits. Should any of these sounds be defective and require correction later, not only the alteration of muscular movements will be necessary, but the building up of new auditory, kinæsthetic and tactile images associated with them.

Parallel with the development of the sounds of speech there is a rapid growth in understanding, and towards the end of the first year the child's ability to understand is far ahead of his ability to reproduce what he hears. Speech necessarily involves the association of sounds with meaning, and although, at this stage, the child does not differentiate and understand each separate word, he is helped by intonation and the facial expression and gestures of the speaker to appreciate the sense of the whole. Preyer says that, "after understanding has been acquired, normal progress is rapid. The child learns to carry out correct actions, kicking,

blowing, coughing and so on, at command, to point out the
features of his own face, and even to answer more difficult
questions by appropriate gestures, pointing, for example,
as a response to 'Where is Mamma'? He pays more and
more attention to the sounds of his environment, often
producing a long string of meaningless syllables with
expressive intonation, the result bearing some resemblance
to a phrase or sentence in an unknown language, rather
than to the mother tongue."

As powers of perception and muscular co-ordination
increase a stage is reached, sometimes designated the
"echo" period. The child selects the required sounds and
uses them in the correct order, imitating, perhaps after
one or two trial attempts, some word he has just heard.
The association of various descriptive sounds and words
with objects becomes an important process in the development of speech. The child is definitely interested in attaching names to the things in his environment, touching and
handling them, and repeating their names. We now get
the one-word sentence, whereby the child successfully
makes known his wants by the use of one word, generally
combined with a few useful gestures. In a group of 1,142
children it was found that the mean age for the first use
of words was 12 months. There was, however, a wide
range of normality extending from six to 30 months.
(Morley) 1957.

But speech development and the growth of language
involve the ability to use words to express thoughts, and
so, as the mind of the child develops, growth in vocabulary
goes rapidly ahead as he progresses by phrases and ever
lengthening sentences until fluent speech is attained. In
the same investigation it was found that phrases were first
used between 10 and 42 months, the mean age being
18 months. The following table is interesting, illustrating

the growth of vocabulary up to three and a half years of age as reported by different observers:—

Age	Smith		Gerlach		Nice	
	No. of cases	Vocabu-lary	No. of cases	Vocabu-lary	No. of cases	Vocabu-lary
1·0 year	52	3	—	—	—	—
1·5 year	14	22	14	12·5	—	—
2·0 years	25	272	—	—	—	—
2·5 years	14	446	29	263	25	508
3·0 years	20	896	—	—	—	—
3·5 years	26	1222	6	1190·5	11	1338

These figures, though showing considerable variation, still demonstrate that the greatest increase in vocabulary probably occurs between two and a half and three years of age, and is a further argument against postponement of operative treatment in cases of cleft palate after the second year.

In the group of 1,142 children previously mentioned observations on the development of speech also showed that two-thirds of the children, had some defective use of articulate sounds during the early stages of speech development. However, there is considerable spontaneous improvement as shown in Fig. 102.

Such defects of articulation occur during the developing speech of childhood whether or not the child has a cleft of the palate and, in some children persist into school life.

During the whole of this time the pleasure principle is well to the fore, the child obtaining much delight and satisfaction in the outlet of speech, even in its early stages, and in his ever-increasing ability to make contact, through speech, with the people in his environment. This fact should be borne in mind in speech therapy with any young child. If this is to be effective it should follow as closely as possible the line of development of the normal child, and he should obtain the same natural pleasure at each stage of speech development, in the achievement of each new sound acquired, and satisfaction as each difficulty is, in turn, surmounted.

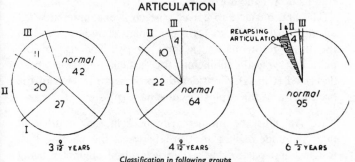

ARTICULATION

Classification in following groups

I. Defective [th] and/or [r] only.
II. Intelligible speech, but defects of articulation
III. Unintelligible speech.

% of children in group of 114 children

Fig. 102

Showing the classification of articulation in the 114 children in the sample group at three age levels and their progress towards normal articulation.

Reprinted from MORLEY, M. E., (1967). *The Development and Disorders of Speech in Childhood.* Edinburgh: Livingstone.

DEVELOPMENT OF SPEECH IN A CHILD WITH CLEFT PALATE

For some time development of speech in a child with a cleft palate proceeds on similar lines to that described above in the case of a normal child. Of the factors necessary for the development of speech he is only deficient in one, the requisite apparatus for normal articulation. He is unable to divide completely the oral from the nasal cavities, so that the first sounds produced in babbling will be nasalised. As the child at this stage is in no way attempting to imitate the sounds of his surroundings, nasalisation is of no importance to him, and such sounds serve to express his feelings and desires quite as satisfactorily as the correct sounds do for the normal child.

The first obstacle to correct speech is encountered when an attempt is made to form consonant sounds other than the nasal resonants m, n, and ng [ŋ]. The use of the palatopharyngeal sphincter for articulation has been described (Ch. II). Consider the processes involved in the production of the explosive consonant [p]:—

(a) Air must be momentarily held in the mouth and pharynx under slight pressure between the cheeks, lips, tongue, and palate, the palatopharyngeal sphincter being closed.

(b) The lips then relax and the air is allowed to escape, producing a slight explosive sound. Until the sound is completed the palatopharyngeal sphincter remains closed.

In a case of unrepaired cleft of the palate the requisite air pressure for producing this sound, as for any other plosive or fricative consonant, is unobtainable, as there is no possibility of preventing the escape of air through the cleft and nostrils. Under these conditions it has been found that the child's speech will probably develop along one of two lines:—

1. He may produce the best sounds of which he is capable, using correct lip and tongue positions, at the same time unavoidably allowing air to escape through the nostrils. The consonants will not be as strong as normal, and in an attempt to improve this state of affairs he may, or may not, contract the muscles of the nostrils, the alæ nasi, in an instinctive attempt to close the anterior nares and prevent

nasal escape of air. Such speech is intelligible but has obvious cleft palate characteristics.

2. Unable to obtain a sufficiently forceful explosive sound in the normal manner, he may produce a similar sound in the larynx, the glottal stop. At the same time he may use the correct lip and tongue positions for the required sound. Fricatives such as s, sh [ʃ], etc., may also be produced by approximation of parts of the speech organs not normally used for this purpose. These will be discussed later. Such attempts sometimes result in at least partially intelligible speech.

So a form of speech will develop, through stages similar to the normal certainly, but with marked deviation from the normal in the result obtained; and, as previously described, it is the continued reproduction of faulty speech movements which steadily and surely builds up those incorrect speech habits which, in later years, are so difficult to eradicate. Also, not only is the ear of the child becoming accustomed to the sound he hears himself producing, but these abnormal auditory images are being inevitably correlated in his mind with the normal sounds he hears around him, and which he is attempting to imitate.

It is due to these facts that the child with a cleft palate is usually completely unconscious of any difference between the sounds he makes and the sounds he hears from others. He only becomes conscious of his defect when he is old enough to realise that he differs from other children in his inability to make himself understood, or when his companions ridicule his attempts at speech. I have questioned many cleft palate patients, and have yet to find one who was able, without training, to recognise any auditory difference between his own and correct articulation. In this way such patients differ entirely from a stammerer, who is, except in rare instances, acutely aware of his speech disability. As the preservation of these faulty speech associations increases the difficulties of patient and speech therapist alike, the age at which treatment is commenced is of the greatest importance.

AGE FOR OPERATION

There are three factors to be considered when deciding the best age for operation. The optimal time will relate to survival, orofacial growth and speech development.

Mortality.—From the point of view of speech development there is every reason for early operation before defective habits become established. As the majority of consonant sounds occurring in speech are in use before the end of the first year it might seem that operation, to be effective functionally, should be performed about six months of age. Many surgeons have successfully operated at this time. Reference to the mortality tables (p. 84) shows that previously, there was increased danger to life at such an early age, but with the advent of antibiotics, modern methods of anæsthesia, and pædiatrics, the rate of mortality amongst children submitted to operation for cleft palate is no longer so important. Recently McCollum, Richardson and Swanson (1956) have reviewed a series of 1,034 children, the majority operated upon between one and two years of age, with no loss of life. Many other surgeons could substantiate these findings. This factor is therefore of much less importance than formerly.

Growth and development.—Although there was a period of time during which it was thought that early operation might damage the maxilla and interfere with growth, many surgeons continued to operate early because they found that the best results, both anatomical and functional, were obtained by early surgery. Most surgeons now accept this fact, and that appropriate surgical procedures do not cause interference with growth.

Treatment has usually commenced with closure of the cleft lip. According to Schultz (1954) the lip should be closed as early as two or three weeks after birth and the palate at two to six months of age. In a bilateral cleft he closes both sides at once rather than follow the usual procedure of closing first one side and then the other a few weeks later. He points out that "the parts being anatomically correct can now react in normal fashion." Other surgeons prefer to operate on the lip when the child is 10 lbs. weight at about the age of three months. In a bilateral cleft of the lip one side is repaired and following an interval of time which allows for some growth, the second side is repaired.

If the repaired lip is tense or too long, however, it may exert an undue restraining influence on the growth and expansion of the alveolar arch. Especially is this so when the alveolus is cleft and the ununited segments are more mobile than when the arch is complete and capable of offering normal resistance to lip and facial pressure. The segments of the arch may be forced together, and as tissue is frequently deficient, the arch will thus be narrowed. Again the segments may be rotated inwards and even overlap, with further narrowing of the anterior part of the palate and of the alveolar arch. Some failure of growth may be attributed to partial failure of dentition with resultant lack of alveolar development, although supernumary teeth may assist growth of the alveolus. The subsequent development of the alveolar arch would therefore seem to depend, at least partially, on the surgical result. Where operative procedures stimulate growth, as already described (p. 138-141) the developing lip will form no mechanical

L

barrier to growth of the maxilla and alveolus, but will help to mould it and assist growth in the required direction through normal muscle action.

Speech development.—In cases operated upon between one and two years of age, when, although speech is not yet established, it may be assumed that the child has already learned some incorrect habits for the production of many consonant sounds, it is found that, given a successful surgical result, normal speech may be attained without the aid of special training. Either the faculties naturally possessed by the child for the purpose of acquiring speech are at this time very active, or the bad habits learned before operation have not obtained a persistent hold (probably both these factors play a part), but from a study of the results in a large number of cases, it is evident that operation alone can, at this age, produce a good speech result. It has been amply proved that the majority of children, following successful operation for cleft palate at one, two, or even three years of age, develop normal speech without any aid beyond that which a child naturally receives in its home surroundings.

It is true that cleft palate speech may continue, and even appear to develop for some time, following successful operation. The child of two or three years of age, who has already used faulty speech before operation, will not suddenly lose the defects acquired on emerging from the anæsthetic. However, fluids will cease to escape through the nostrils, and he will soon be able to indulge satisfactorily in any form of blowing games, blowing trumpets, whistles, and so forth. Such children may be kept under observation for six months, or for a year or two according to their rate of development, during which time it will be noticed that all trace of nasal tone and nasal escape of air gradually disappears, and that faulty sounds are replaced by correct ones. The child eventually speaks normally and naturally, and is never conscious of the previous existence of any defect. (See case histories Nos. 26 to 30.)

There are two exceptions to the above. Firstly there are some children who would have had a defect of articulation even if the palate had been normal. It was shown in Fig. 102 how, at three years nine months, 31 per cent of children representative of the childhood population had defects of articulation and that at approximately five years of age 14 per cent still had articulatory defects, 4 per cent being unintelligible to most people. A certain proportion of children with clefts of the palate may therefore be expected to have an articulatory disability in addition to that due to the cleft. They will have greater difficulty in changing faulty articulatory patterns developed during the early stages of speech development before closure of the cleft. They may also have some difficulty in using the palatopharyngeal sphincter, even when postoperatively this is adequate for speech, and in co-ordinating nasopharyngeal closure with the oral release of air for articulate sounds (see also p. 179-192). These will require assistance, but they are in the minority.

Secondly, operation, at any age, may not succeed in producing a competent palatopharyngeal sphincter, and in these cases also specialised help will be required to train the child to make the best possible use of the condition remaining after operation.

Speech results of later operation.—So far we have been considering the ideal, when surgical treatment has been carried out before the optimum age for the development of speech is passed, and before defective speech habits are fully established. But there are children and adults who, for one reason or another, do not come for operation until later in life. In practice it is found that the longer operation is delayed, other factors being equal, the longer will it be before natural, normal and easy speech is attained, and the greater difficulty will its attainment present.

The majority of children of four and five years of age at the time of operation have, as previously described, acquired faulty habits of speech, but in spite of this many will lose these defects and develop normal speech with very little assistance beyond training in breath direction by means of blowing games. If any articulatory defect tends to persist it can easily be remedied by means of simple exercises, preferably disguised as games, assuming that operation has successfully produced the necessary anatomical and functioning mechanism.

Children a little older, aged six to twelve years, usually require a longer period in which to correct their faults. Conscious ambition where speech is concerned may be lacking at this age, but when correct methods of articulation have once been acquired, the introduction of these into speech, and their constant everyday use, proves easier than at a still later age.

Older children and adults often learn to correct a defect in articulation, in many cases, at a first attempt, but in order that these newly-acquired habits may be used in conversational speech without conscious effort, many months, if not years, of daily practice are required.

If, in any of these cases, it has been impossible to produce a competent palatopharyngeal sphincter and mobile soft palate, the difficulties in speech development are considerably increased, and the result can only approximate to the normal.

Jolleys also studied the speech of the patients he reviewed, and found a significant correlation between speech results and age at operation, those operated upon before two years of age having better speech than those submitted to operation at a later age, but he found no significant relationship to

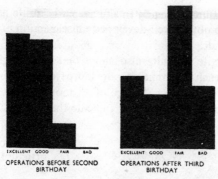

EXCELLENT GOOD FAIR BAD
OPERATIONS BEFORE SECOND
BIRTHDAY

EXCELLENT GOOD FAIR BAD
OPERATIONS AFTER THIRD
BIRTHDAY

Fig. 103.—The Speech results in relation to age at operation.

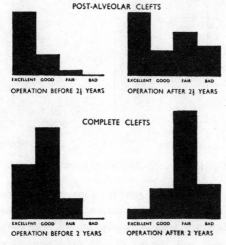

POST-ALVEOLAR CLEFTS

EXCELLENT GOOD FAIR BAD
OPERATION BEFORE 2¼ YEARS

EXCELLENT GOOD FAIR BAD
OPERATION AFTER 2¼ YEARS

COMPLETE CLEFTS

EXCELLENT GOOD FAIR BAD
OPERATION BEFORE 2 YEARS

EXCELLENT GOOD FAIR BAD
OPERATION AFTER 2 YEARS

Fig. 104.—The speech results in post-alveolar and complete clefts of
the palate in relation to age at operation.

the type of operation (Figs. 103 and 104). Jolleys considers
that the muscle fibres, lacking the pull of the muscles on
the other side, become shortened and fail to grow if operation is postponed, and that therefore it is advisable to

provide a functioning soft palate as early in life as possible in order to obtain well-developed muscle action and a good speech result.

Braithwaite's results also show that at any given time normal speech apparently occurs more frequently in children operated upon under the age of 18 months than over this age. This may not, however, indicate the final result but be

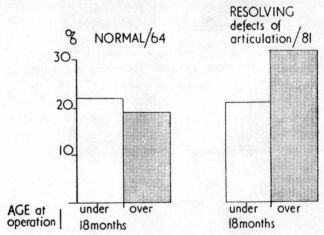

Fig. 105.—Speech results and age at operation.

associated with the fact that the longer operation is postponed the longer it may be before articulatory defects are eradicated either spontaneously or with speech therapy (Fig. 105).

It has been suggested that as growth proceeds subsequent to operation in infancy, nasopharyngeal closure with normal speech, once achieved, may not persist.

Recently, and without appointment, a man aged twenty-one years visited the clinic. He had had a complete left unilateral cleft of the palate and lip. Speech was completely normal. He explained that he had attended for speech therapy at the age of four to six years, but had ceased to attend in October 1939, as his mother was afraid to bring him into the town when an air raid might occur. Operation had been carried out on the lip and anterior palate in the first few months of life, and on the palate at eighteen months. He had not been seen in the interval of fifteen years. In this case the facial structure was in no way abnormal, and he had proportional development of the upper and lower jaws.

This is, however, only one case, and adequate proof requires a follow-up of cases for at least ten to twelve years subsequent to operation.

To obtain further information over 100 patients submitted to operation in infancy between the years 1936 and 1942 were recalled, but contact could only be established with 27. When these patients were reviewed they were aged 14 to 21 years, the average age being 17 years. They were all operated upon in infancy by various surgeons using the Wardill technique.

It was found that only two of these 27 patients had severe defects of articulation with inadequate nasopharyngeal closure, one aged 14 years, and one aged 18 years who was mentally defective, and in whom the repair of the palate had broken down.

Ten patients had developed speech which was completely normal with nasopharyngeal closure. In addition six patients also had nasopharyngeal closure but had slight defects of articulation. Sixteen (59%) of these 27 patients, therefore, had a good speech and functional result, 36% having achieved and maintained normal speech.

Nine patients had a varying degree of incompetence of the palatopharyngeal sphincter, and in two more there was an anterior fistula in the hard palate. Eight of these 11 patients had developed good speech, however, in spite of some slight nasal escape of air. Twenty-four of these 27 patients, therefore (88%), had developed useful speech, although in only ten was it completely normal. At the age when these patients were seen it was considered unlikely that there would be any further spontaneous improvement of articulation.

Ability to maintain nasopharyngeal closure, therefore, persisted in 16 of these 27 patients, but it was not known whether or not the nine patients with some degree of incompetence of the palatopharyngeal sphincter had ever achieved this at any stage following operation.

For psychological reasons early operation is advisable. The aim of all treatment, surgical, orthodontic, prosthetic or speech therapy is to help the individual to face life with an appearance and speech which approximates as nearly as is possible to the normal. A speech aid fitted prior to operation will not only be difficult to adjust in the very young child, but will entail frequent renewals as the child grows, involving not only expense but also emphasizing to the child his abnormality in the pre-school period and early school life, even if the possibility for normal speech development is provided.

Such children will usually require speech therapy in addition, and it should be the aim of all to render this unnecessary where possible. If the requirements for normal speech are not provided early in life, and the child reaches the age when he is aware that others regard his articulation as defective, lack of confidence in what should be an easy and unconscious means of expressing his thoughts may never be entirely eradicated. Much time and effort will also be necessary to change faulty neuromuscular patterns of articulation, which at the age of six or seven years, will be firmly established, in order to develop articulation which is intelligible. McCollum, Richardson and Swanson (1956) have stated that they consider that "the psychological impact of such a gross anatomical defect during the child's early impressionable years must be taken into consideration, and that speech defects will be detrimental to the development of the child's personality if operation is postponed after the period of infancy."

From a consideration of all these factors, therefore, it seems apparent that operation in infancy is desirable, that present day methods render danger to life unlikely, and that such operation will not necessarily interfere with palatal growth but may stimulate and assist development towards the normal whilst the requisite conditions are provided for the natural, spontaneous development of speech.

REFERENCES

BLAKELEY, R. W. (1960). Temporary speech prosthesis as an aid in speech training. *Cleft Palate Bull.*, **10**, 63.

BLAKELEY, R. W. (1964). The complementary use of speech prostheses and pharyngeal flaps in palatal insufficiency. *Cleft Palate J.*, **1**, 194.

BLAKELEY, R. W. (1969). The rationale for a temporary speech prosthesis in palatal insufficiency. *Br. J. Disord. Commun.*, **4**, 134.

BRASH, J. C. (1924). The Genesis and Growth of Deformed Jaws and Palates. *Dental Board of the U.K.*

BURSTON, W. R. (1959). The development of cleft lip and palate. *Ann. R. Coll. Surg. Engl.*, **26**, 225.

FOSTER, T. D. (1962). Maxillary Deformities in Repaired Clefts of the Lip and Palate. *Brit. J. plast. Surg.*, **15**, 182.

GRABER, T. M. (1949). An Appraisal of the Developmental Deformities in Cleft Palate and Cleft Lip Individuals. *Quart. Bull. Nthwest Univ. med. Sch.*, **23**, No. 2, 153.

GRABER, T. M. (1950). Changing Philosophies in Cleft Palate Management. *J. Pediat.*, **37**, No. 3, 400-415.

GWYNNE-EVANS, E. (1952). An Analysis of the Orofacial Structures with Special Reference to Muscle Behaviour and Dental Alignment. *Speech*, **16**, 2, 36.

HARKINS, CLOYD S. (1948) AND BAKER, H. K. Twenty-five years of Cleft Palate Prosthesis. *J. Speech Hear. Dis.*, **13**, 23-30.

JOLLEYS, A. (1954). A Review of Results of Operation of Cleft Palate with Reference to Maxillary Growth and Speech. *Brit. J. plast. Surg.*, 7, 229.

KETTLE, M. A. (1954). The Development of the Orthodontic Problem. *Dent. Practit.*, 5, 23.

McCOLLUM, D. W., RICHARDSON, S. O. AND SWANSON, L. T. (1956), Habilitation of the Cleft Palate Patient. *New Engl. J. Med.*, 254. 299.

McNEIL, C. KERR (1954). *Oral and Facial Deformity.* London: Pitman.

McNEIL, C. KERR (1956). Congenital Oral Deformities. *Brit. dent. J.*, 101, 6, 191.

MOOLENAAR BYL, (1948). *Conference Report on Speech Therapy*, p. 95. London: Tavistock Publications Ltd.

MORLEY, M. E. (1965). *The Development and Disorders of Speech in Childhood.* 2nd Ed. Edinburgh: Livingstone.

PEYTON, W. T. (1931). Dimensions and Growth of the Palate in the Normal Infant and in the Infant with Gross Maldevelopment of the Upper Lip and Palate. *Arch. Surg.*, 22, 704.

PRUZANSKY, S. (1955). *Amer. J. Orthodont.*, 41, 827.

PRUZANSKY, S. (1964). Pre-surgical orthopædics and bone grafting for infants with cleft lip and palate: a dissent. *Cleft Palate Journal*, 1, 164.

SCHULTZ, L. W. (1954). Correct time and sequence for closure of cleft lip and palate. *Amer. J. Surg.*, 87, 651.

SHIERE, F. R. AND FISHER, J. H. (1964). Neonatal Orthopædic Correction for Cleft Lip and Palate patients: a preliminary report. *Cleft Pal. J.*, 1, 17.

SHINN, M. W. (1893). *Notes on the Development of a Child.* University of California Press.

SUBTELNY, J. D. (1955). Width of the Nasopharynx and related Anatomic Structures in Normal and Unoperated Cleft Palate Children. *Amer. J. Orthodont.*, 41, 12, 889.

TODD, T. W. (1931). The Orthodontic Value of Research and Observations in Developmental Growth of the Face. *Angle Orthodont.*, 1, 67.

WALTHER, D. P. (1954). Appliances used in the Orthodontic Treatment of Cleft Palate Cases. *Dent. Practit.*, 4, 385.

WARDILL, W. E. M. (1928). Cleft Palate. *Brit. J. Surg.*, 26, 61.

WEST, KENNEDY AND CARR (1937). *Rehabilitation of Speech.* p. 34. London: Harper.

CHAPTER V

THE ASSESSMENT OF SPEECH

Operation before the development of speech

Operation after the development of speech

Classification of pre-operative speech

Assessment after operation

Examination of the patient

Analysis of typical defects in cleft palate speech

171

THE ASSESSMENT OF SPEECH

BECAUSE the majority of children are now operated upon prior to the development of speech this assessment is usually undertaken post-operatively and at intervals during the subsequent development and progressive improvement of speech. If, however, surgery has been delayed until speech is fully established, a pre-operative assessment may be required. It may also be needed if primary surgery has not been successful and secondary procedures are being considered, and will always be required on referral for, and prior to, speech therapy.

The assessment of speech will be considered here in two groups of patients:—

I. Those submitted to operation on the palate in infancy before speech is fully established, and,

II. Those in which operation was performed later in life after use of speech had developed, or in which early surgery failed to provide the anatomical and physiological requirements for normal articulation.

OPERATION BEFORE DEVELOPMENT OF SPEECH

Closure of the cleft in infancy

Following operation the children should attend the clinic for review every six months and should be seen by a team consisting of the surgeon, the orthodontist and the speech therapist. Where this is not possible the speech therapist can usefully carry out regular observations on the development of speech and report to the surgeon.

Observations should include tests for the degree of nasopharyngeal occlusion, the development of language, and the use of articulation as language develops. Advice to the mother may be useful at any time, but, if surgery has been successful, speech therapy may be postponed until the child is at least four years of age, and then only if adequate progress is not occurring spontaneously.

When assessing the speech of a patient with a repaired cleft of the palate one must consider four main points:—

1. Intra-oral air pressure. This is dependent upon the competence of the palatopharyngeal sphincter and the production of a complete hard and soft palate without breakdown in the suture line or residual fistulas.

2. Vocal tone and resonance balance.

3. Articulation of the consonant sounds as used in speech.

4. Other factors such as (a) disorders of speech which are not related to the cleft of the palate, (b) hearing defect, (c) mental retardation, and (d) the persistence of faulty habits.

1. Intra-oral air pressure.

Some simple but effective tests for intra-oral air pressure are:—

1. Ability to blow through the mouth without nasal escape of air.

2. Ability to sustain air pressure in the mouth with the lips closed and to release it through the lips or through the palatopharyngeal sphincter.

3. The normal articulation of a few simple consonant sounds such as [p], and [ʃ(sh)] in isolation and in a simple syllable.

4. Articulation of k and g if there should be an anterior fistula.

During the first four months after operation some children continue to blow through the nose, with lips closed, rather than through the mouth. Later, if breath direction is not corrected, [s] particularly may develop as a nasal or nasopharyngeal fricative sound. This can occur when there is a competent palatopharyngeal sphincter, but the child chooses the nasal rather than the oral outlet for blowing. It in no way resembles blowing associated with a nasal leak.

The majority of children seen by us in recent years have control of the nasopharyngeal airway and adequate intra-oral pressure for articulation following operation. However, a few children had some nasal escape of air at first, but later developed adequate closure and control with experience. (Case notes Nos. 27, 28 and 30.)

The width of the cleft and the extent of the pre-natal development of the palatal processes varies according to the stage at which growth in embryo is arrested. Where there is insufficient palatal tissue for complete surgical closure of the anterior part of the hard palate, without sacrificing the length of the soft palate, the surgeon may accept a fistula anteriorly, just posterior to the alveolus. Such fistulas usually close spontaneously in the children we have been observing. However, even a small fistula may affect the development of normal articulation by preventing the build-up of the intra-oral air pressure for articulation anteriorly, and particularly for the alveolar consonants such as [t], [d], [s] and [z]. Pressure for the bilabials [p] and [b] and the labio-dentals [f] and [v] may sometimes be obtained by closure of the fistula with the tongue, whilst air pressure for [k], [g] and [ʃ(sh)], produced posteriorly to the fistula, is not affected if the palato-pharyngeal sphincter is competent. If the fistula persists a dental plate should be fitted as soon as is possible to prevent the escape of air into the anterior nasal air-way, and thus avoid the use of faulty patterns of articulation.

2. Vocal tone and resonance. This varies to some extent from day to day, and with infections of the nasal and pharyngeal mucous membranes. Assessment is also dependent upon the subjective opinion of the assessor, and what may be acceptable in one country, or locality, might be considered abnormal and nasal elsewhere. Changes in the oral, pharyngeal and nasal resonance balance occur when the palate is normal, and such changes may be completely independent of typical cleft palate nasality due to a nasal leak and excessive nasality in association with an incompetent palatopharyngeal sphincter.

Good movement of the soft palate and of the pharyngeal wall, especially laterally, would seem to contribute towards a normal resonance balance. Tension in the pharyngeal walls, sometimes evident following a pharyngoplasty, may lead to abnormal resonance, or even a lateral leak of air, the cause of which is not always apparent in lateral radiographs of mid-line palatal movement.

Adenoids may become enlarged during growth in childhood, with or without a cleft palate, with consequent modifications in resonance. Such changes may be temporary and are not usually due to a nasopharyngeal air leak, rather the reverse. Changes in a boy's voice at puberty may also cause changes in resonance which are within normal limits.

Adenoidectomy should be avoided except where it is essential to preserve hearing. Where this has been necessary, temporary nasopharyngeal incompetence has subsequently been observed in a few children with deterioration in articulation, but usually, but not necessarily, with return to normal articulation within a period of time which may extend to six months.

Resonance can usefully be assessed on a 5-point scale where 1, 2 and 3 represent variations in resonance within the normal range. On this scale 4 represents abnormal nasal resonance, due to catarrhal conditions, adenoid growth or pharyngeal tension but without any nasopharyngeal air leak, whilst 5 represents nasality associated with an incompetent nasopharyngeal sphincter and nasal escape of air (See p. 189).

3. Articulation. The spontaneous improvement in the use of articulation in early childhood was shown in Fig. 102. Fig. 106 shows a comparison of the articulation in children with normal palates at three age levels with that of children with cleft palates repaired in infancy at the same age levels.

Although there is a wide range for the age of onset of speech, children born with cleft palates may be later in developing speech than the normal, and articulation cannot be fully assessed until sufficient use of language has developed.

Following the production of a competent palato-pharyngeal sphincter in early life, it is common for the child to pass through a period when articulation is defective, but with gradual spontaneous improvement towards the normal. This period varies in duration, but, other factors being equal, the articulatory defects tend to persist longer in the more severe types of cleft, that is the complete unilateral or bilateral alveolar cleft, or when operation has been carried out later in childhood. Following successful surgery which has provided a complete palate and adequate intra-oral air pressure for articulation we have found a

M

178 CLEFT PALATE AND SPEECH

ARTICULATION

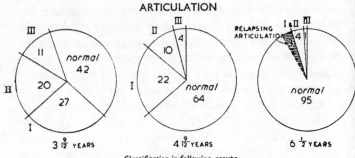

Classification in following groups

I. Defective [th] and/or [r] only.
II. Intelligible speech, but defects of articulation.
III. Unintelligible speech.

% of children in group of 114 children

Showing the classification of articulation in the 114 children in the sample group at three age levels and their progress towards normal articulation.

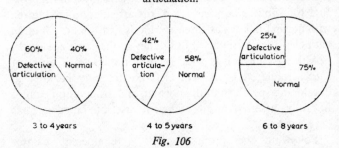

Fig. 106

Showing the classification of articulation in children operated upon for cleft palate in three age groups and the improvement with increasing age.

gradual spontaneous improvement in the use of articulation without speech therapy.

Articulation may be assessed initially on the first words of childhood, which may be "bye bye," "ta ta," "da da," "up" or "car." Later articulation can be assessed as used in single words, short phrases, rhymes, and finally in continuous conversational speech

Where there is inadequate intra-oral air pressure for articulation defective articulation usually persists and becomes increasingly stabilised as use of speech develops. If this is due to an anterior fistula a dental plate may be fitted. If due to an incompetent palatopharyngeal sphincter further surgery may be required.

The stages reached may be assessed as:—

1. normal articulation.

2. resolving defects of articulation: (a) minimal, such as a slight residual distortion of [s], sometimes related only to the use of a temporary orthodontic appliance, (b) more severe defects of articulation.

3. normal articulation for the speech used, but insufficient language development for full assessment.

4. defective articulation due to inadequate intra-oral air pressure resulting from: (a) an incompetent sphincter, (b) a residual fistula.

4. Other defects. (a) *Other disorders of speech.*
The chief of these are (1) dyslalia or (2) articulatory dyspraxia.

1. For example, the child may imitate the articulation of a mother with defective articulation due to a cleft of the palate, or be passing through a period of defective articulation as occurs in many children with normal palates.

2. Again, he may have difficulty in directing and controlling the muscle movements for the reproduction of the sounds used in speech resulting in abnormal articulation due to substitutions, omissions and distortions of the consonant sounds used. Such an articulatory dyspraxia may also cause difficulty in co-ordinating the movements of the palatopharyngeal sphincter with other movements

for articulation, even when the palatopharyngeal sphincter is potentially adequate.

Should the cleft of the palate be associated with other conditions such as cerebral palsy, the child's ability to acquire normal articulation will again be severely affected despite successful surgery.

(b) *Hearing defect.* A severe hearing defect will prevent the imitation of speech, and cause severe delay and limitation in the use of speech. Where the hearing loss is partial the child will not hear the sounds of speech normally. Consonant sounds may be distorted, and he will reproduce these as he hears them. A partial hearing loss due to infection of the middle ear, is unlikely to affect speech unless very severe. It is usually intermittent and tends to occur after the development of speech. It may, however, hinder progress in a child who already has defective articulation.

(c) *Mental retardation.* Although use of language is usually limited and its onset delayed in children who are mentally retarded, articulation may be normal in the limited speech used if operation on the palate has been successful. Where articulation is defective these children will experience greater difficulty in acquiring normal articulation either with or without speech therapy.

(d) *Persistence of abnormal habits.* Whether these are the reflex patterns basic to articulation as described, or faulty patterns of articulation developed before operation on the palate, they will tend to interfere with, and delay, the use of normal articulation.

It is useful to classify the speech results as follows:—

1. Nasopharyngeal closure and adequate intra-oral air pressure.

   (i) Normal speech.

(ii) Defects of articulation with adequate intra-oral air pressure and normal resonance.

    (*a*) Minimal defects of [s] only.

    (*b*) Resolving defects of articulation.

    (*c*) Some consonant sounds normal but insufficient speech development for full assessment.

2. Inadequate intra-oral pressure due to:—(*a*) an anterior fistula; or (*b*) incompetent sphincter.

    (i) Good articulation but some nasal escape of air and /or nasal tone.

    (ii) Poor speech with obvious defects of articulation and/or nasal tone.

3. Associated with other defects or abnormalities such as a congenital hearing loss or mental defect.

OPERATION PERFORMED AFTER SPEECH IS ESTABLISHED

CLASSIFICATION OF SPEECH BEFORE OPERATION

As previously described, a child with a cleft palate will encounter difficulties when beginning to speak, and will develop some form of defective speech if left untreated, the ultimate result depending on the method used by the child to compensate for his inability to produce normal sounds. These cases can be divided into two groups. This classification is based on the type of speech prior to operation, and therefore excludes all those cases on which operation is performed before speech is established. Such cases were discussed in the preceding section. Though in practice it will be found that many patients have faults belonging to both groups, it proves to be a very useful means of classification.

Group A.—Patients in this group use normal relations of tongue, lips and teeth for the production of all sounds, but speech is accompanied by gross nasal escape. Such speech is usually intelligible, but consonants are weak and vowels nasalised.

Group B.—This includes all cases with articulatory substitutions such as the glottal stop, pharyngeal [s], or the replacement of one sound by another, e.g., [k] for [t], and [g] for [d], etc. Some consonants may be produced in normal positions, but will be weak, as in Group A.

ASSESSMENT AFTER OPERATION

(a) Anatomical and physiological.—The results of operation may be divided into three sections, as follows:—

Palate incomplete, function impossible.—As cleft palate surgery progressed these cases have become more and more rare, but there are those in whom the palate may have broken down following operation, with the formation of persistent holes in the hard or soft palates, or resulting scar tissues may have caused contraction of the soft palate, drawing it away from the pharyngeal wall, and making it short thickened and immobile. Such results are sometimes attributable to the poor physical condition of the child at the time of operation, and it is important that he should be in good health if a satisfactory surgical result is to be obtained. In some cases the size of the cleft prior to operation, and the scarcity of tissue may have made the surgeon's task difficult, the result being classed by him as a surgical failure.

Palate complete, function not yet developed.—This includes patients who have been operated upon, and in whom operation has been successful in producing the anatomical mechanism required for speech, but who are still unable to obtain closure of the palatopharyngeal sphincter. This may be due to (1) the fact that operation is too recent, and the muscles have had insufficient time to adapt themselves to their new function; or (2) inability on the part of the patient to learn to use the sphincter mechanism without training. Or again, the sphincter may be competent on blowing but not for speech.

Palate complete, function normal.—In these cases there is a competent sphincter which the patient is able to use on blowing and on speaking.

(*b*) **Speech.**—The speech results of any surgical treatment which is successful in closing the cleft and producing a palatopharyngeal sphincter depends to a great extent on the group to which the patient belonged before operation. Successful operation on cases in **Group A** will, by providing the sphincter mechanism, obviate the chief fault, that of nasal escape. Normal speech may not immediately follow, as the condition of the soft palate, especially its mobility, continues to improve for several months after operation, and the optimum result may not be achieved until six or eight months after operation, or even longer. Even then there are those patients who do not learn spontaneously, but must be taught to make use of the newly acquired sphincter in blowing and in speech. However, cases have been known in this Group where normal speech has been achieved within a few weeks after operation, and without specialised training.

In **Group B** operation, however successful, produces very little improvement in speech. If defective habits are wel established they persist in spite of the best that surgery can do. The patient himself is unable to recognise his own defects and so cannot correct them without help. The tone of the voice may be improved, but the glottal stop and other substitutions remain, and the patient may or may not be able to use the palatopharyngeal sphincter without training.

EXAMINATION OF THE PATIENT

Before commencing any post-operative treatment it is necessary for the therapist to examine each case carefully and try to form some idea as to how much of the speech defect is due to anatomical insufficiency and how much to other contributing causes.

Age at operation.—It is first of all useful to know at what age the operation was performed, and whether the patient was speaking fluently or not at the time of operation. If, as in cases previously described, speech was not established before operation, and if sufficient time has elapsed for its development, the difficulty may be due to the cleft palate, or it may be due to defective hearing or mentality, or other defects of articulation not related to the cleft palate. Such factors may be present in addition to the cleft palate, and the possibility must not be ignored. If speech had been acquired prior to operation the persistence of bad habits must also be included as the probable chief cause of the present defect.

Anatomical condition.—*Palate*—Notice the apparent length of the soft palate, remembering that this is not an accurate guide to the competence of the palatopharyngeal sphincter.

Ask the patient to yawn or to say "ah" [a:] with the mouth open, and notice the degree of mobility of the soft palate as it is, or is not, raised by the action of the levatores.

Examine the palate to see if there is a fistula. Many

of these fistulas remaining after operation close gradually with time, but large defects are a great hindrance to the development of good speech, and, if present, the surgeon should be consulted with a view to referring the patient for dental treatment. If the fistula is in the hard palate a small dental plate can be provided to cover it. This will in no way prevent the tendency of such a fistula to close gradually and spontaneously, but it will obviate escape of air through it into the nasal cavities. Upper incisor teeth may also be fitted to these plates, even for small children, when the cleft has been through the alveolus and the teeth are irregular or missing. In this way the production of many consonant sounds is considerably simplified.

If the patient is already wearing a plate, notice if it fits well. Especially is this important in young children as plates must be renewed from time to time during growth. Sometimes a newly erupted tooth will push the plate out of position and allow air to escape through the fistula in the palate.

Lips, teeth and alveolar ridge.—In the case of a repaired hare-lip, notice how far the patient is able to raise it in order to show his upper teeth. Much difficulty will be experienced in the production of labio-dental sounds such as [f], and [v], also other sounds, if the upper lip is long, tight and immobile.

When a cleft has extended to the alveolar ridge, there may be some deformity in the development of the teeth and missing teeth, especially the upper incisors, are responsible for various difficulties, the sounds [s], [z], [th (θ, ð)], [f]. and, [v] being usually affected. Irregularities in the contour of the alveolar ridge will also affect the production of these consonants. (See note concerning dental plates above.)

Notice if there is any deformity of the alveolar ridge which may be a hindrance to the production of such sounds as [t] and [d]. A palate which is shortened antero-posteriorly, or a narrow or high-arched hard palate, will also make the use of these sounds difficult except in very slow speech. When the palate is shortened the tongue tends to protrude beyond the upper incisors, when it is excessively arched the tongue has difficulty in reaching it for the production of [k,] [g], and [ng (ŋ)].

Competence of the palatopharyngeal sphincter.—The normal use of the palatopharyngeal sphincter has previously been described (p. 41-43 and 46-56) and simple tests have been suggested (p. 174).

Blowing test.—Test the patient's ability to use the sphincter in blowing, noticing any tendency to constrict the nostrils, or resort to tricks such as pressing the upper lip forward and up in such a way as to block the anterior nares.

Hold a polished surface, such as a pocket torch or mirror, or a card upon which is a feather, under the patient's nose while he is blowing to determine how much air, if any, is escaping through the nostrils.

Ability to retain air in the mouth.—Ask the patient to blow out his cheeks, holding the air under pressure in the mouth and pharynx. This is accomplished normally with closure of the lips and palatopharyngeal sphincter. If the palatopharyngeal sphincter is incompetent such intra-oral pressure cannot be maintained unless the nostrils are closed by the fingers to prevent escape of air through the nasopharynx. During a first attempt it is sometimes helpful if the nostrils are nipped by the fingers until the mouthful of air is obtained. Then release the nostrils to see if the patient can maintain the air pressure using the palatopharyngeal sphincter. Make sure that a trick is not used. After filling the mouth with air some patients can successfully retain it by closing the opening from the mouth to the pharynx with the back of the tongue, but under such conditions the air cannot be released through the lips for articulation of a normal [p]. This requires an open oro-pharyngeal isthmus with supporting breath pressure from the lungs. Test also to see if, after maintaining air pressure in the mouth, the patient can so control the palato-pharyngeal sphincter as to be able to release the air either through the nasopharynx, the lips remaining closed, or through the mouth with the nasopharyngeal airway closed.

In recent years other complicated methods have been devised to assess the competence of the palatopharyngeal sphincter. These fall into two groups, those which attempt to assess the amount of nasal emission of air, or the size of the nasopharyngeal orifice, and those based on lateral radiography of the pharynx or cineradiography.

A manometer may be used to measure the pressure of oral blowing and nasal emission of air. The child blows into a tube and pressure is registered on a dial. The child's nostrils are then occluded and he blows again. If naso-pharyngeal closure is adequate the pressure reading should not change. If there is nasal emission of air, a higher reading will be recorded when the nostrils are occluded. Results may, however, be misleading. Blowing with the nostrils occluded when the palatopharyngeal sphincter is competent may cause some discomfort. As a result the child blows less strongly and the pressure reading is lower than when blowing without closure of the anterior nares. It must also be remembered that until the cleft is adequately repaired the child is unable to practice blowing, as do most infants, with any degree of satisfaction, and there are many grades of performance which depend more upon the control of the diaphragm and rib muscles for blowing rather than upon the competence of the palatopharyngeal sphincter.

Other methods have been designed to measure the

emission of oral and nasal air simultaneously during speaking (Quigley, *et al.*, 1964), but is must be remembered that normally there is intermittent nasal emission of air and that during normal speech nasopharyngeal closure is not consistently complete. It is never static, and varies in degree according to the pressure required for each sound.

Methods for measuring velopharyngeal orifice area, that is the size of the nasopharyngeal opening during speech (Warren and Du Bois 1964), again may bear little relation to the speech result. A small puncture in a balloon will prevent its inflation, and it is the existence of, and not the size of the opening, which will affect the potential for normal speech, together with the speed at which the opening and closing movements of the palatopharyngeal sphincter can be accomplished.

In an attempt to provide visual evidence as to the existence of nasopharyngeal closure methods such as lateral radiography of the pharynx and lateral cineradiography have been developed to a high level of technical efficiency by many, among whom are Hoffman, (1964), Kirkpatrick (1964), Subtelny, (1964), and Moll (1965).

When by these methods it is apparent that the soft palate is short, and there is no possibility of nasopharyngeal closure, it is most unlikely that speech could ever approach the normal. Also, when full flexible movement of the soft palate is demonstrated with bunching of the mucosa and thickening of the soft palate at the point of insertion of the levatores towards the posterior pharyngeal wall, it is most probable that nasopharyngeal closure will be adequate for normal articulation. However, a competent palatopharyngeal sphincter is not necessarily demonstrated by contact in the mid-line between the soft palate and the posterior pharyngeal wall, as inward movement of the lateral pharyngeal walls is also an important factor. A lateral view may not therefore indicate what is occurring in other planes, and nasal escape of air may persist in spite of apparent mid-line closure. Again, when radiographic investigations are carried out whilst the patient produces sustained consonant sounds the potential for the normal articulation of sequences of vowel and consonant sounds may not be indicated, each sound being influenced by adjacent sounds.

Since the early part of this century and even earlier the chief reason for surgical treatment has been the achievement of normal speech. The ultimate test of successful surgery is the acceptability of the patient's speech, and no matter what other methods of assessment may suggest, the speech ability is logically the only valid test of success. Frequently the simpler tests, within the experience of the young child, produce more reliable results than the more complicated procedures. The variations in speech of those with normal palates are considerable, and "normal" speech in the cleft palate patient is that which is acceptable to those in the child's environment and considered by the trained ear to be within the normal range.

It is important to remember that, although variations in the size of the nasopharyngeal airway will cause variations in the type of defective speech, which are inconsistent and also influenced by other factors, adequate pressure for normal articulation requires a competent palatopharyngeal sphincter, just as momentary bilabial closure is required for the articulation of [p] and [b].

Speech attainment.—The assessment of speech requires that two factors be considered:—

1. Vocal tone and resonance on vowel sounds.
2. Articulation.

The assessment of vocal tone is based on experience and

a knowledge of, and comparison with, what is considered to be within the normal range for any age group. Although subjective, such an assessment can give a useful indication of the quality of the voice and the balance of resonance and may be classified on a five-point scale as follows:—

The normal, clear tone of a young child . 1

Some increase in nasal resonance . . 2

Further increase in nasal resonance but still within the range of normal variation . 3

Excessive nasal resonance, but without nasal emission of air 4

Nasal emission of air influencing resonance with marked nasal tone 5

In this classification 1, 2 and 3 are variations within the range found in children with normal palates. The two types of abnormal resonance represented by 4 and 5 occur where there is a marked defect typical of cleft palate. Whereas excessive nasal resonance, group 4, affects mainly vowel sounds and vocal tone, nasal emission of air is most apparent on the plosive and fricative consonant sounds. When making these assessments consideration must always be given to the locality and country in which the patient lives, the language he speaks, and temporary variations due to nasal infections.

A cleft of the palate, or an incompetent palatopharyngeal sphincter will affect the normal resonance balance. The mouth, nasopharynx, oropharynx and nostrils form one cavity, depending upon the extent of the cleft, with acoustic properties differing essentially from the normal. There is nasal escape of air and increased nasal and nasopharyngeal resonance. Vowel tone is affected, having the well-known nasal quality. Variations occur in relation to the extent to which the oral and nasal cavities are separated, and according to the patient's ability to control the outlet of air through the nasopharyngeal airway.

There are naturally occurring modifications in resonance during growth. Excessive development of adenoid tissues, particularly the former, and chiefly in children aged seven to twelve years, affects resonance in those with repaired cleft palates as it also does in those with normal palates. In the adolescent boy there is growth of the larynx, mainly in the antero-posterior direction; in the girl, the increase in length is in the vertical direction, and in both there are changes in pitch, vocal tone and resonance, Such normal variations must be considered when assessing the speech of the cleft palate patient.

Articulation.—Long and elaborate word tests for the assessment of articulation are not necessary. It is more important to note how the patient is attempting to articulate consonant sounds and to compensate for his disability, than to attempt to assess his speech ability on the number of consonants produced correctly, in varying positions in certain single words. Asking the patient to repeat a few one-syllable words will give an initial indication as to the degree of the defect and the problems requiring treatment. Suggested words could be: pie, boy, tie, door, car, go, fire, see (or see-saw), shoe, chair, jam, letter, red (or road), you (yes or yellow), water.

The use of consonant sounds in conversational speech should then be noted, whether or not medial and final consonants are being used and the variations due to changes in position of the sounds in words and to the influence of adjacent consonants. Use of consonant blends can also be noted during speech. If the child is at first too shy to converse readily, assessment may be made whilst he is playing with other children, perhaps in the waiting room, saying a well-known rhyme, repeating a rhyme line by line after the therapist, or repeating a story, phrase by phrase.

It may also be useful to test the patient's ability to repeat simple words, as above, when the nostrils are compressed with the fingers to prevent nasal escape of air. Consonant sounds which the child has been unable to articulate are sometimes produced easily with this assistance.

It may be found that the patient can blow without nasal escape but is unable to obtain complete nasopharyngeal closure during speech. This may happen when the soft palate is immobile, the rapid opening and closing of the palatopharyngeal sphincter being impossible, although complete closure is achieved on sustained effort. Or again, it may be due only to lack of co-ordination. The patient has learnt to use the sphincter for blowing, but old neuro-muscular habits persist on speaking.

Following examination, the physiological result of operation and the type of speech can be classified as below.

I. **Type of cleft**

II. **Age of patient**

III. **Age at operation**—(*a*) Lip   (*b*) Palate

IV. **Stage of speech development at the time of operation on palate**

V. **Examination:**

    1. Condition of soft palate.

    2. Condition of hard palate.

    3. Lips.

    4. Teeth.

    5. Alveolar ridge.

6. Competence of the palatopharyngeal sphincter.
   Blowing test.
   Ability to hold air in the mouth under pressure.
   Other tests.

7. Speech.
   (*a*) Vocal tone and resonance.
   (*b*) Articulation.
       Results of tests for consonant sounds.
       Results when nostrils are occluded.
       Sounds used in conversational speech.

VI. **Classification**—(*a*) **Anatomical and physiological.**

1. Palate incomplete—function not possible.
2. Palate complete—function not developed.
3. Palate complete—function normal.
   (*b*) Speech:
       Group A.
       Group B.

We shall now consider in detail the principal faults in each Group which must be corrected before normal speech can be attained.

ANALYSIS OF TYPICAL DEFECTS IN CLEFT PALATE SPEECH

Group A cases

(*a*) *Function of palatopharyngeal sphincter not developed.*
   The chief faults in this group are:—

1. Weak plosive and fricative consonants.
2. Nasal escape of air.

N

3. Nasal grimace.
4. Nasopharyngeal snort.
5. Nasal tone.

1. **Weak consonants.**—Weak plosive consonants are due to lack of air pressure in the mouth. They are, however, formed with correct relations of tongue, lips and teeth, and are accompanied by the sound of air escaping through the nose. Fricative sounds are also weak and often accompanied by a secondary fricative sound produced in the nostrils which have been contracted in an attempt to lessen the amount of air escaping in that direction. A nasal [s] is usually the most obvious. In some cases the tongue is placed so as to form a complete block to any outlet through the mouth, or the lips may be closed, and the sound [s] is then made entirely in the nose. More often, however, there is a combination of an oral attempt with the addition of nasal escape. [f], [v], [th (θ, ð)], [sh (ʃ)], [zh (ʒ)], [z] are all affected to a greater or less extent. The sounds [l], [r], [h], [y (j)] and [w], owing to their formation, require less air pressure than most, and are usually affected least in any type of cleft palate speech. The speech attainment in this group will largely depend on the proportion of air which the patient is able to direct through the mouth as compared with that escaping through the nose, and may be partly determined by the extent of the cleft. Habits of breath direction vary from the patient who, when asked to blow, closes his mouth and does so entirely through the nose, to those who in spite of a cleft palate or incompetent sphincter are able to direct the greater proportion of air through the mouth with sometimes an approach towards normal articulation. As the nasal outlet cannot be fully controlled, the amount of air pressure available for articulation will depend largely on the degree of opening of the oropharyngeal

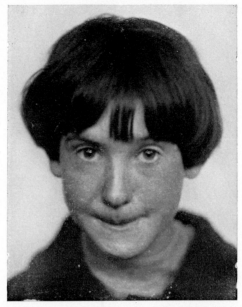

Fig. 107.—Typical nasal grimace on production of nasal[s].

isthmus and also on the position of the tongue in the mouth. If it is raised at the back more air will be deflected into the nasal airways. Relaxation of the base of the tongue, that is particularly of the genioglossus, hyoglossus, mylohyoid, and of the palatoglossus, will increase the diameters of the oropharyngeal isthmus and hence the amount of air which may be directed through the mouth.

The amount of air passing into and through the naso-pharynx is also influenced by the degree of pressure used for articulation. Light contact of lips, or of tongue against the alveolus may produce a clearer consonant sound with less nasal escape than when forceful articulation is attempted. For the same reason nasal escape of air is less obvious on vowel sounds or certain consonants where there is less obstruction to the air stream as it passes through the mouth, causing less backward pressure.

2. **Nasal escape of air.**—As previously described, the weakness of the consonants is due to lack of air pressure in the mouth and the escape of air through the nose. [m] [n], and [ng (ŋ)] are the only sounds in the English language on which air may pass through the nose, and then in the form of vibrations and not in a continuous stream as in breathing. This nasal escape of air produces a hissing or fricative sound in the nose, or sometimes a snorting sound in the nasopharynx additional to the speech sounds.

3. **Nasal grimace.**—The alæ nasi are contracted in an attempt to close the nostrils anteriorly in compensation for inability to obtain nasopharyngeal closure, and a typical grimace is produced (Fig. 107). This narrowing of the nostrils may accentuate the fricative sounds produced when air escapes through the nose.

4. **Nasopharyngeal snort.**—This is produced by the passage of air through a sphincter which is closed but not so tightly as to prevent the passage of air as on snorting.

It occurs seldom, and can accompany any consonant sound, but is most frequently associated with the production of fricatives, especially [s]. It may occur when adenoids are present, and also when the soft palate is rigid due to scar tissue, but the patient has obtained considerable development of the muscles of the pharynx by conscientious practice in an attempt to achieve nasopharyngeal closure. Such muscular development, though useful in some cases, is seldom a satisfactory substitute for a flexible soft palate. Again, this nasopharyngeal snort may occur *temporarily* during the development of the use of the palatopharyngeal sphincter.

5. **Nasal tone.**—This is a deep, hollow tone associated with the production of vowel sounds, and with an absence of true nasal resonance. (Resonance 5.) There is nasal turbulence due to escape of air, and the condition is sometimes known as rhinolalia mixta. It may be due to an immobile soft palate, a too capacious nasopharynx, an excesssively high arch in the palate, or deformity in the nasal cavities, and persists in such cases perhaps in spite of the patient's ability to snort. Other causes may be faulty production of vowel sounds owing to a misplaced tongue, speaking with almost closed lips, and teeth, or a wrong habit of breath direction, and in such cases can often be improved by training.

The ear recognises a certain type of nasal resonance as normal. There is a balance between oral, nasal, pharyngeal and other resonance tones which varies individually within normal limits and can be modified temporarily by nasal obstruction, sinusitis or a sore throat. McDonald and Baker (1951) offer an hypothesis that there is a "characteristic balance or ratio between oral and nasal resonance which depends on the relative sizes of the posterior openings into the nasal passages and the oral cavity." This is probably variable and depends to some extent on tongue position. It is possible to change the type of resonance when humming a sustained note if the back of the tongue is alternately raised and lowered.

House and Stevens (1956) studied vocalisation and resonance and found the dimensions of some portions of the nasal tract exhibited wide variations from individual to individual, and varied with time for any given individual. They describe the vocal tract as extending from the glottis to the lips, and state that its cross-section is small compared with the wavelengths of sounds up to 4,000 c.p.s. They considered the variability in dimensions in various parts of this tract, and described the oral cavity as being the most variable portion. It is there that resonance is modified so that the various vowel sounds may be differentiated. The amount of damping of sound was found to be less in the vocal tract than in the nasal tract, although again the degree of damping in the nasal tract was found to vary from one individual to another. Because of this they believe that the principal influence of nasal coupling is to modify the output of the vocal tract. They also state that as there is greater impedance in the oral cavity of the vocal tract for the vowel [i:(ee)] than for [ɑ:(ah)] the resonance will be modified to a greater extent for the former than for the latter with any given degree of nasal coupling.

Abnormal resonance in cleft palate patients occurs mainly on the vowel sounds, although the voiced consonants are also modified. From recent clinical observations normal resonance in post-operative cleft palate patients has been found to be most closely associated with good movement of the pharyngeal walls and particularly with movement of the lateral pharyngeal walls, and it has been extremely rare to find a child who has any abnormality of resonance. This is apparent within six months after operation, and before the use of articulation has fully developed or whilst it is still defective. The development of such normal vocal tone and resonance has been attributed to the type of operation performed (pp. 121, 124). McCollum, Richardson and Swanson (1956) in a review of 1034 primary cleft palate repairs in infancy have also stated that "lateral pharyngeal acitivity exhibited by the non-nasal speakers in this study indicates that there is considerable compensatory activity to diminish the transverse diameter of the pharynx."

Nasality is increased if there is insufficient opening of the mouth during speech. This may be associated with a long, tight, or inert upper lip following some types of operation for cleft lip, poor movement of the lower jaw, or a blocking of the oral cavity either at the back by the raised tongue, or anteriorly by a tongue which rests habitually against the upper incisor teeth or between them, and to insufficient space in the mouth for normal activity of the tongue and soft palate. In some patients this may be related to abnormal shortening of the maxilla with a protruding lower jaw.

Surgical interference with the muscles of the pharynx may interfere with the essential mobility of the posterior and lateral walls, and operations such as suturing a pharyngeal flap to the palate may cause interference with the adjustments for normal resonance which can never thereafter be changed. In such cases nasal tone may persist when there is little or no nasal escape of air.

Abnormal resonance in cleft palate may therefore be classified in at least three groups. Firstly, there may be variations within the normal range (Resonance 1, 2, or 3). Secondly, the vocal air stream continues to be directed mainly into the nasopharynx due to the persistence of faulty habits of jaw movement, of tongue position or of palatal movement when nasopharyngeal closure is anatomically possible, or there may be obstructions in the naso-pharynx or abnormality of nasal contours, with little or no movement of the pharyngeal walls, which may cause a permanent imbalance of resonance (4). Thirdly, resonance may be associated with gross nasal escape of air in spite of a good oral airway when the palatopharyngeal sphincter is incompetent (Resonance 5.) (See p. 190).

(b) *Function of palatopharyngeal sphincter normal.*—These cases should require no speech therapy. Operation has provided a competent sphincter, which the patient has learned to use, and he now speaks without nasal escape of air. Contraction of the anterior nares being unnecessary, the nasal grimace will probably have disappeared, and consonant sounds which were weak before operation should be normal. Occasionally it is found that some slight defect may persist in the production of the sound [s], or [s] in conjunction with another consonant, as [sp], [st], and [sk]. This defect sometimes continues when there is no trace of nasal escape elsewhere and speech is otherwise normal. (See Case 1.)

Group B cases

(a) *Function of palatopharyngeal sphincter not developed* Faults in this group are many, and include:—

1. Nasal escape of air.
2. Nasal tone.
3. Nasal grimace.
4. Nasopharyngeal snort.
5. Glottal stop.
6. Pharyngeal fricatives.
7. Incorrect articulation, substitutions.

1. **Nasal escape.**—This is less obvious in Group B than in Group A, though the subconscious feeling of loss of

pressure due to inability to close the sphincter is responsible for the substitution of the glottal stop and pharyngeal sounds. Some patients, having learned during treatment to articulate the plosive and fricative sounds correctly, change from Group B to Group A, and unless the sphincter mechanism becomes competent there is then a period when nasal escape becomes more obvious until nasopharyngeal closure is achieved. If this is anatomically impossible no further progress can be made, but Group A speech is more intelligible than that in Group B, and may be almost normal.

2 and 3. **Nasal tone and the use of the nasal grimace** have been described under Group A. The nasal grimace occurs less frequently in this group than in Group A, as the air stream is usually interrupted in the larynx or pharynx and the patient does not therefore try to prevent nasal escape of air by contraction of the nostrils.

4. **Nasopharyngeal snort.**—This may occur here as in Group A, or may be present temporarily during treatment.

5. **The glottal stop** (phonetic symbol ʔ).—This is a sound by no means limited to cleft palate patients, and may sometimes be heard in educated English speech, e.g., Asia ʔ and Africa, the ʔ ether, etc. [eiʃe ʔ ənd æfrikə. ðəʔi: θə] and in dialect. It is caused by the abrupt opening of the vocal cords which have been drawn together by hypertension in the laryngeal muscles, closing the glottis completely. When expiratory air reaches the glottis increased breath pressure must be used to separate the vocal cords before tone is produced. The greater the tension in the muscles, the greater will be the force required to open the glottis, and the louder the explosive sound which results. In cases where the glottal stop is very forcible the hypertension of the laryngeal muscles may be such as to bring together the ventricular bands, as on exertion. Describing the function

of the vocal cords and the ventricular bands, Negus says: "The ingress of air into the glottis is prevented by approximation of the true vocal cords, but these have little power to prevent its egress. The false cords, or ventricular bands, on the contrary, have very little power to prevent ingress of air into the lungs, but when the edges are brought together they act as valves and offer great resistance to the egress of air; they are, therefore, to be regarded as the chief factors in the closure of the glottis during exertion," as in coughing. Again he says: "In the higher apes and man they (the ventricular bands) can come into firm contact and cause the air stream to be shut off, and they can then be used for phonation. . . . The muscles which close them are the members of the sphincteric group."

It is this sound which is so often used by a cleft palate patient as a substitute for plosive sounds which, due to the defect, cannot be made correctly, the patient feeling subconsciously that this is the only position where the breath stream can be interrupted to obtain the requisite pressure for a plosive sound. The more determined the child is to make himself understood, the more will he tense his laryngeal muscles to produce a forcible plosive sound.

The glottal stop is, therefore, usually substituted for any or all of the plosive consonants, [p], [b], [t], [d], [k] and [g], and may also be used for other consonant sounds. In some cases correct lip and tongue positions are used in conjunction with the glottal stop. Such speech can be at least partially intelligible, and in one case in my experience, though a very forcible glottal stop was used for every plosive sound, speech was so intelligible that no stranger had any difficulty in understanding every word spoken. In such cases the use of the glottal stop often ceases, at least in the production of individual sounds, if the patient prevents nasal escape by nipping the nostrils, or when nasopharyngeal closure is obtained following operation.

6. **Pharyngeal fricatives.**—The use of the glottal stop for the production of plosive consonants is usually accompanied by the substitution of some fricative sound made in the pharynx or larynx for the normal fricatives [s], [z], [sh (ʃ)], [th (θ, ð)], [zh (ʒ)], [f] and [v]. These may be described as "pharyngeal sounds." [s] is the sound most frequently produced in this way. In all cases it can be made with the mouth open, when there is no possibility of a fricative sound being produced between the tongue and palate or teeth. There are apparently at least two varieties with corresponding slight differences in the sound. In some cases [s] can be made with the tongue slightly protruding, whilst in others the tongue must be drawn back, and the sound then appears to be produced by vibrations set up between the back of the tongue and the pharyngeal wall. In the former case it resembles the sound [h], but made with increased friction between overtense vocal cords, and is a sound of higher frequency than the one produced between the back of the tongue and the pharyngeal wall. This fricative sound may be produced by air passing between the arytenoids as in whispering. Wyllie (1894) described whispering as follows: "Whereas in vocal speech the air passes the glottis through a narrow chink between the vibrating cords, in whispering the greater part of the air is made to pass through a triangular opening in the posterior part of the glottis, between the projecting parts of the arytenoid cartilages whose bodies remain apart, although their vocal processes are more or less closely approximated. This fricative noise plays in whispering exactly the same part that is played in vocal speech by the sonorous tones of the voice." "When the voiced sound [h] is used," according

to Negus, (1929) "the arytenoids come into contact at the tips of the vocal processes while the bodies remain apart and leave a triangular aperture between them." Through this opening air escapes with a fricative sound.

Again, if the ventricular bands may be used for the production of the glottal stop, it is possible that this laryngeal fricative sound may be produced by friction between these approximated bands. Negus describes how "it is possible for the folds to vibrate and to interrupt the air current in a rhythmical manner, with the production of rough tones of lower pitch than those produced by the vocal cords, when the air pressure is the same in each case."

But however produced, although a patient may have little difficulty in making a normal [s], of all defective cleft palate sounds this pharyngeal or laryngeal subsititution for [s] is the most difficult to eradicate from speech, and tends to persist the longest in conversation.

The other fricative consonants may be produced in a similar manner, with or without the correct tongue and lip positions, or they may be entirely omitted.

7. **Faulty articulation.**—Inability to produce certain consonants, due to the anatomical deformity of the mouth, may result in the substitution of another consonant instead of the glottàl stop, or in the adoption of some abnormal position of tongue or lips in an attempt to form the required sound. The following faults are among the most common:

   (i) [t] may be used as a substitute for [k], and [d] for [g], and *vice versa.*

   (ii) [n] is used for [t] and [d].

   (iii) [m] may be used for [p] and [b].

   (iv) [n] is occasionally found instead of [ng (ŋ)], or [ŋ[for [n] in other cases.

(v) [k] and [g] may be made by contact between the back of the tongue and the posterior pharyngeal wall, or, in some cases, h is used as a substitute.

(vi) [f], [v], [th (θ, ð)] may be bilabial when the upper incisor teeth are missing, or the upper lip cannot be raised sufficiently.

(vii) [t] and [d] may be interdental, that is, made with the tongue tip protruding beyond and making contact with the edge of the upper incisor teeth. This may be due to a narrow or shortened hard palate following operation on a complete cleft, and consequent inability of the tongue to make the rapid and easy contact with the alveolar ridge required for the production of these sounds.

During the last seven years the spontaneous development of articulation has been observed in children following primary repair of the cleft palate in infancy. The articulation in these children differs particularly in two ways from that of children with defects of articulation but no cleft palate. Firstly, a greater proportion of cleft palate children have defective articulation of the consonant [s], and the substitutions used differ markedly from those used by other children with this defect. Secondly, the child with no cleft palate usually substitutes tongue tip consonants for those made with the back of the tongue, as [t] or [d] for [k] and [g]. The cleft palate child, on the other hand, uses the back of the tongue more readily than the tip and frequently substitutes [k] or [g] for [t] and [d]. The consonants [k] and [g] may also be substituted for other anterior consonants, whilst fricative consonants, particularly [s] are often made with the tongue approaching the [k] position rather than the [t] position.

The following table (Fig. 108) shows the substitutions used

Consonant substitutions for [s]	Cleft Palate		Normal Palate	
	60 children with repaired cleft palates seen 20 years ago	88 children with repaired cleft palates seen during last 7 years	88 children with normal palates and defective articulation of [s]	58 children with defective [s] from a group of 1142 children, 162 of whom had defective articulation
Not attempted	10	5	8	3
Anterior w	—	—	—	1
f	—	—	1	1
θ [th]	—	2	8	3
ts	—	—	1	—
t	1	3	43	33
weak attempt	—	9	—	—
slight defect	—	8	—	—
Medial l	—	—	—	1
ʃ [sh]	—	17	5	6
ɟ (lateral) [s]	—	11	13	6
ç (fricative in k position)	2	18	3	1
Posterior s (nasal)	20	5	2	—
Nasopharyngeal	—	2	—	1
h	—	—	4	2
Pharyngeal	27	8	—	—
Total	60	88	88	58
Anterior substitutions	1.6%	25%	60%	65%
Medial substitutions	3.3%	52%	24%	24%
Posterior substitutions	78%	17%	7%	5

Fig. 108—Table showing defective articulation of [s] in children with clefts of the palate and children with normal palates.

for [s] in four groups of children. The first group is that of 60 post operative cases of cleft palate observed twenty years ago. The second group consists of 88 children who had a primary cleft palate repair in infancy. They were observed at regular intervals whilst articulation was developing spontaneously during the last seven years. At some stage during this development these children had defective articulation of [s]. In the third group are 88 children, aged three to seven years, forming a consecutive series of children referred for treatment with defective articulation and with a defective [s] but with normal palates. The fourth group is that of 162 children out of 1142 who had defects of articulation. Of these 58 had defective articulation of [s]. They were observed over a period of six years during an investigation into the development of speech. (Morley 1957).

Of the 60 children in the first group all had a defective [s]. In the second group 88 of the 155 children in whom this sound could be assessed had defective articulation of [s], or 57%. In the fourth group 58 of 162 children with defective articulation failed to articulate [s] normally or 35%. From these figures children with repaired cleft palates would seem to have more difficulty in the articulation of the consonant [s] than those with normal palates.

Comparing the two groups of children with cleft palate it will be noted that with modern surgery and early operation the proportion of pharyngeal substitutions for [s] has been very much reduced (45% and 9%). In both groups, however, there is a deficiency of anterior substitutions for this consonant when compared with children with defective articulation and normal palates. It has also been noticed that during the development of articulation there is usually a gradual change in the substitutions for [s] always in the forward direction. A child who at first has a pharyngeal [s] may pass through transitional stages when a fricative [k], a lateral [s] or [sh (ʃ)] is used until normal articulation of [s] is reached. The figures given indicate the substitution for [s] at the time when this sound could first be assessed.

Many children also had a weak [s] which again appeared to be a transitional stage, and in at least 8 children there was a very slight defect in the articulation of this consonant. The difference from normal was so slight that it was probably not outside the normal range, and it could not be classified as a substitution. Nevertheless the frequency of the sound produced could not be described as standard to the trained ear. The [s] sound may also vary during its development towards normality, and two or more substitute sounds may be heard in the child's conversational speech during the one interview.

The question arises as to the cause of the pronounced deficiency of anterior consonant sounds in the speech of the child who has had a cleft palate, and of the type of substitutions used for [s]. In some it may be due to a narrowed dental arch, a shortened maxilla, abnormal dentition or irregular alveolar contours. Clinical observations have so far, however, failed to produce convincing evidence that these factors are the chief cause. Children with dental arches and dentition approaching normal have defective articulation of the anterior consonants, whilst a few with grossly abnormal development of the alveolus or maxilla developed normal articulation of [s] and other alveolar and anterior consonant sounds. This was particularly noticeable in the past, as such cases are now rarely seen.

Berry (1949) pointed out that the alveolar consonant sounds were most affected in children with repaired cleft palates and stated that 65% of cases lacked requisite mobility and muscular co-ordination of the tongue for the normal production of sounds. This was assessed on the child's ability to point the tongue and elevate the tip. Matthews and Byrne (1953) however, tested 19 children with cleft palate and 19 controls and found that "the results of this study do not support the hypothesis that children with cleft palates have an over-all inferior tongue flexibility."

Nevertheless it seems probable that the existence of the cleft palate has in some way influenced the development of the movements of the tongue tip resulting in an increased use of posterior or medial substitutions rather than the more usual anterior substitutions.

These may date even from prenatal life and also from compensatory activity to assist sucking in infancy. Normally the tongue is relatively large and lies between the maxillary plates in the early stage of development. Later the floor of the mouth descends with the tongue allowing the palatal plates to fuse about the ninth week of embryonic life. In cleft palate the tongue may retain its higher position, especially in early post-natal life. Later it may take a more normal position in the mouth. On the contrary McKee (1956) found in a radiographic study of tongue position that the tongue tended to be carried higher in the mouth in non-cleft palate persons than in those with cleft palates.

It is probable that it is the positioning and activity of the tongue in the early months of life which will influence the control of the tongue tip for articulation at a later stage of development. Wood Jones (1946) has described the infantile tongue as being blunt and flat along its anterior free margin and states that it has no elongated pointed tip. "During the whole period of sucking the function of the tongue is merely that of acting as a piston by raising and lowering the floor of the mouth and so effecting changes in the buccal pressure that lead to suction. There is no office such as steering food particles about the mouth, cleansing the teeth, licking the lips or framing the sounds of speech, demanding a free, mobile, pointed tip of the tongue at any time during infancy. It is only when infancy is passed that the elongated exploring tip of the tongue is developed." It is possible that the existence of a cleft palate may delay the development of activity of the tongue tip longer than in the normal child. In alveolar clefts the tongue is unable adequately to compress the nipple against the alveolus and compensatory sucking habits may develop, the back of the tongue being raised automatically in an endeavour to occlude the cleft, at least partially, in order to obtain the requisite negative pressure. Again the expiratory air stream through the mouth must rarely reach as far forward as the alveolus with any degree of normal pressure, and the child is unable to indulge in the normal habits of infancy such as blowing saliva bubbles, or producing the bilabial or alveolar sounds which occur frequently in the normal babbling of infancy. Some audible activity may be obtained posteriorly through compensatory adjustments, or nasal sounds only may be produced.

Clinical observations also suggest that there is delay in developing normal maturity of the movements of the tongue tip, with greater activity of the mid and posterior parts of the tongue blade in many of these children with cleft palates, and that this may be the result of the palatal cleft and its influence on the pattern of tongue movements developed.

(b) *Function of palatopharyngeal sphincter normal.*—Due to the fact that operation has produced a competent sphincter which the patient has learnt to use, some of the faults just described will have been corrected. There will be no nasal escape, thus the nasal grimace will not be used. However, it will be found that most of the articulatory defects still persist, including pharyngeal fricatives and the glottal stop, though nasal tone may be much reduced.

o

REFERENCES

BERRY, M. F. (1949). Lingual anomalies associated with palatal clefts. *J. Speech Hear. Dis.*, **14**, 4, 359.

HOFFMAN, F. A. (1964). Cineradiographic system design. *Cleft Pal. J.*, **1**, 382.

HOUSE, A. S. AND STEVENS, K. N. (1956). Analog Studies of the nasalisation of vowels. *J. Speech Hear. Dis.*, **21**, 218.

JONES F. WOOD (1946). *Buchanan's Manual of Anatomy*, 7th Ed. London: Bailliere.

KIRKPATRICK, J. A. (1964). Roentgen evaluation of velopharyngeal closure. *Cleft Pal. J.*, **1**, 388.

MCCOLLUM, D. W., RICHARDSON, S. O. AND SWANSON, T. L. (1956). Habilitation of the Cleft Palate Patient. *New Engl. J. Med.*, **254**, 299.

MCDONALD, E. AND BAKER, K. (1951). Cleft Palate Speech. An Integration of Research and Clinical examination. *J. Speech Hear. Dis.*, **16**, 9.

MCKEE, T. L. (1956). A cephalometric radiographic study of Tongue Position in Individuals with Cleft Palate Deformity. *Angle Orthodont.*, **26**, 2, 99.

MATTHEWS, J. AND BYRNE, M. C. (1953). An experimental Study of Tongue Flexibility in Children with cleft palate. *J. Speech Hear. Dis.*, **18**, 1, 43.

MOLL, K. L. (1964). Cineradiography in research and clinical studies of the velopharyngeal mechanism. *Cleft Pal. J.*, **1**, 391.

MORLEY, M. E. (1965). *The Development and Disorders of Speech in Childhood*. 2nd Ed. Edinburgh: Livingstone.

NEGUS, V. E. (1929). *The Mechanism of the Larynx*, p. 392. London: Heinemann.

QUIGLEY, L. F., SHIERE, F. R., WEBSTER, R. C. AND COBB, C. M. (1964) Measuring palatopharyngeal Competence with the nasal Anemometer. *Cleft Pal. J.*, **1**, 304.

SUBTELNY, J. D. (1964). Physio-acoustic considerations in the radiographic study of speech. *Cleft Pal. J.*, **1**, 402.

WARREN, D. W. AND DU BOIS, A. B. (1964). A pressure Flow Technique for Measuring Velopharyngeal Orifice Area during Continuous Speech. *Cleft Pal. J.*, **1**, 52.

WYLLIE, J. (1894). *The Disorders of Speech*, p. 35. Edinburgh: Oliver and Boyd.

CHAPTER VI

TREATMENT I
GENERAL CONSIDERATIONS

———

Conditions which influence the prognosis

Co-operation between patient and therapist

Group work and individual treatment in cases
of cleft palate

When should speech therapy commence?

TREATMENT I
GENERAL CONSIDERATIONS

THE aim of any treatment for cleft palate is to produce normal speech, and by this is meant not merely intelligible speech, but speech which will defy any phonetician to discover the fact that the patient has ever had a cleft palate, and which is, in addition, natural and free from self-consciousness. This is a high standard, and in many cases one can only approach it as nearly as anatomical or other conditions will permit. But, at the same time, speech which does not reach this standard cannot be described as normal. This does not necessarily mean perfect English diction, but just that the defects attributable to cleft palate, and described in the previous chapter, have been overcome. There are, of course, local differences in speech, such as the use of the glottal stop, which in some parts of the country is dialectal, and in common use; it is not then a defect typical of cleft palate. In other districts, or in other social environments, it occurs rarely except in connection with cleft palate. Normal speech then should be defined as speech which is intelligible, natural, free to the trained ear from defects typical of cleft palate, and equal to that of the patient's environment.

CONDITIONS WHICH WILL INFLUENCE THE RESULT OF TREATMENT

(i) The anatomical and physiological result of surgical treatment, including the development and mobility of the pharyngeal muscles.

(ii) The intelligence of the patient.

(iii) Acuity of hearing.

(iv) The level and type of speech development at the time of operation.

(v) The degree of stabilisation of the faulty neuro-muscular patterns of speech and the patient's ability to inhibit these and incorporate normal articulation in fluent speech.

(vi) The age when speech therapy commences.

(vii) The environment and personality of the patient.

(i) **The anatomical and physiological result of surgical treatment.**—This includes the condition of the palate, the competence or otherwise of the palatopharyngeal sphincter, the condition of the upper lip if the cleft has been complete, the teeth, and to some extent the condition of the nasal cavities. The anatomical result of operation has already been discussed, and methods have been described to test the efficiency of the sphincter. Where it has been impossible at operation to produce a competent palatopharyngeal sphincter, and some anatomical deficiency remains, normal physiological function will be impossible, and in some cases this may be due at least in part to lack of movement in the pharyngeal walls rather than to a deficiency in the palate. In such cases speech therapy is required to help the patient to make the best possible use of the condition resulting from operation. Difficulties in obtaining sufficient air pressure for clear articulation will be increased when there is persistent nasal escape, although exercises for development of the muscles concerned in the sphincter mechanism will help to lessen this defect to some extent. The instinctive use of the glottal stop will tend to recur again and again when it is felt by the patient that a sufficiently forceful plosive sound is unobtainable elsewhere, and this even when the individual sounds can be made alone with the correct use of the vocal cords.

In some cases good speech is acquired by much practice, and remains good while the patient is at the clinic, but he lapses badly when not under observation, the effort required for good speech being greater than he can sustain continuously. It is in this connection that ambition and perseverance on the part of the patient are so important until correct habits are firmly established. Wardill has described a patient of his who was considering matrimony. Her speech became normal, but when seen some months later, after the marriage was an accomplished fact, she had reverted to the worst type of cleft palate speech!

However, in many cases with some anatomical deficiency speech becomes good, remains good, completely intelligible, and may even appear to be normal to any but the acute ear of the speech expert. Should little progress be made with speech therapy, then a secondary operation should always be considered, and the surgeon consulted to see if he thinks there is a possibility of improvement from further surgical treatment. If so, speech therapy, at least in Group A cases, may be postponed until after operation. In Group B an attempt may be made to teach correct articulatory habits if nasal escape is prevented by compressing the nostrils with the fingers during practice. In this way such cases may improve until they can be classed as Group A. No further improvement is then possible, as there is no functioning sphincter to prevent nasal escape of air through the open nasopharynx and the nostrils until the secondary operation has been performed.

Should a secondary operation be considered inadvisable the dental surgeon may be able to fit an obturator to compensate for the inadequate sphincter, and in some cases this proves a successful means of obtaining nasopharyngeal closure.

If neither of the foregoing alternatives are possible the best the therapist can do is to train the patient to direct his voice and breath so that the maximum amount possible passes out through the mouth and the minimum through the nose. It has been observed that the speech of a cleft palate patient sounds better on the telephone than when speaking face to face. It is thought that this may be due to the fact that the part of voice which passes out through the nostrils does not impinge directly on the microphone, being directed in a more downward direction than that part proceeding from the mouth, and thus being to some extent eliminated. If so, this illustrates the value of exercises designed to minimise as far as possible the proportion of the air and speech sounds which passes up into the nasopharynx and out through the nose.

(ii) **Intelligence.**—Though intelligence in certain cases may be below normal the speech defect in cleft palate patients is not the result of retarded intellectual development, as in some cases of dyslalia. Unless the intelligence is much below the average it will affect chiefly the length of time required to obtain the highest standard of speech of which the patient is capable. The speech defect itself, with its resultant handicap in preventing normal intercourse with other people, and hindering progress at school, may be responsible for much apparent mental retardation in children. In such cases the general improvement which takes place as better speech develops is very noticeable.

If intelligence is definitely subnormal defective speech may persist when all individual sounds can be correctly articulated, and there is no trace of nasal escape or other defect typical of cleft palate. This occurred at one stage in the treatment of a child of seven years. She was mentally retarded, and, with a perfect anatomical and physiological result so far as the cleft palate was concerned, made very slow progress in learning to speak normally. There was here an additional factor, and even had the palate been normal the child would not have developed correct speech without assistance. This additional factor may be determined when analysing the patient's speech if it is remembered that the child with slow and faulty speech development, irrespective of any palate defect, often has more difficulty in pronouncing final consonant sounds than initial ones. His progress follows the line of speech development of the average child, in that initial consonant sounds make their appearance before final and medial sounds, but it is retarded. In such a child the defect is described as dyslalia, and this ommission of final and medial consonants may occur when the majority of them can be articulated correctly in the initial position. In the cleft palate patient, the cause of the defect being purely mechanical, the difficulty is concerned with the articulation of the individual consonant, and such a patient often finds it easier to place such a sound, when required, at the end of a syllable rather than at the beginning.

Given a successful surgical result the backward child may gradually and spontaneously develop speech according to his mental capacity, whilst in other cases control of palatal and pharyngeal movements may be inadequate with persistent nasal speech, such as is found in some backward children who have no cleft palate.

In mentally backward adult patients, however, speech therapy may show little result owing to the patient's inability to co-operate in eradicating faulty habits and the substitution of more normal articulation in spontaneous conversation.

Where a successful operative result has not been achieved

the prognosis in the case of the mentally retarded patient is poor, as they lack the determination and intelligence required to compensate for their physiological disability.

(iii) **Acuity of hearing.**—Children born with a cleft palate appear to be more prone than the normal child to catarrhal conditions of the pharynx and infections of the middle ear, which sometimes result in slight deafness. However, it is unusual for the hearing to be impaired sufficiently to make it an important factor in hindering speech re-education, although this possibility should be borne in mind if progress is slow. Slight deafness or variable hearing may increase the length of time required for treatment, as the patient is unable to benefit to the same extent from hearing the normal speech of people in his environment, but it is unusual for it to affect the final result.

Should the hearing loss be persistent and prove to be a handicap in school, or be found to retard progress under speech therapy, it should be thoroughly investigated with a view to medical treatment. If the condition is chronic and fails to respond to treatment, the child should then be fitted with a hearing aid, which may enable him to compensate for his hearing loss.

A congenital failure of inner ear development may be found in a few children with resulting difficulty in hearing and discriminating the consonant sounds, particularly when, as is usual, such a hearing loss is greater for the higher than for the lower frequencies of sound. Such children may be late in developing speech, and articulation will be defective, the degree of defect depending on the extent of the failure to hear normally, and irrespective of the speech defects due to the cleft palate.

(iv) **The level and type of speech development at the time of operation.**—As previously described, the neuro-muscular patterns of articulation are being established during the babble period of speech development, and neuromuscular control of the lips, tongue, palatal and pharyngeal muscles from the time of the first cry. Crying, sucking and swallowing provide exercise for the development of normal function in these muscles, and compensatory habits developed by the cleft palate child form the basis for faulty use of the muscles concerned with articulation at a later stage. Following operation more normal reflex swallowing will develop spontaneously through eating and drinking, but abnormal function of the palatopharyngeal sphincter may persist in blowing and also in association with articulation.

(v) **The degree of stabilisation of the faulty neuromuscular patterns of speech.**—In some children articulatory habits become stabilised at an early age, and are consequently more difficult to change. This applies in greater degree in the case of children where primary operation has been unsuccessful, and in the case of those where operation has not been performed until later childhood or adult life. The type of speech then developed, whether it be Group A or B, will affect the time required for the establishment of normal speech. This has been fully discussed, and appropriate exercises for treatment will be found in Chapter VII.

Again, the faculty of speech is not developed to the same degree in each individual. Some are much more interested in words and language and have the ability to acquire languages other than their own with ease and rapidity, whilst some children even have difficulty in learning to speak their own language, and when speech does begin to develop it may be unintelligible for some years unless adequately treated. This faculty for acquiring language and speech is probably at its maximum acuity in early childhood when it is required for the development of speech. A small child who, given the opportunity can easily pick up a second language from a foreign nurse, would experience much greater difficulty in accomplishing the same process a few years later in school, or in adult life, when conscious effort is required as well as the use of reasoning, comparison and memory. This ability to develop speech depends on factors such as auditory perception, memory span and ability to control and co-ordinate the various parts of the speech mechanism, and just as some people naturally have a greater aptitude for mathematics, or music, than others, so some have a greater ability to discriminate and reproduce spoken sounds and to express themselves in speech.

Although dysarthria, as seen in children with cerebral palsy, or isolated dysarthria, is rare in association with cleft palate, articulatory apraxia, or a basic difficulty in reproducing accurately the sounds of speech, may hinder the spontaneous development of normal articulation, or even the use of the palatopharyngeal sphincter in speech. Such apraxia may also occur in children with no palatal defect.

One child, aged two and a half years, substituted a nasopharyngeal sound for the consonants [s] [sh(ʃ)] [t] [d] [ch(tʃ)] and [j (dʒ)] although he had no anatomical defect and had normal co-ordinations of the palatopharyngeal sphincter for all other sounds. Another child, aged 4 years, nasalised certain vowel sounds, particularly [i:(ee)] and [ay(ei)]. Consonants were affected according to their relation to these vowel sounds, plosives being made with a plosive sound through the palatopharyngeal sphincter, and fricatives by a fricative or snorting sound in the same position. Ability to do this indicates the ability to close the sphincter completely, in addition to the fact that all other sounds were produced normally. Initial consonants were affected more frequently than those in the final position in words. Both these children were of high intelligence but the defect did not easily respond to treatment. The reason for the development of abnormal articulation of this type is not clear, but we have considered it to be an articulatory apraxia. Such an apraxia may occur in some children or adults with cleft palate who then find it more difficult than is usual to change their faulty neuromuscular patterns developed prior to operation.

(vi) **The age at which speech therapy commences.**—Age is a factor to be considered in relation to the duration of faulty speech habits, and their degree of stabilisation as mentioned above. In a child of four to six years, once he can articulate each consonant sound correctly, normal speech generally follows spontaneously within a few months with very little further assistance. As the age increases the child usually has less difficulty in producing any given sound by imitation, or with the help of instructions from the speech therapist, and when he is old enough to read and write he has the additional advantage of possessing visual as well as auditory images of the sounds he is attempting to make. But as this difficulty decreases, the ability to use such sounds spontaneously in conversational speech with the eradication of old and faulty habits is acquired slowly and only with much practice. These points are discussed more fully later in the chapter.

(vii) **Personality and environment.**—In cases of cleft palate the speech defect is entirely due to mechanical causes, and is not the result of, nor necessarily accompanied by, the emotional problems which may be associated with a stammer. Nor is there any interference with the natural outflow of speech sounds, or feeling of inhibition associated with the desire on the part of the patient to express himself in language. It must be remembered that to the child with a cleft palate his speech is the same as that of the people around him, and he may reach the age of six, seven or even eight years before he is consciously able to recognise any difference, and then only through training. Indeed, in some cases, usually those belonging to Group A with intelligible speech only marred by nasal escape, the patient may never be aware that his speech is in any way defective. (See cases 1 and 8, Chapter VIII.) However, the child discovers that he differs from others in that he cannot make his speech intelligible to anyone, with the possible exception of his mother and his own family. It is here that he is faced with a problem which he is unable to solve without help. In the majority of these cases the result appears to be bewilderment and eventual acceptance of the fact that there is a difference between himself and others. There may be withdrawal from social contacts and a tendency to avoid speech, even refusal to speak at all, whilst in others an aggressive attitude may develop with much forcible use of the glottal stop when this inability to convey his thoughts and wishes to others is realised. Unless something is done to help the child to remedy the defect, matters will become worse as he grows older and develops an increasing sensitiveness to his abnormality. In many cases where operative procedures have been delayed normal self-confidence has been replaced by a feeling of inferiority associated with a subconscious fear of speech, this condition being intensified by the fact that the patient has not the knowledge nor the ability to do anything to remedy matters unaided. Once speech therapy commences, following operation, and the patient realises that some progress is being made, the whole outlook changes. A positive optimistic attitude replaces the previous hopeless fear of speech when he finds himself able to utilise his energies in the right direction. There are cases, however, where much nervous tension, resulting from fear and self-consciousness relating to speech situations, persists, causing abnormal tension in the laryngeal muscles and those of the lips and tongue. This hypertension is a great hindrance to progress. Exercises for relaxation of these muscles alone may then be insufficient, and general muscular relaxation must first be taught and practised as a preliminary to correction of the speech defects.

Illustrating these difficulties is the case of a girl who was first brought to the surgeon at the age of twelve years, the mother having been under the impression that this was the earliest time at which operation could be performed. When told that operative treatment should have been carried out much earlier she brought along a younger child, aged four years, who also had a cleft palate. Both were operated upon. At the end of the year the younger sister was speaking normally (see Case 18), but the elder, after two years of speech therapy, still had some nasal escape, and a second operation was performed. This second operation was completely successful anatomically, and all speech sounds were then normal, but nervous tension, resulting from fear and self-consciousness, persisted. Although she could repeat rhymes with no cleft palate speech defect, she relapsed badly in conversational speech. The position was almost comparable to that of a stammerer who can speak normally when in a room alone, but stammers when he tries to converse with another person. Her feelings can be realised from a remark made one day, obviously of tremendous importance to her, that she had spoken to a boy who had recently come to live in her district, and who had noticed no defect in her speech. She had found it less difficult to speak to this boy, because, as she explained, he had never known about her defect. Gradually she gained confidence in her ability to speak normally, but much time and encouragement was required before she completely lost her feeling of inferiority in connection with speech situations.

In another case the father and mother were so ashamed of the fact that their child had a cleft palate that the boy was hidden as far as was possible. In addition the parents had also arrived at the opinion, by what means is not known, that a child with a cleft palate must necessarily be defective in other ways, possibly mentally, and certainly incapable of managing his own affairs, either in the associations of childhood or in later life. Eventually this boy was submitted to operation at twelve years of age and obtained a good physiological result, though there remained some nasal escape. When he first came for speech treatment at the age of thirty-four years he was easily intelligible with only slight nasal escape, but he had developed such feelings of inferiority and social inadequacy that his whole life had been affected, and he had been quite unable to profit from an attempt on the part of his parents to give him a professional training.

However, in contrast to these, one meets many children whose parents have dealt with the situation so wisely that faulty emotional habits due to feelings of social insecurity and inferiority have never developed. These children have been submitted to operation and have in every other respect been treated as normal individuals. Consequently they have taken their place in their own environment, and have proved conclusively that cleft palate is not necessarily associated with any psychogenic disorder.

Even in cases where children have experienced difficulties owing to defective speech it has been found that the majority prove to be individuals who can accept their defects and make a good adjustment to life, finding suitable outlets to compensate for their disability.

One patient (Case 4), a girl of eleven years when speech therapy commenced immediately following operation, not only acquired normal speech, but with the additional disability of congenital absence of the left radius, causing shortening of the forearm and loss of power in the hand, had learned dressmaking. Six months after training ceased she visited the clinic wearing a coat and hat made by herself, her first attempt, and a very successful one. She was then fourteen years old.

Another child, whose speech at the age of seven was almost completely unintelligible, had learned to read fluently in his own cleft palate language, with glottal stop substitutions for all plosive consonants. It was obvious that he understood what he read, though no one else was able to do so. He had had no special help with reading, nor had he been allowed to read aloud in school, but in this way he had proved to himself that he was able to do what the other children of his environment could do, at least to his own satisfaction.

Such cases could be multiplied many times. In any treatment for speech defects, ambition on the part of the patient and determination to overcome difficulties give speech therapy the best possible chance.

How the patient's environment can encourage or discourage him has been described, but it can also be of considerable importance in helping or hindering speech development. Simple exercises, practised even for a few minutes daily, increase the rate of progress, but many patients, especially children from poor homes, have no opportunities for private practice, and the fear of ridicule from brothers and sisters is an obstacle not easily surmounted by a sensitive child. An encouraging atmosphere at home and at school will do much to help matters, and, in the case of young children, a mother who will take advantage of odd moments to assist with simple exercises will make a good result more certain and easier to obtain. But in all training there must be variety to prevent boredom, and work suited

P

to the age, mentality and speech ability of the patient. Well-meant attempts to persuade a child to repeat exercises or rhymes day after day, perhaps on the part of a mother who feels there is some disgrace associated with a cleft palate, and is over-anxious for improvement, may produce nothing but antagonism on the part of the child to the whole question of speech. This must be carefully avoided, even at the cost of relinquishing, at least for a period, the practice of exercises between visits to the clinic.

CO-OPERATION BETWEEN PATIENT AND THERAPIST

This is very important if consistent progress is to be made, and the responsibility for obtaining it rests largely with the speech therapist. An interest in the speech defect is not enough, a sympathetic understanding of the child as a personality being quite as important, if not more so. Older children and adults come to the clinic with a definite object in view, and in most cases enough determination to achieve the desired improvement in speech. If ambition is lacking, or the patient becomes discouraged, little progress will be made. It has been said that praise should not be given where it is not yet due, but if it cannot be given for final achievement, it can be given for progress, however small, and every speech therapist knows the value of such judicious praise in preventing discouragement. Especially with young children work must be interesting and often disguised as play. In all cases exercises must be adapted according to the ability of the patient, but the standard of difficulty should be such that, with a reasonable amount of perseverance, success can be achieved. Half an hour at a speech clinic once a week will result in very slow progress, unless interest in speech is sustained during the intervals between visits. Time spent in gaining this co-operation is never wasted, and only then will the children visit the clinic regularly, not because they must, but because they wish to do so, to show with much pride how they have overcome last week's difficulty.

GROUP WORK AND INDIVIDUAL TREATMENT IN CASES OF CLEFT PALATE

Although speech therapy in cases of cleft palate is usually individual, there are many points in favour of group treatment, and in the years 1934-35 I carried out experiments to compare for myself the value of the two methods of treatment. Group methods were only used with children under twelve years of age. These children were grouped partly according to age and partly according to the treatment most required, the number of children in each group ranging from five to eight.

For eight months treatment was carried out in groups only, then experiments were made with group and individual treatment alternately. One week the children worked together in groups for an hour, the next week each child had fifteen minutes individual treatment.

Much of the treatment for cleft palate speech consisted at that time in exercising the soft palate and gaining correct habits of breath direction by means of blowing games and other exercises. Such games are more enjoyable when played with companions. The spirit of competition is aroused, shyness is forgotten, and many children will practise assiduously at home in order to excel the following week. Care must be taken, of course, to see that no child becomes unduly discouraged, perhaps having greater anatomical or physiological difficulties than the others with which to contend, but that each is able to gain praise for improvement if not for success.

Nursery and other rhymes, or simple plays, can be dramatised, and the chance of being allowed to play a part is a healthy incentive to speech improvement.

There may also be economy in time, as a greater number of children can be treated in groups than is possible in the same time with individual work, though it is probable that this economy is more apparent than real, as the time required before normal speech is acquired is generally prolonged.

One of the chief advantages, in my opinion, is the effect on the outlook of the child who, after feeling different from other children, now finds himself in company with others, many of whom have as much, if not more, difficulty than he has himself. Such contact helps him to understand how his own speech may be unintelligible, as he finds he cannot understand the other children unless they possess articulatory defects identical with his own. The fact that these other children make progress, and that such progress is duly recognised and praised, is also encouraging to a child who has found himself unable to cope with his difficulties alone.

However, in my own work I have found from these experiments that unless training is to be protracted over a long period of years, some individual treatment is necessary. A child using a pharyngeal [s] will, in most cases, continue to use that sound, even when surrounded by a group of children who may all be using the correct [s], for the simple reason that the sound he is making is, to him, identical with the sound he hears from others. He must first be taught to make the correct sound as an entirely new one, and only when it is thoroughly established can it be used in words where he has formerly used the defective sound. Although this may be done in a group, such work is more satisfactory if individual treatment is possible, and the ear training which is necessary to make possible the recognition of the difference between correct and faulty sounds is not helped by hearing many varieties of incorrect sounds around.

If all children in a group possessed the same articulatory defects more could be accomplished in group work, but even then not so satisfactorily as when at least some of the treatment is individual.

At that time a combination of group and individual treatment was being used at the clinic at the Royal Victoria Infirmary. Several children of about the same age were reviewed, and those requiring treatment attended once a week for half an hour for group work over a period of six to eight weeks. During this time they played blowing games of all kinds and also attempted consonant sounds, using paper butterflies, candles, feathers, paper dolls and so forth. In some cases consonant production improved, but where the sound was replaced by the glottal stop or a pharyngeal frica-tive little, if any, progress was made. The child continued to produce the sound in his own way under cover of the sounds made by the rest of the group. However, this period usually produced a marked improvement in the use of the palatopharyngeal sphincter, and subsequently arrangements were made for each child to attend for individual treatment. By that time shyness and all fear of the clinic had been overcome, and he rapidly learned to correct his own particular articulatory defects with individual assistance.

WHEN SHOULD SPEECH THERAPY COMMENCE?

In general speech therapy should follow operation, not precede it. It is possible for a patient to become discouraged if he attempts to correct his faults when he has little possibility of achieving results, and it is difficult for him not to use too much effort in his endeavours to improve. However, if operation is impossible or must be delayed, exercises for correct articulation may be practised if the patient prevents nasal escape by holding the nose or by wearing a small clip. As in the case of those requiring a secondary operation, Group B patients may thus progress to Group A, when operation should be all that is needed to complete the treatment and permit normal speech.

Post operative treatment for the cleft palate child is best carried out when the combined efforts of the surgeon, orthodontist and speech therapist are available, and much time can be saved if speech therapy can be carried out in association with a regular follow up by such a team. It will vary according to the age of the child, and falls broadly into three stages.

1. *Under four years of age.*—Following operation the children should be seen at least every six months, and the first approach towards normal speech should be the child's ability to make use of the palatopharyngeal sphincter in blowing. Vigorous blowing games are not as a rule necessary, but many children continue to blow through the nose with closed lips rather than through the mouth, when a partition has been provided surgically. It must be remembered that they have been deprived of the opportunity in infancy to develop normal neuromuscular co-ordination of the palatal and pharyngeal muscles through crying, sucking, swallowing and babbling, and normal function is not necessarily established immediately, nor in fact for several months in some instances, following a good anatomical operative result.

At this age treatment should be in the hands of the mother. If the child is not using the sphincter mechanism when attempting to blow or speak, blowing games are helpful, and can be carried out at home if suitable suggestions are made to the mother. It may be necessary to hold the child's nose with the fingers until he learns to direct the air stream through the lips or until he learns to make use of the sphincter mechanism. He should also be allowed to attempt to suck fluids through a straw.

At a later stage, if normal articulation is slow to develop, the mother may be shown how to obtain a few consonant sounds and the use of such sounds in simple babble drills, but it is generally sufficient if the child can produce each consonant sound in isolation, for example, as the noise an animal makes (baa - - -), a snake (s - - -), the sound a train makes (ch ch sh - - -), an aeroplane (z - - -), raindrops (p t p t p t - -) and so on. Exercises are usually not necessary at this stage, and as speech develops these "noises" will eventually be incorporated correctly into the words he uses.

2. *Over four years of age.*—With those patients whose speech is well established speech therapy may commence as soon after operation as the surgeon advises, usually after about one month from the date of operation. The palate should then be soundly healed, but its condition, especially as regards movement of the soft palate, will continue to improve for several months.

If early directive treatment with the mother has not been possible, operation has been postponed until faulty articulatory habits have become firmly established, normal use of the palatopharyngeal sphincter has not been achieved, or a fistula in the hard palate has prevented the build up of the oral pressure necessary for articulation, speech will be defective, and regular speech therapy should now be commenced. A child of four years is usually able to co-operate, and with the mother's presence during treatment and help with daily practice at home, normal speech may be achieved before the age for school is reached. It is a definite advantage to the child if he can speak intelligibly when he goes to school. Not only is life rendered much easier in many ways, but he is able to maintain progress with the other children, especially when learning to read. At the same time, it has been found that the introduction of a child to school life is often a great stimulus, providing him with an added incentive towards the acquisition of good speech. The first year at school may, therefore, be a very useful period for speech therapy.

3. In this group are those older children where secondary operation has been necessary, or those children and adults who have retained their faulty habits of speech for one reason or another. In the case of such older children the mothers rarely attend the clinic, and so are unable to assist with home practice. Daily speech therapy may then be necessary, as such children find it almost impossible to make progress without assistance and frequent practice. The adult, however, can appreciate more readily the difference between normal and defective articulation, and can therefore carry out the necessary daily practice alone.

CHAPTER VII

TREATMENT II
FURTHER SUGGESTIONS FOR TREATMENT

Correct breath direction and use of the palato-pharyngeal sphincter.

Correct Articulation—

    Lip exercises—tongue exercises—exercises to obviate nasal tone and improve resonance —ear training—treatment to overcome the use of the glottal stop and pharyngeal and laryngeal fricatives—other articulatory exercises.

The introduction of correct sounds into speech.

    (*a*) Under seven years;

    (*b*) for older children. seven to twelve years.

    (*c*) children over twelve and adults.

TREATMENT II
FURTHER SUGGESTIONS FOR TREATMENT

IN describing methods of treatment for cleft palate speech it is impossible to avoid some generalisations, but it must be obvious to all who have come in contact with these cases that each is a separate problem, combining a different series of defects and presenting a different personality problem. Each case, therefore, must be treated on its own merits. The suggestions which follow are not all required in each case, but all have been found useful in the treatment of at least one patient. What has the desired effect in one case appeals to another not at all, and experiments must be made until a successful approach is discovered and each individual problem solved.

Age is of little importance in determining the choice of exercise, as almost all the following have been used with children and adults, but the language and illustrations used to describe each, and to teach it, must be suited to the development and intelligence of the individual patient.

For example, when explaining the sphincter mechanism to a small child we talk about the breath and voice coming out through the "front door" (the mouth), or by the "back door" (the sphincter), when it goes into a dark passage (the nasopharynx) and out down the nose. We can prevent the air coming out of our noses if we hold them with our fingers, but it is much better to close the back door properly. Children like to watch the therapist's own soft palate moving up and down, and can readily understand how it closes and opens a door at the back.

With older children a demonstration of the contraction

of the orbicularis muscle of the lips (as in whistling) can be used to illustrate how a similar contraction can occur in the nasopharynx, whilst to an intelligent adult one can give a full description of the muscles and movements taking part in the closure of the palatopharyngeal sphincter.

To a child the snort may be described on this basis as air squeezing through the "back door" when it is almost shut, and a similar sound can be demonstrated through the "front door" by forcing breath through lips which are closed, but not too tightly.

In giving these explanations it must always be remembered that *conscious* control of the sphincter *during* speech is almost impossible, and any attempt is certainly undesirable, but the foregoing is useful as an explanation as to why speech is defective, and as a reason for the practice of blowing games and palate exercises. Those which follow, directed to obtaining conscious control of the sphincter, are, therefore, only of value if they ultimately produce automatic co-ordination of the speech mechanism including the palatopharyngeal sphincter muscles. They are practised apart from speech as gymnastics for the development of this spontaneous and unconscious habit.

Treatment for cleft palate can be divided into four steps through which the patient will progress towards normal speech, and the exercises used have, therefore, been grouped accordingly.

1. Correct breath direction involving the full use of the palatal and pharyngeal muscles to produce closure of the palatopharyngeal sphincter.

2. Normal neuromuscualar control and co-ordination of these muscles with those of articulation.

3. Correct articulation of every vowel and consonant sound, and the ability to use each sound initially,

finally and medially, in combination with other consonants, eg., [sp], [sk], [ts], [str], etc., in syllables and words, and at the speed necessary for incorporation in fluent speech. Correct articulation of vowel sounds is considered with regard to nasal tone and not with the alteration of dialectal peculiarities.

4. The introduction of these sounds into speech, entailing the unconscious use of new and correct habits of articulation.

Group A cases, whose only fault is that of nasal escape of air, will require training in section 1, and possibly sections 2 and 4.

Group B,—These cases have articulatory substitutions, or use vowel and nasal resonants only. Those in which function is not yet developed are also unable to make use of the palatopharyngeal sphincter mechanism, and consequently have nasal escape. Such cases will need exercises from the four sections. Those patients who have already learnt to use the sphincter mechanism should only need exercises from sections 2, 3 and 4.

In cases where nasal escape persists, it has not been found necessary to postpone the use of exercises in sections 3 and 4 until those in sections 1 and 2 can be successfully carried out. As described in discussing the advisability of preoperative treatment, if undue effort is avoided, articulatory exercises can proceed parallel with exercises for control of the sphincter. If difficulty is experienced in obtaining sufficient pressure, due to nasal escape, the patient may compress the nostrils with the fingers, and, when the correct sound is achieved, should aim to produce the same sound, with the same auditory and tactile sensation, without holding the nose. This indirect attack is sometimes useful in obtaining function of the palatopharyngeal sphincter.

Again, it is not intended to suggest that it is necessary to postpone the use of simple rhymes until every sound can be articulated correctly. Such rhymes can be useful if only one sound is correctly articulated whenever it occurs, but when faulty sounds have been learnt in a rhyme it should be discarded and new rhymes substituted for the practice of other consonants.

In all cases daily practice is necessary, but one long period each day does not produce such good results as several short ones, especially with young children. If the patient is not old enough to carry this out without assistance, the co-operation of the mother or other adult is enlisted. It has been found useful for the mother to attend with the child, when she is shown how the required sounds are obtained, or how palate exercises are performed, and she is asked to carry out a few such exercises and simple sound drills with the child for not more than five to ten minutes at a time, perhaps two or three times each day. The mother is in a position to carry out these exercises with the small child during play, or at odd moments during the day, and it has been found that this assistance is of great importance in fixing new speech habits and in developing normal speech. At the same time parents are asked not to correct faulty pronunciation of words used by the child in conversation. Not only is such correction wearing to the mother, but it is extremely exasperating to any child to be interrupted in the natural expression of his thoughts for correction of his articulation. Such treatment does more harm than good. The word corrected is very often one which is too difficult for the child to pronounce correctly without further treatment, and in any case such correction is unnecessary. Concentration on the exercises given eventually establishes normal speech habits; after a preliminary period of two to three months it is found that conversational speech improves spontaneously in the great majority of cases.

Where is does not, or in the case of adults, more conscious practice of the use of new sounds, in reading and in speech, may be necessary.

It must be stressed that all treatment must aim to develop the normal neuromuscular patterns for articulation and not to teach speech, or words, especially to young children. Treatment follows the principles involved in motor learning, namely *inhibition* of the faulty patterns already acquired, *facilitation* of the required normal movements, *association* through experience of these movements for articulation with those for other sounds, such as vowel sounds, and also association of the muscle movements with new sensory impressions, auditory, kinaesthetic, and tactile. When these stages have been achieved there must be *stabilisation* of the newly acquired motor and sensory patterns until they can be used spontaneously and without conscious control at the speed required for conversational speech. Only then should an attempt be made, or the child expected to incorporate these normal sounds in speech.

Such exercises fall into four groups. Firstly, those for achieving good breath direction with the use of the palatopharyngeal sphincter. Secondly, exercises for co-ordination of the palatopharyngeal sphincter and the movements for articulation. Thirdly, exercises for correct articulation; and fourthly, exercises for improving resonance.

EXERCISES FOR DEVELOPING CORRECT BREATH DIRECTION AND THE USE OF THE PALATO-PHARYNGEAL SPHINCTER.

In the majority of children operated upon in early life such exercises are now usually unnecessary and use of the palatopharyngeal sphincter is established soon after operation and persists. A few children, however, still direct the air through the nose rather than through the mouth when a functional partition has been provided and the air stream may be diverted either way at will.

If the child nips his nostrils and then attempts to blow it may be at once obvious that he is in some difficulty and at first he may not find it easy to direct the air through the only outlet now available. However, he will eventually find a way to accomplish this, if only to avoid the slight discomfort experienced when the air stream is deflected into the nasal airways through which there is then no outlet.

Blowing exercises are now rarely necessary, but may be useful in adjusting the tongue position to obtain the least resistance to the air stream, or voice, passing through the vocal tract. Where there is still an anatomical deficiency it is especially important that the maximum amount of air should be directed through the mouth, thus minimising the nasal escape of air, and for this purpose some blowing games or exercises may be useful.

These exercises may also assist in the development of increased mobility and compensatory movements of the posterior and lateral pharyngeal walls and of the soft palate, and may assist the adequacy of nasopharyngeal closure and help to achieve the best possible functional result. Much may be done in this way, though the result may not always be permanent. Two cases in my experience obtained complete nasopharyngeal closure after much exercise. In one case the speech was normal (Case 12), but in the other the soft palate was immobile, and some nasal tone persisted without nasal escape of air. Both were discharged, but when seen again after an interval of twelve months, both had nasal escape. Apparently, in relaxing their efforts, this extra development of muscle had disappeared, everyday speech being insufficient to maintain it. Though still good, their speech could not be classed as normal.

It cannot too often be stressed that all such exercises should be carried out without effort, and it is for this reason that competitive blowing games are now little used. They may, however, be adapted for breath direction as described.

1. **Whistling.**—If this is impossible owing to nasal escape the patient should nip his nose until he has learnt to whistle, and should then aim to produce the same result, using the palatopharyngeal sphincter. When once acquired this is a very useful and natural method of exercising the muscles of the soft palate and sphincter. Where it has been possible to observe the normal palatal movements in patients through a defect in the face it has been noticed that palatal and pharyngeal movements for whistling and blowing resemble those for speech but differ from those for swallowing. Such exercises may therefore contribute towards normal control of the nasopharyngeal outlet for speech.

2. **Wind instruments.**—Pleasure may perhaps be combined with exercise if the patient can learn to play a simple wind instrument. Mouth organs are useful, though they may not be appreciated by the family.

3. **Suction games.**—Silver paper fish may be picked up and carried, using suction through a straw, hard peas may be utilised in the same way, and small, celluloid dolls lifted and bathed in water (Ferrie). To obtain sufficient suction the palatopharyngeal sphincter must be closed. When this is impossible it has been found that a few children will learn to draw in air simultaneously through the nose and mouth, in which case the exercise serves no useful purpose, but

Q

it illustrates once again that the intelligent child will find a way, whenever possible, to compensate for his deficiencies.

4. **Humming.**—Humming, a tune or on a monotone, is a useful exercise in that it may help to develop muscle. As previously described (p. 49), the sphincter is almost closed during this act, the soft palate being well raised. It also helps to obtain relaxation of the laryngeal muscles and to clear nasal tone.

5. **Yawning**—This stretches and exercises the muscle of the soft palate.

   (i) Breathe in on the yawn position and out on a vowel shape without sound.

   (ii) Breathe in on a yawn position and out on a voiced vowel sound.

   (iii) Think the yawn position, raising the soft palate and depressing the back of the tongue, and voice a vowel sound. Test with a mirror held under the nose to detect nasal escape, if any.

6. **Conscious movement of the soft palate.**—Watch the movement of the soft palate in a mirror whilst repeating ah, ah, ah, [ɑ: , ɑ: , ɑ:], with the mouth wide open, relaxing the palate between each vowel sound. Raise the palate as high as possible. Sustain the vowel sound ah [ɑ:], and still watching the movement in a mirror, lower and raise the soft palate, noting the variation in tone when the palate is raised and lowered.

7. **Alternation of vowel and nasal resonant.** *e.g.*, ah ng, ah ng . . . [ɑ: ŋ, ɑ: ŋ], (*a*) aloud, (*b*) whispered. Let the patient use a mirror and watch the movement of the soft palate.

8. **Holding air under pressure in the mouth.**

(i) Blow out the cheeks and explode the air through the lips. When possible, this exercise produces a certain amount of massage of the soft palate. It is also useful to demonstrate the need for a closed palatopharyngeal sphincter.

(ii) When the sphincter is too incompetent to permit this, ask the patient to nip the nostrils with the fingers, blow out the cheeks and then remove the fingers without allowing the air to escape through the nose. (Be sure, however, that he does not accomplish this by raising the back of the tongue, thus shutting off the mouth from the nose, in an attempt to compensate for an open sphincter.)

(iii) Ask the patient to hold his nose with his fingers and blow. Whilst continuing to blow he should remove his fingers, attempting to do this without any alteration in the direction or force of the breath stream.

(iv) Let the patient blow down the nose, and then try to raise the palate and close the sphincter in an attempt to interrupt the nasal air stream.

(v) Practice alternately the oral and nasal emission of air so that the patient consciously experiences the difference in sensation. Also hold the air under pressure in the mouth and release it alternately first through the mouth and then through the nasopharynx.

Exercises for co-ordination of the palatopharyngeal sphincter and the muscles of articulation.—If nasal escape persists in speech after operation, and blowing games and simple palate exercises have failed to ensure the use of the palatopharyngeal sphincter, further training will be required to encourage correct co-ordination between the sphincter mechanism and the muscles concerned with articulation. In many cases the patient can blow without nasal escape, and can hold air under pressure in his mouth, showing the presence of a competent sphincter, but when asked to say [p] or [pah (pɑ:)] he relaxes the sphincter before relaxing the lips. The air escapes through the nose, leaving insufficient pressure for a good plosive consonant. To train correct co-ordination one should first aim to obtain it with one consonant, and this can usually be accomplished best with [p].

    (i)   (*a*) Hold air under pressure in the mouth and release it through the palatopharyngeal sphincter keeping the lips closed.

    (*b*) Hum - - - (the sphincter being slightly open) - - - then deflect the breath into the mouth, distending the cheeks - - - (the sphincter being closed).

    (*c*) Hum - - - blow out the cheeks - - - hum, etc. alternately.

    (*d*) Hum - - - blow out cheeks - - - release on p. The lips relax to articulate [p] *before* the sphincter opens. It is here that difficulty is experienced as many patients who have an efficient sphincter allow the air to escape down the nose before they open the lips. This exercise may be written:—

    m - - - - - - - - - - - blow out cheeks - - - p.

    (sphincter open) (sphincter closed) (sphincter remaining closed).

(ii) Blow out the cheeks, the sphincter being closed and air being held in the mouth under pressure. Relax the lips to articulate [p]. This exercise omits the hum as in No. (i). If the sphincter is not sufficiently competent, nasal escape may be prevented by nipping the nostrils with the fingers until the patient understands what is required. Repeat alternately holding the nose and without.

(iii) When this can be accomplished easily the patient must develop the ability to alternately open and close the sphincter with increasing rapidity. Exercises involving alternation of a nasal and its corresponding oral sound are used, at first quite slowly:—

m - - - pah, m - - - pay, m - - - pee, m - - - po, m - - - poo.

The hum is sustained and sufficient intra oral pressure is built up before the lips are relaxed. In all cases the plosive consonant must be as strong as possible. In the early stages, if difficulty is experienced, the nostrils may be nipped for the production of the [p], but not, of course, during the hum. This exercise may be repeated using m - - - bah, etc., n - - - tah, etc., n - - - dah, etc., ng - - - kah, etc., and ng - - - gah, etc.

(iv) When control of the opening and closing of the sphincter has been acquired the exercises should be practised more rapidly and with repetition, so that the speed of the muscle movements approximates to the speed required in normal speech. The following exercises should be practised as rapidly as is possible with maintenance of normal pressure on the plosive consonants:—

m - - - pah - - - m - - - pah - - - m - - - pah,
m - - - pay - - - m - - - pay - - - m - - - pay, etc.

[n] and [ng] should also be used in this exercise in conjunction with [t], [d], [k], and [g].

(v) Omit the nasal resonant and practise using the plosive consonant alone, slowly at first, and subsequently more rapidly with repetition:—

Pah, pay, pee, po, poo and pah, pah, pah, pay, pay, pay, etc.

The consonant sound should be exaggerated in this exercise by the use of good oral air pressure, but never by forcing from the larynx. Such exercises can be used with any consonant, plosive or fricative, if desired.

(vi) Practise using [p] as a final sound with a vowel as ahp [ɑː p]. ɑː - - - pause whilst air is held in the mouth under pressure - - - p, exploding the air gently through the lips.

These exercises are most easily practised with the consonants [p] and [b], but when the habit of correct co-ordination has been acquired with the bilabial consonants it can usually be incorporated quite easily into the articulation of other consonants. They are of most use where there is the possibility of palatopharyngeal closure.

EXERCISES FOR CORRECT ARTICULATION

Where nasopharyngeal closure is adequate following surgery, treatment will consist in developing the use of normal consonant sounds as described through the processes involved in motor learning, possibly including the alteration of other neuromuscular habits of movement and co-ordination such as those of the palatopharyngeal sphincter itself. Although it may be difficult to achieve normal articulation of consonants if the palatopharyngeal sphincter

is incompetent such practice may help to improve nasopharyngeal closure by improving breath direction as the
patient attempts to produce the consonant sounds with the
requisite oral air pressure. As pointed out in 1940, "It
should again be noted that it is not necessary to postpone
the teaching of these sounds (consonants) until the patient
has complete control of the palatopharyngeal sphincter.
The nostrils should be held with the fingers whilst the sounds
are being learnt and the correct sensations acquired. The
subsequent attempt to produce the sounds correctly without
holding the nose is often a great help to acquiring normal
nasopharyngeal closure."[1]

The following points require consideration when attempting to correct faulty articulatory and co-ordination patterns
in a child or adult.

1. **The use of consonant sounds is normally at a level below
and at a speed beyond conscious control.**—As the child
develops speech, whether normally or otherwise, consonant
and vowel sounds become integrated as phonemes in sequential patterns in syllables and longer sequences. These
sequences become increasingly stabilised through motor
activity and sensory feedback, auditory, tactile and proprioceptive. The use of individual phonemes in speech
becomes mainly automatic and not under voluntary control.
The individual is concerned with the thought he is receiving
or expressing and usually has little or no conscious appreciation of the individual sounds he either hears in the speech of
others or uses himself. It is for this reason the child has
difficulty in changing his articulation patterns without help,
especially if they become fully stabilised before surgery.
For this reason also therapy should aim to demand from the

---

[1] MORLEY, M. E. (1940). Types of Cleft Palate Speech and their
Treatment. *Speech.*, 5, 2, 9.

patient as little conscious awareness and control as is possible.

2. **Resistance to change.**—Not only is it difficult for the patient to change articulatory habits no longer under voluntary conscious control, but he will also resist change. For example, when a child has used "tit down" for "sit down", to him the [t] is normal in that particular sequential phoneme pattern in his own speech. The substitution of [s] in his own speech is to him not only auditorily incorrect but the associated tactile and proprioceptive feed-back is also incorrect. The child may be well aware of the defective articulation of such a sequence if used by another, he may be able to hear the difference easily when he himself pronounces "tit" and "sit," but in his own speech he prefers that to which he is accustomed, both in the sequential motor activity and its associated sensory feed-back. Perhaps one may understand the situation to some extent if one considers how one would react were he to change every [s] and substitute [t] in conversational speech, even for five minutes.

It must also be remembered that the faulty phoneme sequences in words and phrases as used by the child are, to him, completely associated with his sensory appreciation of, and with the meaning of the corresponding normal sequences he hears made by others. In other words he hears "sit down" and to him this has the same meaning and significance as "tit down" in his own speech. The child will, however, reject as incorrect "tit down" when spoken by another.

Tests for consonant discrimination in young children are not always reliable. So many factors play a part—interest, attention, co-operation, a situation which requires the identification of single, isolated sounds, which to him is entirely outside his normal experience, and even the fact that he may interpret phonemes used in words correctly, allowing for poor articulation or idiosyncrasy on the part of the tester! The child may say, "Well, it sounded like shrub [ʃrʌb] but I think he meant scrub [skrʌb]."

A test for consonant discrimination in a young child may perhaps best be carried out by repeating to him a familiar rhyme with one incorrect consonant sound. For example: "Humpky Dumpky sak on a wall," etc. Simple sentences may be similarly used, especially as spoken by the child. He will then usually show strong objection and reject such pronunciation.

With very young children, two to three years of age, the development of correct consonant sounds is achieved mainly through imitation. Imitation of animal and other noises can produce a large proportion of the consonants in the phonetic alphabet. When the correct sounds can be articulated separately they are introduced into simple exercises, words and rhymes, as far as possible in the form of play. In this way new habits gradually and automatically replace faulty ones, and self-consciousness and speech consciousness are avoided.

With older children and adults the approach can be more direct. The faulty habits must first be made conscious, and when a correct sound has been produced the patient should compare, not only the difference in sound between the old and the new way of making it, but also the difference in the kinæsthetic and tactile sensations produced in the larynx, tongue and lips. Conscious imitation of the various positions of tongue and lips should be practised, using a mirror. In this way, the senses of hearing, touch and sight all combine in helping to fix the new habits.

The correct use of the organs of speech for all sounds has been described in many books on phonetics, and will not be discussed here, but suggestions which have been found helpful in achieving the production of consonant sounds in cases of cleft palate, including treatment for correcting use of the glottal stop and pharyngeal fricatives, are given below.

The order in which articulatory defects are corrected should depend on the individual patient. It is always advisable to begin with the consonants he can make, if any, and when these have been used in exercises proceed by way of those he can make most easily to those he finds more difficult, as confidence, auditory acuity and co-ordination improve.

Lip exercises.—When difficulty is experienced due to a tight and inert upper lip, exercises for the lip muscles are useful, and in most cases improvement is obtained. If the disability is great, and persists, further operative treatment by a plastic surgeon may be necessary.

Tongue exercises.—These may be useful and control should be practiced using consonant sounds such as tttt, dddd and ta, ta, ta, etc. There may be difficulty due to missing teeth and a deformed upper jaw. The tongue can be very adaptable in occluding lateral gaps, but agility exercises may be useful in obtaining easy and rapid production of [t] and [d], when the palate is shortened antero-posteriorly, and the tongue is inclined to protrude beyond the upper incisors.

It should be noted that with present day surgery both the lip and dental arch approach closely to the normal in many patients, and such exercises as those described may not now be needed. Movements of the tongue, particularly of the tip, may, however, assist both movement and control, and render some of the anterior consonant sounds less difficult to obtain.

Exercises to obviate nasal tone and to improve resonance. —Narrowed, or undeveloped nostrils, or a deflected septum tend to make it more difficult for the patient to avoid nasalised speech of the rhinolalia mixta type.

The acquisition of a satisfactory acoustic balance between oral and nasal resonance is essential and may be difficult to obtain in some patients. However, this defect is now much less common and in the great majority of patients under review at the present time there is no trace of abnormal resonance.

The causes of abnormal nasal resonance have already been described (pp. 176, 196). In some cases the condition may not be capable of alteration, but where the increased nasality is mainly due to faulty direction of expiratory air into the nasopharynx rather than through the mouth, there will be inadequate oral resonance and an excess of nasal tone. This may be improved by exercises.

(i) Practise relaxation of the tongue on the floor of the mouth, particularly allowing the base of the tongue to relax. Raise and lower the back of the tongue easily.

(ii) Practise a vowel sound such as [ɑ: (ah)] with the tongue as flat and relaxed as is possible for normal vowel resonance. This is especially important for [i: (ee)] and [u: (oo)].

(iii) Watch that the patient does not try to speak with the teeth together or the tip of the tongue impeding the oral outlet, thereby increasing both the nasal escape of air and nasal tone. Exercises for relaxation and movement of the lower jaw may be required.

(iv) Hum on m - - - or n - - -. Use each nostril alternately, closing the other with the finger. Then hum using both nostrils together.

(v) Hum a simple tune on m - - -, or n - - -as in (iv).

(vi) Hum, then easily and gradually open the mouth on a vowel sound, directing the breath through the lips and not up into the nasopharynx.

(vii) If some vowel sounds are less nasal than others work from one which is not nasalised, changing to another vowel sound gradually, without altering the tone.

(viii) Practise a nasalised and unnasalised vowel sound alternately, *e.g.*, ɑ : ɑ̃ : ɑ : ɑ̃ :.

(ix) If a good [z] sound can be produced "buzzing" is useful for clearing nasal tone. The voiced sound produced in the larynx is carried well to the front of the mouth to combine with the fricative sound made between the tongue, alveolar ridge and teeth.

Ear training and the development of normal articulation.—The majority of children with defective articulation such as dyslalia, dyspraxia, or dysarthria have normal perception and discrimination for the sounds of speech although they may have difficulty in reproducing sequences of sounds in speech, and ear training exercises as such may not be necessary. Cleft palate patients in general require these even less than those with other articulatory disabilities since the essential cause of the defective speech is not associated with the sensory or motor nervous pathways related to speech except in so far as development of faulty habits is concerned. It is usually necessary for the child to acquire a new consonant sound at first in isolation through making the required movement. Imitation of the sound auditorily may or may not be sufficient as the child will generally continue to produce his own faulty articulation. Visual imitation of the required movement may then help and the child should be shown how to place his tongue or lips, or the therapist can devise means to assist the required movements using her fingers, the child's finger or a spatula. For example when [t] is substituted for [k] it is often possible to obtain [k] if the child's finger is placed on the anterior upper surface of the tongue. An attempt to produce [t] may then result in [k]. If not a spatula placed edgeways between the incisor teeth and resting on the front part of the tongue blade will prevent the articulation of [t] and assist articulation of [k]. It is generally necessary to teach the required consonant sound as an entirely new one to the child and it may be some time before he can associate this new sound with the same consonant sound as made by others and be able to use it when required in speech. The sound should therefore be first practiced in isolation (or with an unstressed [ə] or [ʌ] until it can be freely imitated without hesitation. Repeating the sound in isolation removes it from the context of established sequences within which it has been used incorrectly until such time as correct motor activity and sensory feedback for the new sound are fully integrated.

Treatment to overcome the use of the glottal stop.—The eradication of the use of the glottal stop can be very difficult, and it tends to persist in speech long after all sounds can be correctly articulated individually. In many cases it occurs between the consonant and a vowel sound. For example, the sound p can be correctly made, but the child finds it impossible to say pah [pɑː]; instead he says p ʔɑː. Sometimes the syllable can be whispered correctly, but any attempt at a voiced vowel sound, necessitating use of the vocal cords, immediately causes hypertension of the laryngeal muscles and the introduction of the glottal stop. It has become an unconscious neuromuscular habit to associate contraction at this level with articulation, and such interruption of the air stream causes lack of oral pressure in the region of the lips and alveolus, with consequent weakening of articulation in these positions. Much time and care may be required before the patient is able to inhibit such contraction at the laryngeal level and obtain the requisite pressure in the normal position for articulation.

Emphasis must be laid upon easy but careful production of all sounds. Effort must be avoided, and for this reason blowing games and exercises must be used with discretion when attempting the production of a consonant sound. Blowing games as such may be useful. The muscles of the sphincter and soft palate are exercised, and the vocal cords and laryngeal muscles relaxed. But when blowing games are combined with the articulation of a consonant sound, as when the patient attempts to blow some object in order to obtain a plosive sound such as [p], those in Group B will be much more likely to produce a forceful glottal stop, until it is realised through experience how the sound can be produced more easily by a gentle, correctly used puff of air through the lips. It is not the blowing, helping as it does good breath direction, but the suggestion of effort required to move the object which produces the wrong effect. Such exercises are of more use with Group A cases, where there is no danger of increasing the use of a glottal stop, and where the attempt to produce a good plosive sound will cause increased movement of the sphincter muscles.

(i) *Humming*.—Starting with a slight puff of air down the nose, let the patient hum gently. If the hum is correctly produced vibrations will be felt on the lips and in the nose, and there will be no feeling of strain in the throat or larynx. Then add vowel sounds gently, without any effort, and with no alteration of laryngeal tension, *e.g.*, m - - - ah - - -. Repeat this exercise, using other vowel sounds.

(ii) *Whispering*.—Breathe in and out easily through the mouth once or twice for relaxation.

Open the mouth for the vowel sound ah [ɑ:], draw in the breath through the mouth and out in a whispered [ɑ:]. Repeat with other vowel sounds, keeping the jaw, lips and tongue as relaxed as possible.

Then use unvoiced consonant sounds with these easy whispered vowel sounds. Use first [h], and [wh (ʍ)]. If [f], [th (θ)] and [s] are correct, these may also be used, e.g., h - - - ah [h - - - ɑ:], wh - - - ah [ʍ - - - ɑ:], f - - - ah [f - - - ɑ:], th - - - ah [θ- - - ɑ:], s - - - ah [s - - - ɑ:]. Repeat, using other vowel sounds. When these syllables can be produced easily attempt voiced consonant sounds, [v], [w], [th, (ð)], [z], with very easy voiced vowel sounds.

(iii) *Closure of the anterior nares to prevent nasal escape.*—In many cases, if the nostrils are compressed with the fingers to prevent nasal escape, a plosive consonant may be obtained quite easily without the addition or substitution of the glottal stop. As pointed out previously, inability to obtain sufficient air pressure in the mouth induces the use of the glottal stop, and where this is possible the consonant may be normal. When the correct production of the sound is established, try to make it without holding the nose.

(iv) *Plosive articulation.*—Allow the patient to fill the mouth with air, the lips being closed but not tense. The air should then be gently released through the lips as for [p]. This may first be accomplished by the movement of the lower lip by the therapist's or patient's fingers just sufficiently to allow the release of air. In this way even minimum effort on the part of the patient is avoided, and the danger of laryngeal hypertension, or associated glottal stop, the patient experiencing the sensation of a normal [p].

(v) *Co-ordination exercises.*—The exercises described on p. 243 (iii) and (iv) are also useful in obtaining correct articulation of consonant sounds without the use of the glottal stop.

Treatment for pharyngeal or laryngeal fricatives.—All exercises to prevent the use of the glottal stop will help to lessen laryngeal and pharyngeal hypertension and the use of these incorrect fricatives. In some patients they may be more easily corrected than the plosive sounds, in which case they should be tackled first. The correction of the glottal stop will be simplified thereafter.

(i) (*a*) Breathe in, close the nostrils with the fingers if nasopharyngeal closure is not efficient, and blow gently through almost closed lips. From this lip position gradually change to the correct relation of teeth and lower lip for [f] and continue to blow in the same manner.

(*b*) Repeat this exercise with one nostril open, and, when successful, with both open. Or gradually reduce the pressure of the fingers on the nostrils whilst the patient is making the sound.

(ii) Attempt other fricatives in the order which the patient finds easiest, starting with one he can make correctly and gradually changing to another, *e.g.*, f - - - s - - -.

(iii) If the patient can whistle, let him begin with this and then change to the required sound, or he may use a slightly sibilant sound as for [ʍ(wh)] and then modify the articulatory position whilst maintaining the air stream and pharyngeal relaxation.

Further suggestions for consonant practice.

(i) *Blowing games.*—Attempt the various sounds, at the same time using the breath to blow a candle flame, a feather, paper butterflies, paper balls, etc. Various sizes of candles are obtainable, the birthday cake size being the best for young children or for those with little blowing power. This exercise is most useful with Group A cases, and must be used carefully when the glottal stop is prominent. (See p. 253.)

(ii) *Plosive consonants.*—Ask the patient to hum, and whilst he is still humming compress his nostrils quickly with the fingers. A good [p] or [b] may be produced involuntarily. If not, ask the patient to say [p] when the hum is interrupted by compression of the nostrils. This exercise is also useful in obtaining [t] and [d] from [n - - -], and [k] and [g] from [ng (η - - -)].

(iii) *To strengthen plosive consonants.*—Exercises based on m - - - bah, as m - - - bah, m - - - bay, m - - - bee, m - - - bo, m - - - boo (m - - - bɑ: , m - - - bei, m - - - bi: , m - - - bou, m - - - bu:), n - - - tah, n - - - dah, and ng - - - kah, ng - - - gah, etc., are useful for obtaining and strengthening plosive consonants, but only when the palatopharyngeal sphincter is functioning at least partially. If there is much nasal escape nip the nostrils for the plosive sound after the nasal resonant has been produced.

(iv) *Articulation of* [t] *and* [d].—Many patients with complete clefts through the alveolus and lip have difficulty in using the tip of the tongue for the articulation of [t] and [d]. In such cases use of the tongue for normal sucking has been impossible and development and control of the muscles of the tongue tip may be deficient. In many cases [k] and [g] are used as substitutes for [t] and [d], even following operation, and it would seem that this occurs more frequently in the cleft palate patient than in the child who develops

R

defective articulation in spite of a normal palate. In cases where normal function of the palatopharyngeal sphincter has been acquired, but an anterior fistula has persisted, normal pressure can be obtained for the articulation of [k] and [g], but not for consonants articulated further forward in the mouth. In such cases the fistula must first be occluded by a dental plate or further surgery. Where [p] is good [t] may be obtained as follows:—

(a) Ask the patient to make the sound [p]—an easy plosive between the lips.

(b) Place the tongue tip between the lips and again try to say [p]. This gives the tactual sensation of a plosive sound made on the tip of the tongue, but not the correct position for [t].

(c) Make a similar sound with the tongue tip in contact with the upper lip only. Repeat with the tongue tip touching the edge of the upper incisor teeth, and finally with the tongue tip behind the teeth, touching the alveolar ridge.

[t] may also be obtained from [n] as described in Exercise (ii).

(v) *Articulation of* [k] and [g].—[k] may be obtained from [t]. Use a spatula about one inch wide, held vertically, not flat, between the incisor teeth. The part of the spatula just inside the mouth rests on the tip of the tongue and prevents it rising to the alveolar ridge. If the patient now tries to say [t] he will almost invariably produce a [k] sound. Sometimes it is sufficient for the patient to place a finger on the tip of the tongue to hold it down behind the lower incisor teeth, and, in the home, the handle of a spoon is a good substitute for a spatula.

[k] may also be obtained from [ng (ŋ)], as mentioned above, Exercise (ii).

(vi) *Hissing and* [s].—It is an advantage to obtain a correct [s] as soon as possible. This sound occurs frequently in speech, and when used normally appears to cause an all-round improvement in other sounds. Hissing practice is also valuable as an exercise for breath direction.

To obtain [s]:—

(*a*) From [t]. t t t t ts - - -. The taps made with the tip of the tongue behind the upper incisor for [t] help to indicate the position for [s] and to centralise it.

(*b*) From [th (θ)]. Whilst the child is articulating this sound press the tip of the tongue gently back behind the incisor teeth, using a drinking straw. A good [s] often results.

(*c*) From [f]. Whilst producing a continuous fricative sound [f - - -], let the patient change gradually from the [f] position to that for [s], the air issuing from between the teeth instead of between the upper incisors and the lower lip.

(*d*) Let the patient hold a drinking straw lightly between the incisor teeth, allowing the short piece (about half-inch) which is inside the mouth to rest on the upper surface of the tongue. Breath must now be directed through the straw, and this must be accomplished by control of the tongue, and not by closing the lips. The breath may be used to make a candle flame flicker or to make bubbles in water.

(*e*) When there is a persistent nasal leak on [s], exercises involving the alternate use of [s] and a nasal

resonant may help to improve the breath direction, as
m - - - sah, m - - - say, m - - - see, etc., and m - - - zah,
m - - - zay, m - - - zee, etc.

(vii) *Consonant practice using a straw.*—Let a drinking straw rest on the lower lip and blow a sound through
it into a glass of water, as [p]. This is more useful for
unvoiced consonants, as more bubbles are produced
than with the voiced sounds. The position of the straw
will need adjustment for different consonants, being
held lightly between the teeth for [s] and [z], resting on
the edge of the upper incisors for [t] and [d], between
the lips for [b] and [p], and resting on the upper
surface of the tongue for [k] and [g]. Bubbles appear
in the water if the sound is correctly produced. There
is no bubble when the glottal stop is used, and little
or none when there is nasal escape.

However, the unit of speech is the syllable and as
soon as is possible the new sound should be associated
with vowel sounds in simple syllables.

(viii) *Syllable exercises.*—When they can be correctly
and easily articulated, introduce the consonant sounds
into exercises such as pah, pay, pee, po, poo [pɑ:,
pei, pi:, pou, pu:]. For fricatives the consonant is
sustained as f - - - ɑ, s - - - ɑ, etc. The consonant sound
is gradually shortened until the child can use fɑ and
sɑ. Consonants in the final position in words may be
used as ahp, ayp, eep, ohp, oop (ɑ: p, eip, i: p, oup,
u: p]. Ah [ɑ:] is usually the easiest vowel for a cleft
palate patient. The soft palate is not raised quite so
high as it is for oo and ee [u: and i:], and there is less
resistance to the passage of air through the mouth,
the tongue being flat. This vowel is, therefore, practised
first. Repeat with other consonants. The aim should be

initially to associate the new sound with various vowels in single syllables repeated after the therapist. When, after repeated sensorimotor experience, the child can reproduce these single syllables easily, each may be repeated after the therapist three times. This represents the simplest linguistic sequence or phrase where one consonant alternates with one vowel as pɑ, pɑ, pɑ, pei, pei, pei, and so forth. These exercises are repeated using other consonants which can already be produced automatically in isolation until the newly acquired sounds can be used in simple phrases, as indicated, fully stabilised, automatic and carried out without conscious thought.

(ix) *Initial consonants.*—Many cleft palate patients find it easier to use a consonant sound finally than initially, for example ahp [ɑː p] is easier than pah [pɑː]. In these cases first practise syllable drill with the consonant used finally as in Exercise (viii). When this is easy try ahp - - - ah, ahp - - - ay, ahp - - - ee, ahp - - - o, ahp - - - oo [ɑː p - - - ɑː, ɑː p - - - ei, ɑː p - - - iː, ɑː p - - - ou, ɑː p - - - uː]. The break between the [p] and the following vowel sound should be reduced until they are joined smoothly, and the stress is then gradually transferred from the initial vowel to the final one until the former disappears completely. This can be used with any consonant sound.

(x) *Word practice.*—This is rarely necessary in young children if the syllable drills described in Exercise (viii) have been sufficiently practised. Where, however, a few words are spoken with persistent defective patterns of articulation they may be corrected individually. Such practice may be more necessary in the older patient with long established defects of articulation.

INTRODUCTION OF CORRECT SOUNDS INTO SPEECH

Once the child is able to use the simple syllable phrases automatically, at a speed equivalent to that required for normal conversational speech, he should be helped to use them in normal linguistic sequences.

(i) This may be carried out for the young child by allowing him to repeat simple rhymes, at first line by line after the therapist. The rhyme should incorporate as much use of the newly acquired sound as possible and other consonants, not yet at the automatic level, should be ignored. Eventually the child will repeat the whole rhyme himself.

(ii) He may also repeat stories after the therapist, phrase by phrase. At first these should be limited to two, three or four syllable phrases depending upon the consonant difficulties involved for the individual child. The aim should be for the child to incorporate into such phrases any consonant sound which he can already use automatically at speed, as in the syllable-phrase exercises.

(iii) Daily practice is required until such time as these consonants, used with increasing ease and consistency in rhymes and stories, begin to appear spontaneously in the child's conversational speech. He himself is largely unaware of the change which is occurring.

For older children, seven to twelve years.

The same procedure is followed but reading aloud may follow or be substituted for repeating stories.

(i) For children who can read, a graduated series of well-illustrated reading books may be used. It is sometimes useful to let the patient be responsible for every word containing a certain sound, the therapist reading the remainder.

(ii) Simple rhymes and jingles help to fix new habits of speech, and form an intermediate stage between reading, where visual memory is a help to auditory memory, and spontaneous speech.

(iii) Rhymes involving frequent repetition of certain words, such as "This is the house that Jack built," and the story of the Old Woman and the Pig who would not jump over the stile, are interesting and useful in the more advanced stages, and can also be used as a basis for conversation practice.

For adults and older children.

(i) Treatment here can be more direct. Reading aloud is useful to fix the new habits, also rhymes of increasing difficulty. In the early stages all difficult words should be practised separately until they can be incorporated correctly in reading at normal speed. For example one child with a [k] for [t] substitution had difficulty with a much used word "water," pronounced by him "wɑːkə." He could use [t] normally in syllable drills and also repeat "ter, ter, ter" but wa-ter still became wa-ker. In such cases it is justifiable to practice a single word in isolation. The difficulty experienced indicates the sequential nature of familiar sound patterns and the difficulty in changing one unit of that sequence pattern.

(ii) Another useful exercise is to read through a paragraph several times, concentrating on a different consonant sound each time, until all can be used correctly.

(iii) If group work is possible, in addition to individual treatment, play reading adds interest at this stage.

(iv) Conversation practice with correction of faulty

sounds is most important. Descriptions of street scenes, short stories, books read, films seen, directions for finding a certain street or building, holidays, etc., eventually leading to normal discussion and conversation.

(v) Exercises for pitch and inflection may be required in a few cases where monotonous tone persists, although it is generally found that this improves naturally by imitation during the gradual process of training. If not, exercises for treatment may be found in any recognised book on voice production.

(vi) In some patients articulation is better in singing than in speaking and singing may be of some use in helping to establish normal muscular co-ordination. This may be due to the fact that singing has not been so firmly associated with defective neuromuscular co-ordination in early preoperative life, but because singing requires in any case somewhat different muscular control from that required for speech it may not be possible to transfer the improved articulation in singing into speech.

This process of incorporating correct speech into everyday conversation requires more time, and is usually more difficult, than any other part of the training with adults. Time and daily practice are important factors, and extra periods of training can in no way compensate for the subconscious processes which must slowly but surely play their part in the change from old to new habits.

CHAPTER VIII

CASE HISTORIES

Speech development in Group A cases.

Speech development in Group B cases.

Development in the use of the palatopharyngeal sphincter.

Natural development of speech with little training.

Varying difficulties hindering rate of progress.

Difficulties in speech development when the soft palate is immobile.

Improvement produced by a second operation when speech therapy is unable to obtain normal speech.

Observations on the post operative development of speech without speech therapy.

265

CASE HISTORIES

THE following case histories are quoted to illustrate speech development in cases of cleft palate after operative treatment.

In over 300 post-operative cases of cleft palate which I have had the opportunity of observing in connection with my work during recent years it has been found, except in rare instances, that speech therapy is unnecessary in the case successfully operated upon at the right age, that is, before faulty speech habits have become firmly established. The cases described here are those not submitted to operation until after this age, or are surgical failures in that operation was unable to produce the functional mechanism necessary for normal speech, or again those in which the speech "sense" or general intelligence of the child was insufficient to enable him to acquire normal habits unaided.

Though no two cases are completely similar, they have been grouped to demonstrate as far as is possible the various points already described as follows:—

Speech development in Group A cases.

Speech development in Group B cases.

Development in the use of the palatopharyngeal sphincter.

Natural development of speech with little training.

Varying difficulties hindering rate of progress.

Difficulties in speech development when the soft palate is immobile.

Improvement produced by second operation when speech therapy is unable to obtain normal speech.

Observations on the post-operative development of speech without speech therapy.

SPEECH DEVELOPMENT IN GROUP A CASES

Case 1. (*Hilda B.*)—Post alveolar cleft of the soft palate only.
Operation was performed at eighteen years of age.

She was first seen at the Clinic two months after operation. The soft palate was mobile and long. She was unable to snort, and there was gross nasal escape on blowing and in speech. All consonants were articulated normally except for weakness due to nasal escape. [s] was very nasal. She was working and unable to attend for treatment at that time.

Speech therapy commenced fourteen months later. She could now snort strongly, but there was still much nasal escape on blowing. Speech was only slightly improved. Although not unintelligent, she had made no attempt to use the sphincter mechanism.

She attended the Clinic each week, and a month later could blow without nasal escape, although it still persisted in speech, and was specially noticeable on [s], [sp], [st], and [sk]. She attended regularly for six months, by which time all sounds could be articulated without nasal escape except [s] combined with [p], [t], and [k]. Reading was otherwise normal, but there was carelessness in speech. She now ceased to attend the Clinic.

Eighteen months later, three and a half years after operation, she was seen again. Speech was quite normal with care, but a tendency to rather lazy use of the speech organs resulted in occasional slight nasal escape, unnoticeable to the casual observer.

Case 2. (*Alan A.*)—Alveolar left unilateral cleft.

Lip operation in infancy, palate operation at two and a half years, a 4-flap with pharyngoplasty.

He was brought to the Clinic at four and a half years of age, two years after operation, and referred for speech therapy. The palate was excellent, the hard palate being complete, the soft palate long and mobile, but nasal escape was very obvious, and blowing was weak. Speech was Group A, all consonants being formed correctly except for nasal escape. He was able to snort.

For six weeks he attended with other children in a group for blowing games, and then for individual treatment. Blowing gradually became stronger and nasal escape less, but it was still noticeable in speech, even after seven months attendance.

He was very shy and self-conscious, and at one time all speech practice at home had to be suspended. At this time he developed scarlet fever and was in hospital. Whilst there he refused to speak, nor did he speak on returning home, and nothing could be obtained at the Clinic. It was felt best to leave him to recover with time, and no training except blowing games at home was given for three months. At the end of this time he still refused to speak at the Clinic except in a whisper, but the grandmother reported that he was talking well at home. A month later he returned, and this time had completely recovered, and was talking quite happily and without nasal escape or cleft palate defect.

One wonders in this case whether the self-imposed silence was in any way helpful in overcoming a bad habit, or whether the movement of the soft palate and function of the sphincter had merely continued to improve with time and exercise.

SPEECH DEVELOPMENT IN GROUP B CASES

Case 3] (*Margaret R.*)—Post alveolar cleft of the soft, and two-thirds of the hard palate.

She had an unsuccessful operation at four years of age, and a further 4-flap operation with pharyngoplasty at twenty-seven years.

Speech therapy commenced four weeks after operation. She had some nasal escape on speaking, and blowing, and was unable to snort. Speech was Group A-B; all consonants were made in the correct positions escept [s], which was a very strong pharyngeal sound. The remaining consonants were weak.

She learnt to snort at her first visit, and to make an [s] near the normal position, but this required very great care or it slipped back into the pharynx. She also had difficulty in acquiring co-ordination of the sphincter with articulation, and relaxed the lips for an explosive sound such as [p] *after* relaxing the sphincter mechanism. After three weeks [s] was good except for nasal escape, co-ordination was improving, and she could whistle.

Five weeks later blowing was good, without nasal escape, and she could use the palatopharyngeal sphincter in speech. She was discharged four months after operation with normal speech.

Case 4. (*John G.*)—Alveolar right unilateral cleft, including lip and palate.

The lip was repaired in infancy by one surgeon and the palate at twelve years by another. The operation included pharyngoplasty.

Speech therapy.—He first visited the Clinic six months after operation. At operation it had been found impossible to close the hard palate completely, and a large hole remained, closed by a temporary plate which did not fit well. The soft palate was mobile. He could snort, but blowing tests were valueless until another plate was fitted. Speech was Group B and unintelligible. [s], [z], [sh(ʃ)] were pharyngeal fricatives. [th (θ, ð)], [l], [f], [v], and [p]— some attempt with nasal escape. [b], [t], [d], [k], and [g] were all replaced by the glottal stop.

Two months later dental treatment was completed, and speech therapy commenced. There was still nasal escape on blowing. Eight weeks later he could blow without obvious nasal escape, though there was a little under pressure, as on inflating a balloon. Air could then be heard passing through the sphincter. All sounds could now be articulated normally, except for slight nasal escape. Six months later reading was normal except for an occasional missed consonant, but speech was careless. This boy had no assistance in his home surroundings, which were very poor with a low speech standard.

He now started work as an errand boy, and was unable to visit the Clinic except at rare intervals.

When last seen, three years after operation, he could whistle well, speech was fairly good, and easily intelligible, but not normal, as he lapsed into occasional use of the glottal stop when forgetful.

Case 5. (*Joyce T.*)—Post alveolar cleft of the soft palate and one-third of the hard palate.

Operation, at ten years of age, was a 4-flap repair with pharyngoplasty.

Speech therapy commenced five weeks after operation. The soft palate was long and mobile. She was unable to snort, and there was nasal escape on blowing. Speech was Group B. [s] was pharyngeal. [t] and [d] were lateral. [sh (ʃ)], [ch (tʃ)] and [j (dʒ)] were omitted entirely. The remaining consonants were normal except for nasal escape.

Progress in this case was steady, but not rapid. Eleven months after beginning treatment, the palatopharyngeal sphincter was functioning normally. [t] and [d] were not always correct in speech, and [ch (tʃ)] required care. A month later, one year after operation, all sounds were correct, and could be used in speech. The chief remaining fault was nasal tone, and an occasional trace of nasal escape. Much of this nasal tone appeared to be due to lack of flexibility in jaw and tongue, so treatment was now concentrated on relaxation and humming exercises to improve this condition. She visited the Clinic for a further eighteen months at intervals, and at the end of this time was discharged, as speech was then normal and free from conscious effort.

Case 6. (*Margaret P.*)—Alveolar bilateral cleft.

The lip operation was performed in infancy, but she did not come for operation on the palate until she was six years old. Operation, a 4-flap with pharyngoplasty, produced a long, mobile soft palate, but there remained a narrow, slit-like opening in the hard palate about half an inch long. This closed rapidly and spontaneously.

Speech therapy commenced two months after operation. Speech was Group B, with nasal escape and no snort. [p], [b], [t], [d] were back palatal-tongue stops; [k] and [g] were not quite correct; [s], [z], [sh (ʃ)], [j (dʒ)], [ch (tʃ)] were pharyngeal; [f]=[th (θ)].

She was given blowing games and soon learnt to snort. In two weeks she could blow without nasal escape. Four weeks later she could pronounce several consonants without nasal escape. After a further two months she was able to use all consonants correctly in speech. She attended for a further month and was then discharged with normal speech seven months after operation and five months after commencing speech therapy. This child's progress was unusually rapid.

Case 7. (*David W.*)—The cleft was alveolar bilateral, including the lip and palate.

The lip was repaired at ten months by one surgeon, and the palate at the age of five years by another, this operation being the 4-flap repair with pharyngoplasty. On the fifth day following operation he developed scarlet fever and was removed to another hospital. Nevertheless the palate healed well, and only a small hole remained in the hard palate, which gradually closed spontaneously. The upper lip was long, tight and inert.

Speech therapy commenced three months after operation. He could snort, although there was a little nasal escape on blowing. Speech was Group B, no consonants except nasal resonants being used.

After two visits he could blow without nasal escape, and could articulate [p], [b], and [s], but only when he held his nose. Three months later speech was becoming intelligible. All consonants were good except [ch (tʃ)], and [j (dʒ)], and, due to the condition of the lip, [f] and [v]. There was still slight nasal escape and contraction of the nostrils (nasal grimace). Attendance at the Clinic was infrequent for the next seven months, by which time speech was good, although somewhat lazy; slight nasal escape persisted, but without nasal grimace. Speech was now Group A

Two months later, two years and three months after operation, speech was normal with care and in rhymes, though inclined to be indistinct when talking quickly. The condition of the lip was a definite hindrance to good speech. When seen again twelve months later speech was normal with no cleft palate defect.

s

Case 8. (*Thomas D.*)—Post alveolar cleft of the soft and most of the hard palate.

Operation, at eleven years of age, was a 4-flap repair with pharyngoplasty. (He had had a previous operation at eight years by another surgeon.)

Speech therapy commenced two months after operation. The soft palate appeared short, but was fairly mobile. He had a good snort, but gross nasal escape on blowing. Speech was group B, except for a strong pharyngeal [s], and all fricatives, except [s], were omitted.

Six weeks later he could whistle, although with some nasal escape, and could produce one sound [p], without using the glottal stop when holding his nose, In another six weeks [p], [b], [t], [d], and [s] could be articulated, though the glottal stop still accompanied these sounds unless he held his nose. He could blow and whistle well, but with some contraction of the alæ nasi, so apparently the sphincter was not quite competent. Much difficulty was experienced with [k] and [g], and it was seven months later before all speech sounds were articulated correctly, though still with some nasal escape.

Speech was now intelligible, and a determined father would not agree to further visits to the Clinic, as he wished the boy to concentrate on school work and learning to play the piano!

DEVELOPMENT IN THE USE OF THE PALATOPHARYNGEAL SPHINCTER

As has been described, many patients do not learn to use the palatopharyngeal sphincter spontaneously following operation. Such cases require some help. The following five cases have been chosen, as they illustrate differences in the attainment of nasopharyngeal closure.

USE OF THE SPHINCTER WHICH DEVELOPED QUICKLY WITH HELP FIVE YEARS AFTER OPERATION.

USE OF THE SPHINCTER ONLY OBTAINED GRADUALLY AFTER A LONG PERIOD OF TRAINING.

ABILITY TO USE THE SPHINCTER ACQUIRED SUDDENLY WITH COMPLETE COMPETENCE IN THREE DAYS.

USE OF THE SPHINCTER DEVELOPED BY EXERCISE AND LOST AGAIN.

SPHINCTER CONTROL NEVER ACQUIRED IN SPITE OF ABILITY TO SNORT.

USE OF A SPHINCTER WHICH DEVELOPED QUICKLY WITH HELP FIVE YEARS AFTER OPERATION.

Case 9. (*Billy G.*)—Alveolar cleft, bilateral and complete (lip and palate).

Lip operation in infancy by one surgeon. Palate operation, including pharyngoplasty at three years and eight months by another surgeon.

Speech therapy commenced five years after operation. The soft palate was mobile, but he could not snort, and blowing was accompanied by gross nasal escape. The upper lip was scarred and immobile, and the palate was shortened antero-posteriorly, the lower teeth protruding well beyond the upper incisors. He was a mouth breather, probably due to the anatomical difficulty in closing the mouth, and certainly not due to obstruction in the nasopharynx. Speech was Group B. [b] and [p] were replaced by [m]; [t] and [d] by [n]; and [k] and [g] by the glottal stop. No fricatives were attempted.

After two weeks he could inflate a balloon with very

little nasal escape, and six weeks later the sphincter was functioning normally in blowing and in speech. Thus in two months he learnt to make use of the sphincter muscles, although during the five years following operation he had made no attempt to do so.

When last seen, speech was good but not normal, as he sometimes substituted the glottal stop for [t] and [d], which were difficult to produce correctly with the rapidity required in speech.

USE OF THE SPHINCTER ONLY OBTAINED GRADUALLY AFTER A LONG PERIOD OF TRAINING

Case 10. (*Laureen L.*)—Post alveolar cleft of the soft and part of the hard palate.

Operation at eight years, following previous operation by another surgeon, was the 4-flap repair with pharyngoplasty.

Speech therapy commenced five months after operation. The soft palate was long, but only slightly mobile. There was a weak snort, but much nasal escape on blowing. Speech was Group A and completely intelligible, all consonants being correctly articulated, but weak owing to nasal escape. She had never been conscious of any difference between her speech and that of others, therefore incentive towards improvement was lacking. Her mother was able to help her at home with blowing games and exercises, so she was only seen once a month.

After six months nasal escape was somewhat less, but progress was slow. It was decided to postpone further treatment for several months, but blowing games were continued at home.

Eleven months later she returned, and now took more interest in the exercises, although still unconscious of any defect in her manner of speaking. After a further six months of occasional visits, there was definite improvement, and nasal escape was only obvious when speaking quickly and carelessly. The soft palate was more mobile, though it was noticed that the left side was functioning much better than the right side. This was possibly due to scar tissue holding the palate and preventing the complete action of the levator on the right side, and was apparently the cause of the persistent nasal escape.

After another six months under observation, with continued practice at home, speech was normal except for the occasional occurrence of a slight nasopharyngeal sound through the sphincter on [s]. Movement of the soft palate had improved again though the right side remained less mobile than the left. It was then three years after operation.

See also Case 1.

ABILITY TO USE THE SPHINCTER ACQUIRED SUDDENLY WITH COMPLETE COMPETENCE IN THREE DAYS

Case 11. (*Patricia B.*)—Very wide post alveolar cleft of soft and hard palate.

Operation at eleven years was the 4-flap operation with pharyngoplasty.

She was physically small for her age, being one of triplets. The other two, both girls, had normal palates.

Speech therapy commenced three weeks after operation. The soft palate was long. She had a good snort, but much nasal escape on blowing. Speech was Group B, [s] being pharyngeal, and all plosives, except [p], which was weak, were replaced by the glottal stop.

She attended twice a week and one month later could articulate all sounds correctly but with nasal escape. The soft palate was now mobile, the snort good, but blowing was still impossible without nasal escape.

Another month of palate exercises and blowing produced little improvement. One day I asked her to hold her nose and blow, and then to let go while still blowing. By her expression it was obvious that she had discovered where the fault lay, as the air rushed through the nasopharynx when she no longer held her nose. After practising this for three days, she returned with perfect use of the palato-pharyngeal sphincter, and no trace of nasal escape on blowing or in speech. This was the first time I had tried this exercise, and, although I have used it since, never, so far, with immediate success.

Very little further training was required. When seen two years after operation, speech was normal except for a very occasional use of the pharyngeal [s].

USE OF THE SPHINCTER DEVELOPED BY EXERCISE AND LOST AGAIN

Case 12. (*Doris M.*)—Alveolar left unilateral complete cleft. Very wide with little tissue.

Lip repaired in infancy by one surgeon. Palate operation at eleven years by another surgeon. Veau flaps were used with hamular fracture and pharyngoplasty.

Speech therapy commenced three weeks after operation There was a fistula in the hard palate which was closed by a dental plate. She was unable to snort, and blowing was accompanied by gross nasal escape, the outlet through the mouth being entirely obstructed by the tongue, and the air directed through the nose. Speech was Group B.

After ten weeks conscientious practice, she was able to snort, but nasal escape still persisted on blowing. It was fifteen months later before blowing was free from nasal escape. Speech was then very good, the only defect being an occasional pharyngeal [s]. She was discharged.

Two and a half years later, she returned to hospital for further dental treatment, and it was noticed that the palatopharyngeal sphincter was incompetent. Speech was Group A, with persistent, though slight, nasal escape.

Nasopharyngeal closure was only obtained in this case by conscientious practice, probably with considerable muscular development. Apparently ordinary speech was insufficient to maintain this increased development.

SPHINCTER CONTROL NEVER ACQUIRED IN SPITE OF ABILITY TO SNORT

Case 13. (*Edna St.*)—Alveolar left unilateral complete cleft.

Lip repaired in infancy by one surgeon. Palate repaired by 4-flap operation with pharyngoplasty at fourteen years of age by another surgeon.

Speech therapy commenced four months after operation. The soft palate appeared to be long and mobile. There was a small fistula remaining, which was covered by a dental plate. She was unable to snort, and had gross nasal escape on blowing. Speech was Group A.

Three weeks later, blowing had improved and was almost free from nasal escape. There was a weak snort.

After nine months speech had improved, although nasal escape persisted, being more obvious on [s]. She then left the town and was away a year, returning to the Clinic whilst home on holiday. Though the soft palate was apparently long and mobile, and she could now snort strongly, obvious nasal escape still persisted in speech, no further improvement having taken place during the year she had been away

As she was going away again, further treatment was impossible.

NATURAL DEVELOPMENT OF SPEECH WITH LITTLE OR NO TRAINING

It happened, owing to varying circumstances, that very little training was possible in each of the following cases, yet improvement in speech was steady and natural.

Case 14. (*Edna S.*)—Alveolar left unilateral complete cleft.

The lip was successfully repaired at seven months by one surgeon. Operation was performed on the palate, with pharyngoplasty, at five years of age by another surgeon.

Speech therapy commenced five months after operation. There was a small fistula in the hard palate covered by a plate. The soft palate was long and mobile. There was no snort, but only slight nasal escape on blowing. Speech was Group B, except for [f], [v], [p] and [b], which were produced as in Group A with nasal escape. [s] was pharyngeal, and the glottal stop was substituted for all other consonant sounds except the nasal resonants.

After five visits (one a week), she was able to imitate any sound, and could use them in rhymes and in games. There was noticeable nasal escape in speech, although little on blowing.

She then developed measles, followed by whooping-cough, and did not return for three months. Speech was then found to be good. There was occasional use of the glottal stop in conversation, but not in rhymes. There was slight nasal escape on [s] only. No further training was considered necessary.

When last seen seven months later, one year after operation, speech was normal and natural.

Case 15. (*Austin S.*)—Alveolar left unilateral complete cleft.

Lip repaired in infancy by one surgeon Palate operation

with pharyngoplasty at seven years of age by another surgeon.

When first seen, four months after operation, the soft palate was mobile, and he could inflate a balloon without nasal excape. Speech was Group B. The glottal stop was used for [t] and [d], and a pharyngeal fricative for [s], [sh (ʃ)] and [ch (tʃ)].

He was unable to visit the Clinic for treatment, but was seen again seven months later. He could then make a correct [t], but was not using it in speech.

Two years later, speech was good, and would have been normal, but for the persistent use in speech of a pharyngeal [s], [sh(ʃ)] and [ch(tʃ)]. He *could* make the correct sounds, but was not using them. Attendance for treatment was still impossible.

Case 16. (*Norman B.*)—Post alveolar cleft of the soft palate and two-thirds of the hard palate.

Operation, 4-flap with pharyngoplasty, was performed at four years of age.

Speech therapy.—He first visited the Clinic four months after operation. He had a competent palatopharyngeal sphincter in blowing and in speech. The soft palate was long and mobile. All consonant sounds were omitted in speech except [p], which was correct and without nasal eseape.

He lived in a rather remote village and was unable to visit the Clinic regularly. Six weeks later he was seen again, but there was no improvement in speech. [t] and [k] were attempted.

Four months later he returned. He had now started school, but was said to be receiving no assistance of any kind with his speech, nor was the mother able to help at home. [t] was now being used in speech, but there was no

[k]. Although previously no attempt at [s] had been heard, he was now developing a pharyngeal fricative. He learnt to make a normal [s], but did not use it in speech.

So far, speech development had been slight, but he now began to make rapid progress, and three months later, on his next visit, [p], [b], [t], [d], [k], and [g] were all normal and being used in speech. [s], [sh (ʃ)], [ch (tʃ)], and [j (dʒ)] were, however, strong pharyngeal fricatives, although [s] could be made correctly.

After another four months interval, he returned using normal speech, free from all cleft palate defects, except for pharyngeal fricatives as before. He could make these sounds correctly, but could not use them in conjunction with a vowel without an intervening pharyngeal sound.

During the summer he visited the Clinic five times, but the pharyngeal sounds persisted in speech.

Four months later he was in hospital for ten days with appendicitis, and some speech treatment was possible on the last three days. It was found that there had been considerable improvement, normal fricatives being used in a great many words. With treatment on three consecutive days and some practice whilst in hospital, it was expected that speech would become normal without further treatment.

Seen again seven weeks later, speech was normal and he was quite unable to make a pharyngeal [s] on request.

In the last two cases, and in many others, it will be noticed that the pharyngeal fricative sounds, especially [s], tend to persist as defects when speech is otherwise normal.

Case 17. (*Jack H.*)—The cleft was alveolar, left unilateral and complete.

Lip operation in infancy by one surgeon. Repair of the palate by the 4-flap operation with pharyngoplasty at five years of age. Speech at the time of operation was Group B.

He was not seen again until two years after operation. There was no nasal escape. Speech was good and he had corrected all his articulatory faults except that [k] and [g] were replaced by the glottal stop, and [s], when used finally or medially, was a posterior fricative, being made with the sides of the tongue in contact with the back upper teeth. Initially, [s] was correct.

It was found impossible to obtain [k] by imitation, as the glottal stop was always produced, but it was obtained almost immediately by asking the child to say [t] with the tip of the tongue held down with spatula. We called it the "clicky" sound, and it was not until four visits later that it could be associated with the [k] sound and imitated. [s] could then be correctly used in any position in words.

Two weeks later [k], and [g] which had developed spontaneously with the [k], could be used in rhymes, and [s] was correct when it occurred in speech.

He attended for three weeks longer for practice in rhymes and speech games, and was then discharged with normal speech.

Case 18. (*Aline W.*)—Post alveolar cleft of the soft and part of the hard palate.

Operation, the 4-flap combined with pharyngoplasty, was performed at four years of age.

Speech therapy commenced six month after operation. She could snort but had bad nasal escape on blowing. The palate was long and mobile. Speech was Group B. No fricatives were attempted, and all plosives were replaced by a very determined glottal stop.

Six weeks later she could blow without nasal escape, but there was no improvement in speech, and it was three months after treatment commenced before any consonant sound could be articulated without the glottal stop.

Attendance had been irregular, due to the mother's ill-health, and in this case there was considerable psychological difficulty, and extreme physical tension where speech was concerned. It was therefore necessary to proceed slowly and with care. [p], [t], and [s] were learnt first, but not until four weeks later could they be used initially with a vowel sound without the introduction of the glottal stop. Consonant sounds now began to be acquired quickly with little, and in some cases without any, help, although not yet being used consistently in speech.

Only occasional visits to the Clinic were possible, but as confidence increased, speech rapidly improved. One year after operation the only remaining defect was omission of the final [s] and the substitution of [f] for [th (θ)], and [v] for [th (ð)].

On her next visit to the Clinic, two months later, and fifteen months after operation, speech was normal and natural, and she was discharged.

VARYING DIFFICULTIES WHICH HINDER PROGRESS

Case 19. (*Eleanor F.*)—Post alveolar cleft of the soft and one-sixth of the hard palate.

Four-flap operation with pharyngoplasty was performed at eight years of age.

Speech therapy commenced seven months after operation, and continued, with some intervals, for three years. Progress, although extremely slow, was maintained. Mental retardation was a definite factor in this case, the standard of arithmetic being rather more than three years retarded at eleven years, and the standard of reading being also low. No assistance was available at home, consequently more rapid progress was made when she became old enough to practise alone.

The soft palate was long and mobile; in fact, the whole palate was so good that it was almost impossible to tell by observation that she ever had a cleft palate. She had a good snort, but blowing was poor, with much nasal escape. Speech was Group B, [s] and [f] were pharyngeal. No other fricatives were attempted, and all plosives were replaced by the glottal stop.

She attended the Clinic weekly for three months, at this time doing group work with individual treatment on alternate weeks. At the end of this time some attempt could be made to produce [p], [b], [t], [d], and [s] when holding the nose. Nasal escape persisted on blowing.

She was absent for three months from the Clinic, and when seen again, the only possible sounds were [t] and [s] when holding her nose. She attended fairly regularly for another six months with little improvement in speech, and obviously made no attempt to practise between visits. Nine months later the glottal stop was less pronounced, and [s] had become nasal instead of pharyngeal. All sounds could be articulated when holding the nose except [k] and [g].

A year later, two and a half years after operation, she at last learnt to use the sphincter when blowing, although nasal escape and the use of the glottal stop persisted in speech. Three years after operation there was no nasal escape in speech, and she had learnt the difference between a correctly pronounced plosive sound and one combined with the glottal stop, and could then correct her own faults. She was unable to attend further owing to evacuation at the outbreak of war, but it is possible that one day she may be a normal speaker.

Case 20. (*Jessie M.*)—Alveolar left unilateral complete cleft.

Lip operation was performed in infancy by one surgeon. Four-flap operation with pharyngoplasty performed at seven years of age by another surgeon.

Speech therapy commenced three months after operation. The soft palate was long and fairly mobile. There was a tiny fistula in the hard palate, which eventually closed spontaneously. The lip was scarred and rather stiff, but not too long or tight to interfere completely with articulation. She could snort, but had nasal escape on blowing. Speech was Group B. [p] and [b]=[m]; [t] and [d]=[n]; [k] and [g]=[h]. [s] was pharyngeal, and other fricatives were omitted.

In this case slow progress was largely due to lack of ambition with regard to speech, and possibly to fatigue and insufficient physical energy. (She usually visited the cinema three nights a week.) Nevertheless some progress was made. There was an interval of six months when she was unable to visit the Clinic, but ten months after commencing treatment she could articulate all consonants except [k] and [g], but with nasal escape, [s] was oral, though somewhat lateral. After a further ten months she could whistle and nasal escape was only slight. Four months later, with somewhat irregular attendance, all sounds could be used normally in speech with care, and there was only a trace of nasal escape. She attended for still another three months, when all sounds could be used normally in rhymes and reading, and there was no trace of nasal escape. She was discharged two and a half years after operation.

Case 21. (*Joseph J.*)—Alveolar bilateral complete cleft.

Lip repaired in infancy by one surgeon. Four-flap operation with pharyngoplasty at five years of age by another surgeon.

Speech therapy commenced seven months after operation.

There was a fistula in the hard palate covered by a dental plate. This plate also filled the space normally occupied by the upper incisor teeth, these being missing. The soft palate appeared to be long and mobile. He was able to snort, but there was a little nasal escape on blowing. Speech was Group B, [p], [b], [t] and [d] could be articulated, but with nasal escape. [k], [g], [s], [f], [v], [th (θ, ð)] were omitted, although the glottal stop was not pronounced.

The chief difficulties in this case were due to the upper lip, which was long, tight and inert, and the lack of upper incisor teeth.

Progress was interrupted owing to ill-health, but after nine months there was little nasal escape and most consonants could be used normally in speech. The exceptions were [f], [v], and [th (θ, ð)], which were bilabial, owing to inability to raise the upper lip, and [s] and [z] were difficult owing to the structure of the dental plate. Nasal escape was most obvious on these consonants. Speech in conversation was indistinct, though reported to be quite clear when out playing and shouting to other children, or when in a temper. He was an only child, and though by no means slim, the mother spent much time in persuading him to eat. Her own speech was somewhat slurred and rapid, and not very helpful as a pattern for the child.

Five months later there was considerable improvement in articulation and no nasal escape, though nothing further could be done to improve the [f], [v], [th], [s] and [z] until such time as a dental plate, more adapted for speech, could be fitted.

Case 22. (*Fred A.*)—Alveolar right unilateral complete cleft.

Operation of the Langenbeck type, without pharyngoplasty, was performed at three years of age. The lip had been repaired previously.

He was first seen one year after operation. The soft palate was mobile and fairly long, but the nasopharynx was wide. There was no snort and much nasal escape, breath direction being poor. Speech was Group B and was unintelligible. The glottal stop was very pronounced and [s] was pharyngeal.

Blowing exercises were advised, and he was asked to return in six months.

He visited the Clinic again a year later. He then had a weak snort, could blow out his cheeks and say [p], with much contraction of the alæ nasi. After seven visits he could articulate [p] and [t], but could not join them initially to a vowel sound without the introduction of the glottal stop. A month later he could produce a normal [s], but could not use it in speech. Four weeks after this he could repeat the syllables pah, bah, tah, dah, but [k] and [g] were still glottal and [s] was pharyngeal in speech. Blowing was then strong, although there was still some nasal escape. During the next nine months he was only able to visit the Clinic occasionally, at the end of which time speech was still unintelligible, though he could speak fairly well with care.

This boy was not mentally retarded, and is the one previously mentioned who taught himself to read without assistance and was ahead of other children of his age in this respect, except that his reading was only intelligible to himself. Hearing was apparently normal, but ability to imitate sounds was poor. His progress in reading was probably due to very good visual memory. No help was available at home, so it is possible that progress may be more rapid when he is older. He was one of the few cases in which speech definitely deteriorated during intervals of absence from the Clinic; in most cases there is some slight spontaneous improvement.

DIFFICULTIES IN SPEECH DEVELOPMENT
WHEN THE SOFT PALATE IS IMMOBILE

Case 23. (*John F.*)—Alveolar left unilateral complete cleft.

The lip had been repaired in infancy. The palate was operated upon at five years of age, with pharyngoplasty. (There had also been a previous operation on the palate by another surgeon.)

Speech therapy commenced five years after operation. The soft palate was apparently somewhat short and immobile. There was a weak snort, and he could blow up a balloon. The lip was long, tight and inert. Speech was Group B, with nasal escape.

After four months' practice all sustained vowels were made without nasal escape (testing with a mirror). Most consonants were correct, but accompanied by nasal escape. As muscular development took place the nasopharyngeal snort occurred frequently, due to incomplete closure of the sphincter, in conjunction with most consonant sounds. This persisted for four months, and later recurred occasionally.

Speech therapy continued for two years. [f], [v], [th (θ, ð)] were difficult due to the lip condition, but there was much less nasal escape. It was completely absent on sustained blowing, but persisted during speech. He has been seen occasionally since, and ten years after operation speech was intelligible but not easy, some nasal escape persisting with a tendency to use the glottal stop to obviate this.

Case 24. (*Una P.*)—Wide post alveolar cleft of the hard and soft palate.

Repair of the palate with pharyngoplasty was performed at nine years of age, but she had had many previous operations by other surgeons.

T

Speech therapy commenced four years after the last operation. She was then thirteen years of age. The soft palate was apparently rather short and immobile, but she could snort strongly and blow without nasal escape. Speech was Group B. [s] was pharyngeal, and [k] and [g] were replaced by the glottal stop. Other consonants were accompanied by nasal escape.

Speech therapy continued for eighteen months, and nasal escape persisted in speech, though on continuous blowing, as on inflating a balloon there was no trace of this. Speech was good, but not normal, as use of the glottal stop occurred occasionally in rapid conversation.

Apparently a palatopharyngeal sphincter may be competent for continuous effort, but if the soft palate is scarred and immobile there is difficulty in obtaining the rapid opening and closing of the sphincter required for speech.

IMPROVEMENT PRODUCED BY A SECOND OPERATION WHEN SPEECH THERAPY IS UNABLE TO OBTAIN NORMAL SPEECH

Case 25] (*David H.*)—Alveolar left unilateral complete cleft, repaired at four months by the "Lane" operation.

The nasopharynx was wide, with much deformity of the palate. Speech was Group A-B. [s] was nasal and there was nasal escape on all consonants. [b] and [p]=[m], [n]=[ng (ŋ)], [k] and [g] were substituted for [t] and [d]. [l]=[y (j)].

A further operation was carried out at seven years of age, including pharyngoplasty.

Speech therapy commenced two weeks after operation with daily lessons. There was no snort and gross nasal escape persisted, but at the end of a fortnight most consonants could be articulated when holding the nose, though [sh(ʃ)], [ch(tʃ)], [l] and [z] were not always correct.

Treatment in this case was only possible at long intervals and was therefore intensive for short periods. He returned four months later, nasal escape still persisted, and he was again using [ng (ŋ)] for [n], and [y (j)] for [l], all consonants being weak. After ten daily visits there was some further improvement, especially in rhymes, although nasal escape was no less, and speech was usually rapid, careless and often unintelligible. He then left the country, but continued to carry out a course of exercises with his mother.

A year later he returned, and had treatment for another two months. At the end of this time, two years after operation, speech was normal except for nasal escape, and he could sometimes read without this being obvious. It was decided to perform a further operation.

When seen three weeks after this operation, speech was much improved, nasal escape being only obvious on [s], and two weeks later he could blow and speak without any trace of nasal escape. Speech was not always careful, chiefly due to lack of confidence rather than to indifference, but no further training was possible or thought to be necessary.

He went to a public school, and two years after the second operation speech was reported to be completely free from all cleft palate defect.

OBSERVATIONS ON THE POST-OPERATIVE DEVELOPMENT OF SPEECH WITHOUT SPEECH THERAPY

Case 26. (*M.A.*)—Unilateral complete alveolar cleft, left. Operation on the lip was at eight months and on the palate (Braithwaite) at one year five months. When

T*

first seen one month after operation no speech was
used.

At 2 years—Using a few words; has nasopharyngeal
closure. Sounds heard in speech—(k) (g) (t) (d) (p) and
(b) were normal, (s) was nasal.

At 3 years—Speech normal escept [s] [ʃ(sh)].

At 3 years 6 months—Normal speech.

Case 27. (*R.B.*)—Unilateral complete alveolar · cleft.
Operation (F.B.) on the lip at 1 year 8 months, and
on the palate at 2 years 2 months.

At 2 years 3 months—Crying not nasal. Blows via the
nose with mouth closed. Speech has excessive nasal
resonance.

At 3 years 4 months—Articulation weak with nasal
escape of air.

At 4 years—Nasopharyngeal closure for blowing. Some
nasality and inco-ordination in use of sphincter for articulation. No [s] or [ʃ(sh)]. Mother advised to encourage
blowing.

At 4 years 3 months—Good nasopharyngeal closure for
all consonants except (s).

At 5 years—Normal articulation.

Case 28. (*M.F.*)—Postalveolar cleft. Operation (F.B.) on
the palate at 13 months.

At 1 year 7 months—Nasal blowing. Says "Mum"
only. Normal resonance on vocalising.

At 2 years 6 months—Blowing still slightly nasal. Talking
now, resonance 5 with nasal escape of air.

At 3 years—Blowing not nasal. Language developing—
articulation weak due to nasal escape of air.

At 4 *years*—Normal articulation, some excessive nasal resonance on vowels. (Had a cold.)

At 5 *years*—Speech normal.

Case 29. (*B.M.*)—Postalveolar cleft. Operation (F.B.) on palate at 16 months.

At 17 *months*—Vocalising—vowel tone good.

At 2 *years*—Speaking well but not using (s). Other sounds normal.

At 2½ *years*—Occasionally has a nasopharyngeal (s). Otherwise normal.

At 3½ *years*—Normal speech.

Case 30. (*E.C.*)—Unilateral complete alveolar cleft. Operation (F.B.) on lip at 6 months and on the palate at 18 months.

At 1 *year* 1½ *months*—Blowing nasal, no speech.

At 5 *years*—Normal speech.

At 5½ *years*—Tonsils and adenoids removed. Now has articulation with nasal emission of air.

At 5 *years* 8 *months*—Articulation improving again—slight nasal escape of air only.

At 7 *years*—Normal speech.

AUTHOR AND SUBJECT
INDEX

AUTHOR INDEX

297

SUBJECT INDEX

299